AMERICAN MAPS 1795-1895

A GUIDE TO VALUES

Frontis engraving from Colton's American Atlas. This image was also used as the frontispiece in Johnson's New Illustrated Family Atlas.

AMERICAN MAPS
1795-1895

A GUIDE TO VALUES

WALL MAPS, FOLDING MAPS, ATLASES & MAPS FROM ATLASES

A PRICED LISTING OF MAPS OF AMERICA, THE UNITED STATES AND TERRITORIES BY AMERICAN COMMERCIAL CARTOGRAPHERS 1795-1895

K. A. SHEETS

ANN ARBOR
1994

AMERICAN MAPS 1795-1895
A GUIDE TO VALUES

ISBN NO.

K. A. SHEETS
PO BOX 7024
ANN ARBOR, MI 48107

Engraving from David Burr's Universal Atlas, NY, 1836

ABOUT THE LISTINGS

The purpose of this book is to provide a convenient preliminary reference work about 19th century American maps, their makers, and their values.

Generally, we have included only maps and atlases which have appeared for sale, at auction, in shops, and from specialized delaers, in the past twenty years. However, this is not a comprehensive listing of maps offered for sale during that same period. .Manuscript maps and excessively rare printed maps have not been included. Listed are folding maps, wall maps and maps from atlases published by commercial firms during the period 1795-1895. We have tried to list the most significant maps published by the most significant publishers from this period. We have not included county maps, maps from county atlases; county atlases; U.S. Government publications; maps from School and juvenile Geographies; maps from periodicals; harbor maps, and coastal charts. These maps are certainly worthy of interest, but were beyond the scope of the present volume. We hope to include them in a future volume.

The prices listed represent our estimation of current (1994-1995) retail value for an exemplar of the listed item in near fine condition. The listed price is meant to suggest a range of prices for the listed item or like items. Condition and edition should affect value. As with all antiquarian items, the actual value is that agreed upon by a willing seller and a willing buyer.

The listings include the name of the publisher, the title of the map as it appears on the map, the place and date of publication, dimensions (in inches), the name of the atlas in which the map appeared if the map is ex-atlas, and reference information about the map, or the atlas in which it appeared, and our estimation of retail value.

Tanner, Henry S.**Georgia and Alabama.** Phila, 1819-23. 20 x 27. Ex-atlas. HC Engraving. From *American Atlas.* See Phillips (M)93. **$850.00**

Publisher. Generally, the publisher's name as it appears on the map or within the atlas.
Title. Generally, the title exactly as it appears on the map.
Place. The place of publication as it appears on the map or within the atlas.
Date. Generally the date of publication as it appears on the map or within the atlas. Many maps published in the 19th century bore the same date of publication for decades: a map originally published in 1855 might display this date as late as 1875, although the map may have been revised. We have tried to list the range of dates in which a map was published, i. e., 1856-59.
Dimensions. Generally, the dimensions of the printed image, height first. However, many descriptions from other sources give the dimensions of the sheet, or give length first, or are simply inaccurate. In an ideal world, we think, dimensions of the printed image would be given to the nearest half inch or half centimeter, height first, followed by the sheet dimensions in parentheses: 16 x 13 (18 x 15). **The dimensions given here (which are all in inches) should be regarded as approximate.**
Type. Ex-atlas, folding map, wall maps, separately issued map. Many folding maps were also issued as wall maps. Some ex-atlas maps were first issued as folding maps, or later revised and issued as folding maps.
Medium. Engraving (on copper or steel), HC engraving (hand colored engraving), lithograph after engraving (many maps after 1860 were engravings transferred to lithographic plates), lithographs, cerographs, wax engraving. Many maps combined two or more of these processes, or combined lithographic color with hand color.
Comments. Atlas, if the map is ex-atlas, additional title information, additional reference information.
Price. A retail price for a near fine exemplar of the listed map.

Reference. References to listing number or page number in standard reference works. See bibliography. The most commonly cited references in the listings are **Phillips (A)**, Phillips, P. L. *A List of Atlases in the Library of Congress,* Washington, 1901, (entry number given) **Phillips (M)**, Phillips, P. L. *A List of Maps in the Library of Congress*, Washington, 1901 (page number given), **Ristow**, Ristow, Walter W. *American Maps and Mapmakers Commercial Cartography in the Nineteenth Century*, Detroit, 1985, (page number given), **Schwartz & Ehrenberg,** Schwartz, S. I. and Ehrenberg, R. E. *The Mapping of America,* NY, 1980, (page number given), **Karpinki**, Karpinski, L.C. Map *Bibliography of Michigan and Great Lake Region*, Lansing, 1931 (page number or entry number given), **Howes**, Howes, Wright *U.S.IANA*, NY, 1962 (entry number given).

Maps showing and naming more than one state or territory are indexed by both (or all) subjects in the Subject Listing. The S. A. Mitchell **Map of Ohio and Indiana**, for instance, is listed under both Ohio and Indiana in the subject list. Within subject, the listings are arranged in chronological order. Within the Publisher Listing, the maps are listed by publisher, subject, and date. Wall maps and folding maps are listed by publisher in a separate section, as well as by subject in the Subject Listing. Atlases are listed by publisher in the Atlas section.

• Within the listings, illustrated maps are indicated by a dot. Most of the illustrated maps have been reproduced at 50% of actual size.

For the most part we have relied on the information printed on the map itself, although a map by S. A. Mitchell, for instance, with a copyright date of 1868 on the map, might actually have been published in 1877, or earlier, or later. Many maps (and atlases) were in a constant state of revision. Some publishers, like Johnson & Ward, periodically issued revised versions of maps which were sent to subscribers or sold by mail. It is not unusual to find two differing states of the same map in an atlas, and neither is it unusual to encounter two differing states of the same map with the same date of publication or copyright. Often, information within the map itself is the only reliable guide to date of publication. The addition of place-names and revised boundaries may give the most accurate information as to when the map was actually published.

We have not had an opportunity to physically examine each and every map listed, but we have taken care to be as accurate as possible. We have relied heavily on dealer catalogs, auction catalogs and auction records, as well as standard reference works, for the listing information. Different cataloguing standards can produce differing descriptions of the same item. We have tried to be consistent in organizing this information, but encourage readers to compare information with catalog and cartobibliographical listings if the map itself cannot be examined. The map itself is the best source of information. Specialist dealers are an excellent resource for information about individual maps as well as map prices.

Errors are inevitable and we encourage readers to consult other reference works, as well as this one, in conjunction with a particular map, price, or cartobibliographical feature.

Acknowledgements

Particular thanks are due to John Dann and David Bosse of the William L. Clements Library, F. J. Manasek of G.B. Manasek, Inc. and Susan Bay. Grateful thanks are also due to the map dealers and collectors who have shared information, opinions, and catalogs.

ILLUSTRATIONS

1 Colton, G. W. Frontis from *Colton's American Atlas* Frontis

2 Carey & Lea *Geographical, ...Historical Map of Arkansas Territory* Phila 1822-23 *From A Complete Historical, Chronological and Geographical American Atlas* 19

3 Lucas, Fielding *Plan of Baltimore* Baltimore 1840 Folding Map 21

4 Colton, J. W. & G. W. *Boston and Adjacent Cities* NY 1855-56 *Colton's Atlas of the World* 23

5 Johnson & Ward *Johnson's California, Territories of New Mexico and Utah* NY 1864 *From Johnson's New Illustrated Family Atlas* 25

6 Johnson & Browning *Johnson's New Military Map of the United States* NY 1861 *From Johnson's New Illustrated Family Atlas.* 27

7 Mitchell, S. A. *Map of Kansas, Nebraska and Colorado* Phila 1861 *From A New General Atlas* 29

8 Johnson & Ward *Johnson's Nebraska, Dakota, Colorado, Montana & Kansas* NY 1862 *From Johnson's New Illustrated Family Atlas* 31

9 Carey, Matthew *Delaware* Phila 1795 *From The American Edition of Guthrie's Geography* 33

10 Tanner, Henry S. *Florida* Phila 1833 *From The Universal Atlas* 35

11 Tanner, Henry S. *A New Map of Georgia With Its Roads and Distances* Phila 1833-36 *From A New Universal Atlas* 37

12 Bradford, T. G. *Missouri, Illinois and Iowa* Boston 1835 *From A Comprhensive Atlas* 38

13 Carey & Lea *Geographical, Historical Map of Illinois* Phila 1822 *From A Complete Historical, ...Geographical American Atlas* 39

14 Greenleaf Indiana Brattleboro 1842 *From A New General Atlas* 41

15 Morse & Breese *Indiana* NY 1842 (Cerograph) *From The Cerographic Atlas* 43

16 Tanner, H. S. *Iowa* Phila 1841 *From A New Universal Atlas* 45

17 Johnson & Browning *Johnson's Nebraska & Kansas* NY 1861 47

18 Carey, Matthew *Kentuckey* Phila 1804 *From the Pocket Atlas* 49

19 Carey, Matthew *Louisiana* Phila 1814 *From The General Atlas* 51

20 Carey, Matthew *The District of Maine* Phila 1814 *From the General Atlas* 53

21 Carey, Matthew *Massachusetts* Phila 1805 *From The Pocket Atlas* 54

22 Carey & Lea *Geographical, ...Historical Map of Michigan Territory* Phila 1822-23 *From A Complete Historical, ...Geographical American Atlas* 55

23 Lucas, Fielding *Mississippi* Baltimore 1840 *From A General Atlas* 57

24 Finley, A. *Missouri* Phila 1832 *From A New General Atlas* 59

25 Tanner, H. S. *A New Map of Missouri...* Phila 1841 *From A New Universal Atlas* 61

26 Mitchell, S. A. *Map of Missouri* Phila 1847 *From A New Universal Atlas* 63

27 Colton, J. W. & G. W. *Missouri* NY 1855-56 *From Colton's Atlas of the World* 65

28 Carey, Matthew *The State of New Hampshire* Phila 1796 *From The General Atlas* 67

29 Arrowsmith & Lewis *New Jersey* Phila 1804 *From New and Elegant General Atlas* 69

30 Arrowsmith & Lewis *New York* Phila 1804 *From New and Elegant General Atlas* 70

31 Tanner, T. R. *Strangers' New York City Guide* NY 1842 Folding map 71

32 Carey, Matthew *North Carolina* Phila 1814 *From the General Atlas* 73
33 Lucas, Fielding *North America* Baltimore 1823 *From A General Atlas* 74
34 Arrowsmith & Lewis *Ohio* Phila 1804 *First separate map of the new state. From A New and Elegant General Atlas* 75
35 Tanner, Henry S. *A New Map of Ohio...* Phila 1833 *From The Universal Atlas* 77
36 Scott *Pennsylvania* Phila 1795 *From the United States Gazeteer* 79
37 Carey, Matthew *A Map of the Tenasee State Formerly Part of North Carolina* Phila 1796 *From Guthrie's Geography* 83
38 Bradford, T. G. *Texas* Boston 1835-36 *From A Comprehensive Atlas* 85
39 Colton, J. W. & G. W. *Texas* NY 1856 Folding Map 87
40 Melish, J. *United States of America* Phila 1820-22 *From Lavoisine's Genealogical, Historical and Chronological Atlas* 88
41 Melish, J. *United States* Phila 1819 Folding map From *Advice to Emigrants* 89
42 Thomas, Cowperthwait & Co *A New Map of the United States of America* Phila 1850-52 *From A New Universal Atlas* 91
43 Arrowsmith & Lewis *Vermont* Phila 1804 *From New and Elegant General Atlas* 94
44 Reid *The State of Virginia...* NY 1796 95
45 Johnson & Browning *Johnson's Washington & Oregon* NY 1861 11 x 14 *From Johnson's New Illustrated Family Atlas* 97
46 Thomas, Cowperthwait & Co *Map of the State of Wisconsin* Phila 1850-55 *From A New Universal Atlas* 103
47 Title page and contents page from Fielding Lucas' *General Atlas...*Baltimore, 1823. 147
48-49 Title page and contents page from the second edition of Carey & Lea's *A Complete Historical Chronological And Geographical American Atlas.* Phila 1823. 149-50
50 Title page from *Mitchell's New Universal Atlas.* Phila, 1848. 151
51-52 Title page and List of Maps from *Colton's Atlas of the World.* NY, 1856. 153-54
53-54 Title page and List of Maps from *Johnson's New Illustrated Family Atlas* NY 1861 155-56
55-56 Title page and List of Maps from *Mitchell's New General Atlas* NY 1863 158-58

Most of the illustrations are 50% of actual size

• *Within the listings, illustrated maps are indicated by a dot*

The maps illustrated as nos. 3, 9-11, 13, 18-21, 28-32, 34-39, 41, 43-44, were provided courtesy of the William L. Clements Library. All other illustrations are items from private collections.

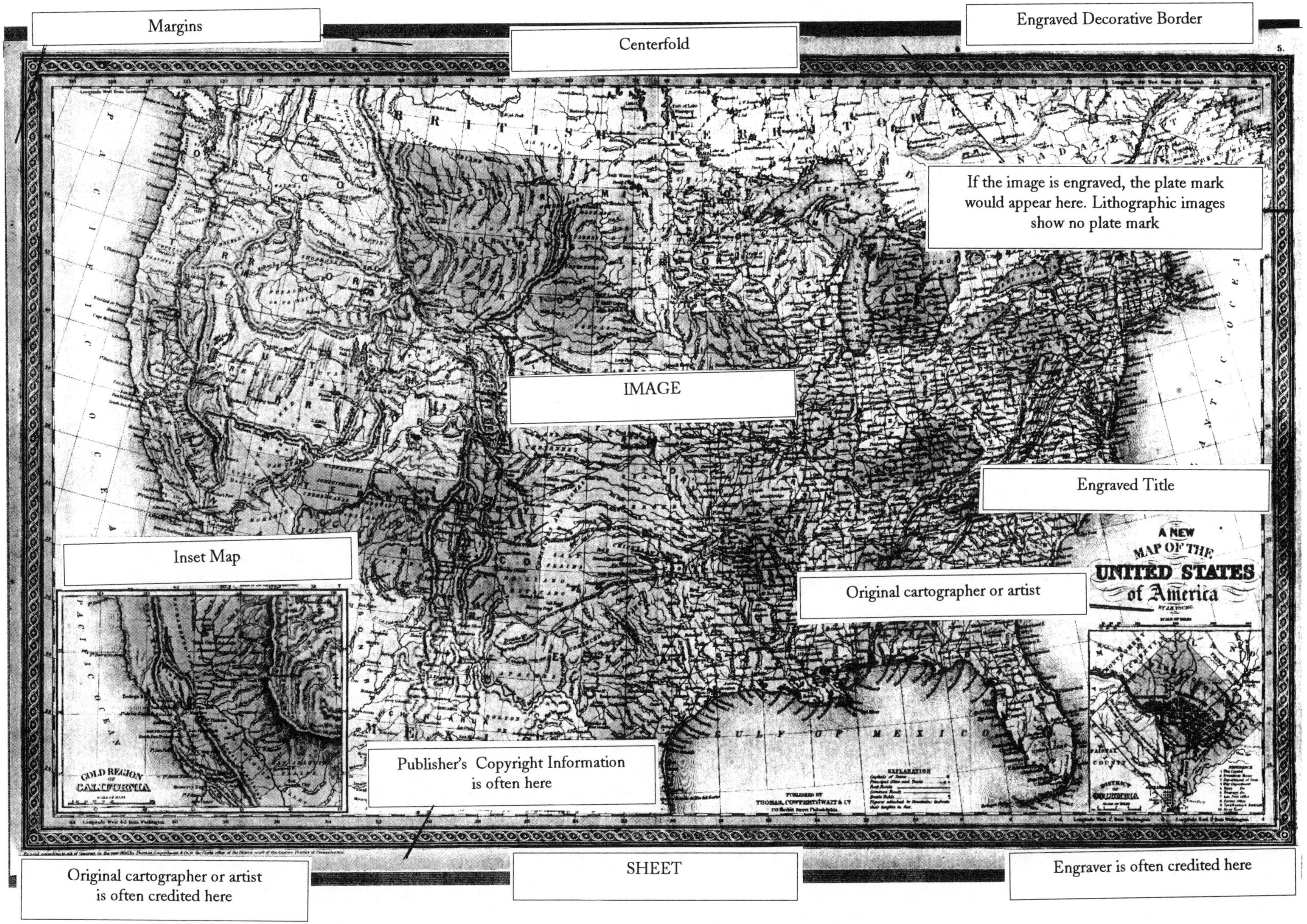
Margins
Centerfold
Engraved Decorative Border
If the image is engraved, the plate mark would appear here. Lithographic images show no plate mark
IMAGE
Engraved Title
A NEW MAP OF THE UNITED STATES of America
Original cartographer or artist
Inset Map
GOLD REGION OF CALIFORNIA
PACIFIC OCEAN
GULF OF MEXICO
Publisher's Copyright Information is often here
Original cartographer or artist is often credited here
SHEET
Engraver is often credited here

UNITED STATES TERRITORIAL ACQUISITIONS

		Square Miles
1783	Treaty of Paris	827,844
1803	Louisiana Purchase	920,000
1819	Florida Purchase	59,268
1845	Annexation of Texas	371,063
1846	Oregon Treaty	255,000
1848	Mexican Cession	522,568
1853	Gadsden Purchase	45,535
1867	Alaska Puchase	577,390
1898	Annexation of Hawaii	6,449
1899	Spanish Cession	114,326
	(Phillipnes & Porto Rico)	3,550

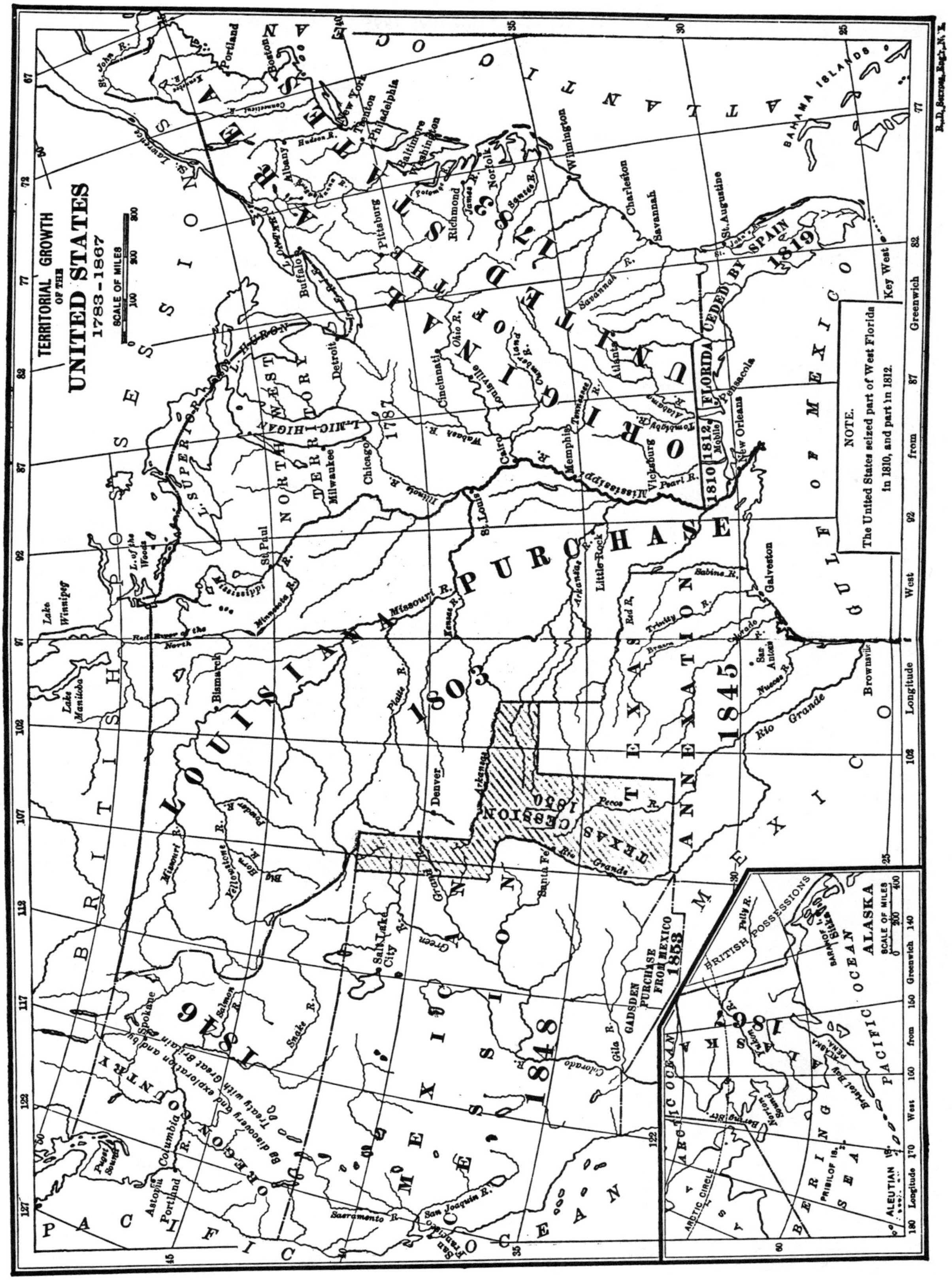

Map reprinted from Cornman & Gerson, *Topical Survey of United States History*

References cited in the Listings

References to listing number or page number in standard reference works. See bibliography. The most commonly cited references in the listings are **Phillips (A)**, Phillips, P. L. *A List of Atlases in the Library of Congress,* Washington, 1901, (entry number given) **Phillips (M)**, Phillips, P. L. *A List of Maps in the Library of Congress*, Washington, 1901 (page number given), **Ristow**, Ristow, Walter W. *American Maps and Mapmakers Commercial Cartography in the Nineteenth Century*, Detroit, 1985, (page number given), **Schwartz & Ehrenberg,** Schwartz, S. I. and Ehrenberg, R. E. *The Mapping of America,* NY, 1980, (page number given), **Karpinki,** Karpinski, L.C. Map *Bibliography of Michigan and Great Lake Region*, Lansing, 1931 (page number or entry number given), **Howes**, Howes, Wright *U.S.IANA*, NY, 1962 (entry number given).

LIST OF MAPS BY SUBJECT

• *Illustrated*

Alabama

Alabama became a state in Dec. 1819

Tanner, Henry S. **Georgia and Alabama** Phila 1819-23 20 x 27 Ex-atlas HC Engraving *From American Atlas* $850.00

Carey & Lea **Geographical, ...Historical Map of Alabama** Phila 1822-23 17.5 x 22 Ex-atlas HC engraving *Complete Historical, Chronological and Geographical American Atlas Phillips (A) 1373a Phillips (M)92* $225.00

Lucas, Fielding **Alabama** Baltimore 1823 14.5 X 11.5 Ex-atlas HC engraving *From A General Atlas Phillips (A) 742* $250.00

Finley, A. **Map of Louisiana, Mississippi, and Alabama...** Phila 1827 17 x 20 Folding Map HC engraving $850.00

Finley, A. **Alabama** Phila 1829 8.5 x 11 Folding Map HC engraving *Cloth or leather folder Phillips (A)752* $600.00

Tanner, Henry S. **A New Map of Alabama With its Roads and Distances** Phila 1833-36 10.5 x 13.5 Ex-atlas HC engraving *From A New Universal Atlas Phillips (A)774* $225.00

Mitchell, S. A. **Map of the States of Louisiana, Mississippi and Alabama** Phila 1835 17.5 x 21.5 Folding Map HC engraving *Cloth or leather covers* $600.00

Burr, David H. **Map of the State of Alabama** NY 1836 15 x 12 Ex-atlas HC engraving *From The Universal Atlas Phillips (A) 1379a* $175.00

Bradford, T. G. **Alabama** Boston 1838 14.5 x 11.5 Ex-atlas HC engraving *From An Illustrated Atlas* $150.00

Bradford & Goodrich **Alabama** Boston 1838-42 11.5 x 14 Ex-atlas HC engraving *From Universal Illustrated Atlas Phillips (A) 783* $150.00

Mitchell, S. A. **A New Map of Alabama With its Roads and Distances** Phila 1847 14 x 11 Ex-atlas HC engraving *From A New Universal Atlas* $95.00

Thomas, Cowperthwait & Co **A New Map of Alabama With Its Roads and Distances** Phila 1850-55 14.5 x 12 Ex-atlas HC engraving *From A New Universal Atlas* $95.00

Colton, J. W. & G. W. **Alabama** NY 1855-56 15 x 18 Ex-atlas Lithograph after engraving *From Colton's Atlas of the World Phillips (A)816* $95.00

Desilver **A New Map of Alabama With Its Roads and Distances...** Phila 1856-57 14.5 x 11.5 Ex-atlas HC Engraving *From A New Universal Atlas Phillips (A)823* $125.00

Morse & Gaston **Alabama** NY 1857 6.5 x 5 Ex-atlas Cerograph *From Diamond Atlas Phillips (A)824* $60.00

Johnson & Browning **Johnson's Georgia & Alabama** NY 1861 17 x 23 Ex-atlas Lithograph after engraving *Johnson's New Illustrated Family Atlas* $75.00

Asher & Adams **Georgia & Alabama** NY 1872 16.5 x 22.5 Ex-atlas Lithograph *Asher & Adams New Statistical and Topographical Atlas Phillips(A)1272* $75.00

Gray **Gray's New Map of Alabama** NY 1880 28 x 17.5 Ex-atlas Lithograph after engraving $75.00

Colton, J. W. & G. W. **Map of the State of Alabama** NY 1885 36 x 27 Folding Map Lithograph after engraving *Cloth folder. Separately issued.* $325.00

Bradley **County Map of Georgia and Alabama** Phila 1887 12.5 x 20 Ex-atlas Lithograph *From New General Atlas See Phillips (A)920* $65.00

Alaska

Alaska Purchase 1867. Became a state in 1959

Colton, J. W. & G. W. **Northern America** NY 1855-56 15 x 18 Ex-atlas Lithograph after engraving *From Colton's Atlas of the World Phillips (A) 816* $95.00

Colton, J. W. & G. W. **Northern America, British, Russian, and Danish** NY 1856 15 x 18 Ex-atlas Lithograph after engraving *From Colton's Atlas of the World* $95.00

Mitchell, S. A. **(Alaska) Northwestern America ...Territory Ceded by Russia ...** Phila 1867 11.5 x 14 Ex-atlas Lithograph after engraving *From A New General Atlas Phillips (A) 850* $100.00

Colton, J. W. & G. W. **Map of the Territory of Alaska** NY 1886 13 x 16 Ex-atlas Lithograph after engraving *From Colton's General Atlas* $85.00

Rand McNally & Co. **Official 24 x 36 Map of Alaska** Chicago 1897 24 x 36 Folding Map Wax engraving $200.00

Americas

See North America

Carey & Lea **Geographical, ...Historical Map of Americas** Phila 1822-23 17.5 x 22 Ex-atlas HC engraving *Complete Historical, Chronological and Geographical American Atlas Phillips (A) 1373a* $250.00

Arizona

Arizona became a state in Feb. 1912

Mitchell, S. A. **Arizona and New Mexico** Phila 1867 11.5 x 14.5 Ex-atlas Lithograph after engraving *From A New General Atlas Phillips (A) 850* $75.00

Lloyd, H. H. **Map of Utah, Arizona, New Mexico, Kansas, Colorado & Indian Territory** NY 1870 16.5 x 27 Ex-atlas Lithograph after engraving *Issued as a supplement to state and county atlases* $225.00

Colton, J. W. & G. W. **New Mexico and Arizona** NY 1873 17 x 25 Ex-atlas Lithograph after engraving *From Colton's General Atlas Phillips (A) 866* $150.00

Mitchell, S. A. **New Mexico and Arizona** Phila 1874 13 x 11 Ex-atlas Lithograph after engraving *From A New General Atlas* $75.00

Colton, J. W. & G. W. **Colton's Map of New Mexico and Arizona** NY 1877 20 x 24 Folding Map Lithograph after engraving *Cloth or leather folder* $450.00

Mitchell, S. A. **County and Township Map of Arizona and New Mexico** Phila 1881 15 x 22 Ex-atlas Lithograph after engraving *From a New General Atlas Phillips (A) 895* $85.00

Bradley **Arizona and New Mexico** Phila 1886 14.5 x 22 Ex-atlas Lithograph *From New General Atlas See Phillips (A) 920* $75.00

Bradley **County and Township Map of Arizona and New Mexico** Phila 1887 14 x 22 Ex-atlas Lithograph *From New General Atlas See Phillips (A) 920* $85.00

Rand McNally & Co. **Arizona** Chicago 1887 19 x 13 Ex-atlas Wax engraving *From Indexed Atlas of the World* $85.00

Arkansas

Arkansas became a state in June 1836

• Carey & Lea **Geographical, ...Historical Map of Arkansas Territory** Phila 1822-23 17.5 x 22 Ex-atlas HC engraving *Complete Historical, Chronological and Geographical American Atlas Phillips (A) 1373a Illustrated* $475.00

Lucas, Fielding **Arkansas Territory** Baltimore 1823 11.5 X 14.5 Ex-atlas HC engraving *From A General Atlas Phillips (A) 742* $350.00

Burr, David H. **Arkansas** NY 1835 11 x 13 Ex-atlas HC engraving *From The Universal Atlas Phillips (A) 1379a* $175.00

Bradford, T. G. **Arkansas** Boston 1838 11 x 14 Ex-atlas HC engraving *From An Illustrated Atlas* $100.00

Bradford & Goodrich **Arkansas** Boston 1842 11.5 x 14 Ex-atlas HC engraving *From Universal Illustrated Atlas Phillips (A) 783* $125.00

Greenleaf **Arkansas** Brattleboro 1842 11 x 13 Ex-atlas HC engraving *From New General Atlas Phillips (A) 784* $175.00

Tanner, Henry S. **A New Map of Arkansas With Its Canals, Roads...** Phila 1842 14 x 11.5 Ex-atlas HC engraving *From A New Universal Atlas* $150.00

Morse & Breese **Arkansas** NY 1844-46 12 x 14.5 Ex-atlas Cerographic prtd color *From North American Atlas Phillips (A) 1383* $100.00

Mitchell, S. A. **A New Map of Arkansas With Its Canals, Roads Distances** Phila 1848 15 x 12 Ex-atlas HC engraving *From A New Universal Atlas* $95.00

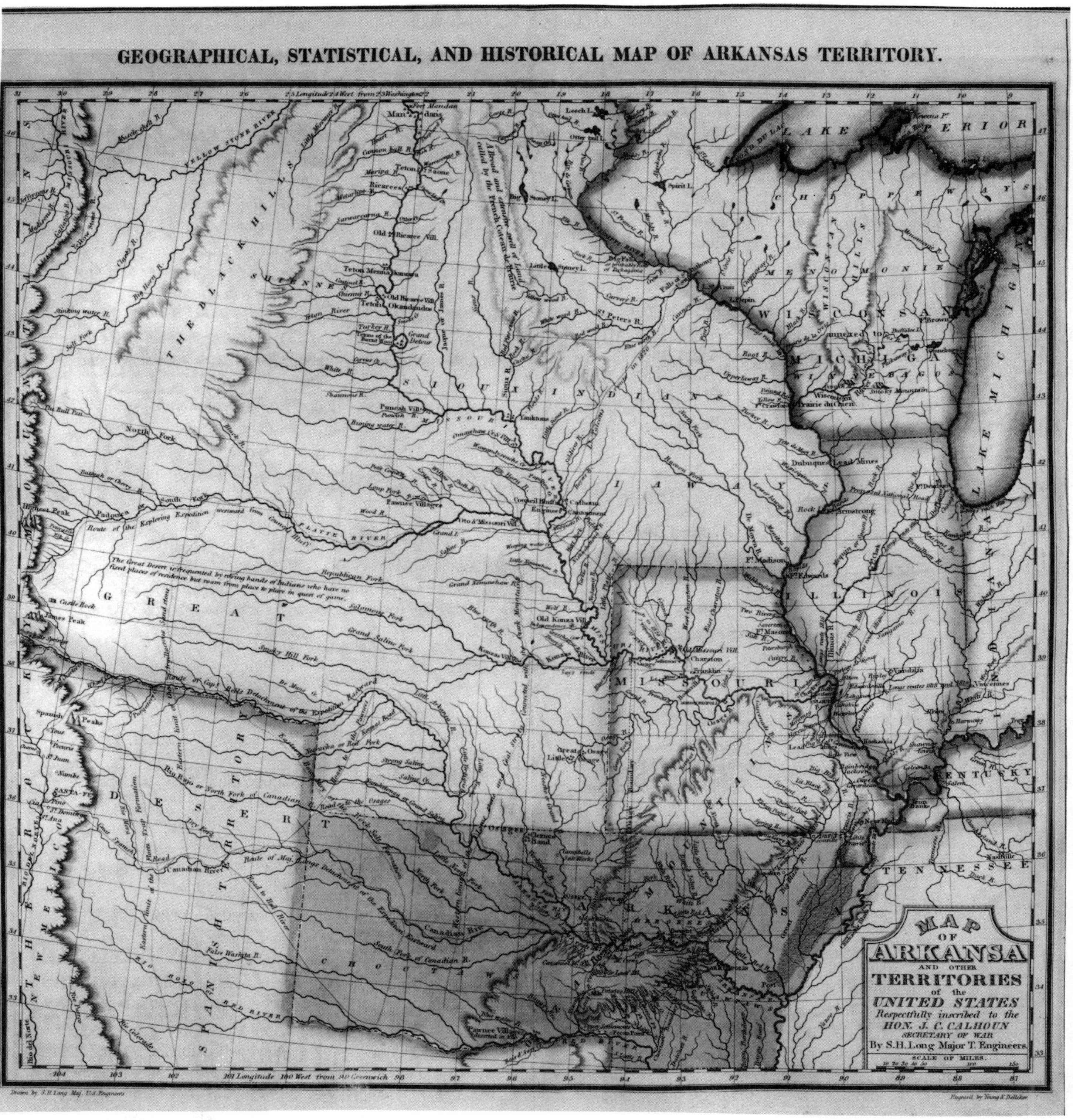

Carey & Lea ***Geographical, ...Historical Map of Arkansas Territory*** *Phila 1822-23 17.5 x 22 Ex-atlas HC engraving From A Complete Historical, Chronological and Geographical American Atlas Phillips (A) 1373*

Thomas, Cowperthwait & Co**A New Map ofArkansas With Its Canals, Roads...**Phila185414.5 x 12Ex-atlas HC engraving*From A New Universal Atlas Phillips (A)813*$95.00

Colton, J. W. & G. W.**Arkansas**NY1855-5615 x 18Ex-atlasLithograph after engraving*From Colton's Atlas of the WorldPhillips (A)816*$95.00

Desilver**A New Map ofArkansas With Its Counties, Towns...**Phila1856-5716 x 13.5Ex-atlasHC Engraving *From A New Universal AtlasPhillips (A)823*$125.00

Johnson & Browning**Johnson'sArkansas, Mississippi, Louisiana**NY186123 x 17Ex-atlasLithograph after engraving*Johnson's New Illustrated Family Atlas* $75.00

Asher & Adams**Arkansas and Portion of Indian Territory**NY187216.5 x 22.5Ex-atlasLithograph*Asher & Adams New Statistical and Topographical Atlas Phillips(A)1272*$85.00

Mitchell, S. A.**County Map of Arkansas, Mississippi and Louisiana**Phila187421 x 13.5Ex-atlasLithograph after engraving*From A New General Atlas* $50.00

Baltimore

Melish, J.**Baltimore, Annapolis and Adjacent Country** Phila18347 x 5Ex-atlasHC engraving $85.00

• Lucas, Fielding**Plan ofBaltimore**Baltimore184014.5 X 20.5Folding MapHC engraving *Illustrated*$475.00

Bradford, T. G.**Baltimore**Boston183811.5 x 14.5Ex-atlasHC engraving*From An Illustrated Atlas* $125.00

Bradford & Goodrich**Baltimore**Boston184111.5 x 14.5 Ex-atlasHC engraving*From Universal Illustrated Atlas Phillips (A) 783*$100.00

Bradford, T. G.**Baltimore**Boston184211.5 x 14.5Ex-atlasHC engraving*Another issue.* $100.00

Colton, J. W. & G. W.**Baltimore**NY1855-5615 x 18 Ex-atlasLithograph after engraving*From Colton's Atlas of the WorldPhillips (A)816*$150.00

Mitchell, S. A.**Plan ofBaltimore**Phila18609 x 11Ex-atlasLithograph after engraving*From A New General AtlasPhillips (A)831*$60.00

Weishampel**New and Enlarged Map ofBaltimore City...**Baltimore187224.5 x 28.5Folding Map Lithograph $500.00

Gray**Gray's New Map ofBaltimore**NY187815 x 12.5 Ex-atlasLithograph after engraving $75.00

Boston

Melish, J.**Boston and Adjacent Country**Phila1818-227 x 4Ex-atlasHC engraving*Engraved for J. Melish's Description of the United States* $85.00

Bradford, T. G.**Boston**Boston184211.5 x 14.5Ex-atlas HC engraving*From An Illustrated Atlas* $175.00

• Colton, J. W. & G. W.**Boston and Adjacent Cities** NY1855-5615 x 18Ex-atlasLithograph after engraving *From Colton's Atlas of the WorldPhillips (A)816 Illustrated*$125.00

Mitchell, S. A.**Plan ofBoston**Phila186013 x 11Ex-atlas Lithograph after engraving*From A New General Atlas Phillips (A)831*$75.00

Railway Map Publishing Co.**Map ofBoston**Boston1877 26 x 20Folding MapLithograph $95.00

Gray**Boston and Adjacent Cities**NY188116.5 x 22Ex-atlasLithograph after engraving $75.00

British Possessions

Carey & Lea**Geographical... Map ofBritish Possessions**Phila1822-2317.5 x 22Ex-atlasHC engraving*Complete Historical, Chronological and Geographical American AtlasPhillips (A) 1373a*$250.00

California

California became a state in Sept. 1850. Mexican Cession 1848

Mitchell, S. A.**Oregon and Upper California**Phila 1845-4916 x 13Ex-atlasHC engraving*From A New Universal Atlas* $375.00

Mitchell, S. A.**Map of the State of California...Territories of Oregon and Utah...New Mexico**Phila1845-5016 x 13Ex-atlasHC engraving *From A New Universal Atlas* $375.00

Lawson, J. T.**Lawson's Map... of the Gold Regionsof Upper California**NY184915 x 21Folding MapHC engraving $2,000.00

( )**Map of the Gold Regions of California** NY 1849 28 x 21Folding MapHC engraving $6,000.00

Mitchell, S. A.**Oregon, Upper California and New Mexico**Phila1849-5016 x 13Ex-atlasHC engraving *From A New Universal Atlas* $375.00

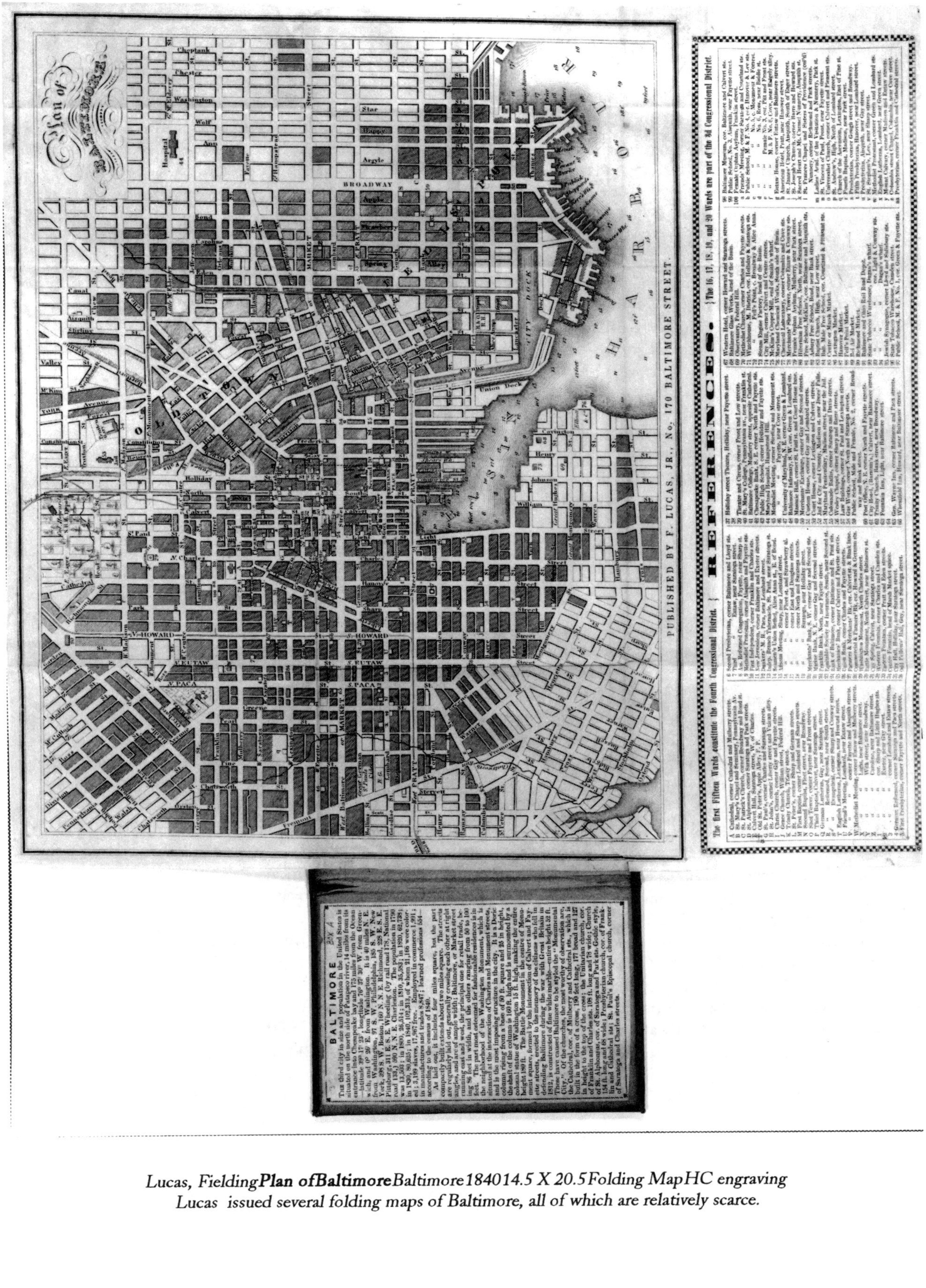

Lucas, Fielding ***Plan of Baltimore*** *Baltimore 1840 14.5 X 20.5 Folding Map HC engraving*
Lucas issued several folding maps of Baltimore, all of which are relatively scarce.

Thomas, Cowperthwait & Co **A New Map of California...Oregon, Washington, Utah & New Mexico** Phila 1850-52 15.5 x 12.5 Ex-atlas HC engraving *From A New Universal Atlas Phillips (A) 807* $475.00

Colton, J. W. **California** NY 1854 15.5 x 12 Folding Map HC engraving *Cloth folder* $1,250.00

Colton, J. W. & G. W. **California** NY 1855-56 15 x 18 Ex-atlas Lithograph after engraving *From Colton's Atlas of the World Phillips (A) 816* $175.00

Desilver **A New Map of the State of California, Territories of Oregon, Washington, Utah & New Mexico** Phila 1856-59 15.5 x 12.5 Ex-atlas HC Engraving *Baltimore: Cushing & Bailey Phillips (A) 823* $400.00

Colton, J. W. & G. W. **California** NY 1857 15 x 12 Ex-atlas Lithograph after engraving *From Colton's General Atlas* $125.00

Colton, J. W. & G. W. **Oregon, Washington, Idaho, California, Utah and New Mexico** NY 1858 13 x 11 Ex-atlas Lithograph after engraving *From Colton's General Atlas Phillips (A) 827* $175.00

Colton, J. W. & G. W. **California** NY 1860 13 x 10 Ex-atlas Lithograph after engraving *Shows 39 counties* $95.00

Johnson & Browning **Johnson's California, Territories of New Mexico and Utah** NY 1861 18 x 24 Ex-atlas Lithograph after engraving *Johnson's New Illustrated Family Atlas Illustrated* $150.00

• Johnson & Ward **Johnson's California, Territories of Utah, Nevada, Colorado, New Mexico...** NY 1864 18 x 24 Ex-atlas Lithograph after engraving $150.00

Mitchell, S. A. **County Map of California** Phila 1864 13.5 x 10.5 Ex-atlas Lithograph after engraving *From A New General Atlas* $95.00

Frey, A. C. **Topographical Railroad & County Map of ... California and Nevada** NY 1868 38.5 x 30.5 Folding Map Lithograph after engraving $850.00

Asher & Adams **Asher & Adams California & Nevada. North (and) South** NY 1872 16.5 x 22.5 Ex-atlas Lithograph *Asher & Adams New Statistical and Topographical Atlas. 2 sheets. Phillips (A) 1272* $175.00

Lloyd, H. H. **California and Nevada** NY 1872 15.5 x 12 Ex-atlas Lithograph after engraving *Issued as a supplement to state and county atlases* $150.00

Colton, J. W. & G. W. **Colton's California & Nevada** NY 1873 25 x 17 Folding Map Lithograph after engraving *Cloth or leather folder* $500.00

Colton, J. W. & G. W. **Colton's California and Nevada** NY 1873 29 x 17 Ex-atlas Lithograph after engraving *From Colton's General Atlas Phillips (A) 866* $125.00

Gray **Gray's Atlas Map of California, Nevada, Utah, Colorado, Arizona & New Mexico** NY 1873 15.5 x 25.5 Ex-atlas Lithograph after engraving *From Atlas of the United States. Based on Colton* $125.00

Mitchell, S. A. **County Map of the State of California** Phila 1873 23 x 15 Ex-atlas Lithograph after engraving *From A New General Atlas Phillips (A) 870* $95.00

Gray **Gray's California and Nevada** NY 1874 27 x 17 Ex-atlas Lithograph after engraving $100.00

Colton, J. W. & G. W. **Colton's California and Nevada** NY 1887 25 x 17 Ex-atlas Lithograph after engraving *From Colton's General Atlas* $100.00

Wilson & Co. **Indexed Sectional Map of Southern California** SF 1895 22 x 38.5 Folding Map Lithograph $500.00

Charleston

Melish, J. **Charleston and Adjacent Country** Phila 1834 7 x 5 Ex-atlas HC engraving $85.00

Colton, J. W. & G. W. **Savanah & Charleston** NY 1855-56 15 x 18 Ex-atlas Lithograph after engraving *From Colton's Atlas of the World* $95.00

Chicago

Colton, J. W. & G. W. **St. Louis & Chicago** NY 1855-56 15 x 18 Ex-atlas Lithograph after engraving *From Colton's Atlas of the World* $95.00

Colton, J. W. **City of Chicago, Illinois** NY 1856 12.5 x 8.5 Folding Map HC engraving *Cloth folder* $850.00

Mitchell, S. A. **Chicago** Phila 1867 13 x 11 Ex-atlas Lithograph after engraving *From A New General Atlas* $65.00

Mitchell, S. A. **Plan of Chicago** Phila 1874 11 x 9 Ex-atlas Lithograph after engraving *From A New General Atlas* $75.00

Gray **Chicago** NY 1876 15.5 x 12.5 Ex-atlas Lithograph after engraving $75.00

Mitchell, S. A. **Chicago** Phila 1879 22 x 14 Ex-atlas Lithograph after engraving *First edition of this map. From a New General Atlas* $85.00

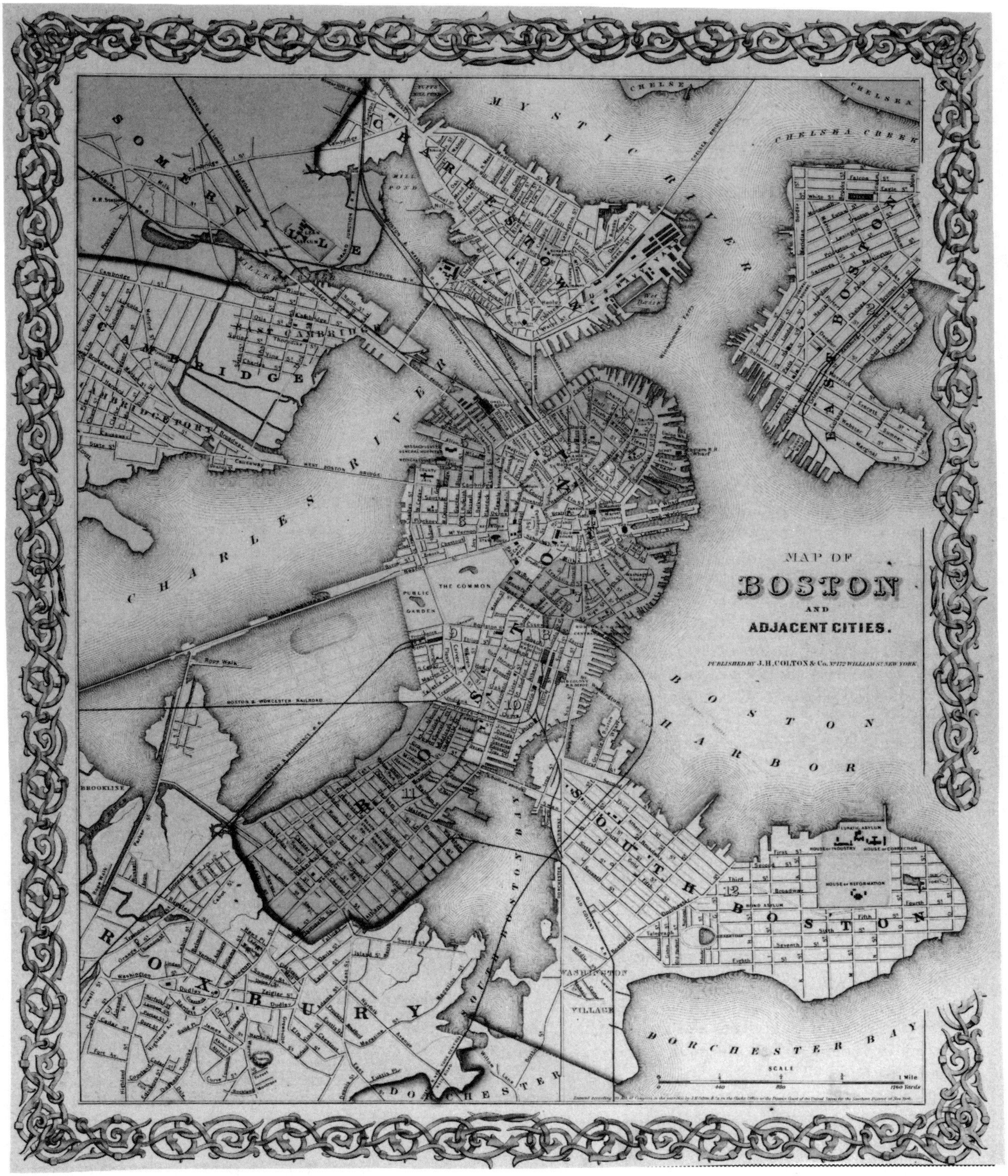

Colton, J. W. & G. W. **Boston and Adjacent Cities** *NY 1855-56 15 x 18 Ex-atlas Lithograph after engraving From Colton's Atlas of the World. A typical example of the city maps from this atlas, often considered the last of the elegantly produced American atlases.*

Cincinnati

Colton, J. W. & G. W. **Pittsburgh & Cincinnati** NY 1855-56 15 x 18 Ex-atlas Lithograph after engraving *From Colton's Atlas of the World* **$95.00**

Mitchell, S. A. **Plan of Cincinnati** Phila 1860 10.5 x 11 Ex-atlas Lithograph after engraving *From A New General Atlas* **$60.00**

Mitchell, S. A. **Plan of Cincinnati and Vicinity** Phila 1874 10.5 x 11 Ex-atlas Lithograph after engraving *From A New General Atlas* **$60.00**

Civil War

Aschbach **Pocket Map Showing the Probable Theatre of War** Phila 1861 15 x 13 Folding Map HC engraving **$800.00**

Disturnell **Army Map of the Seat of War in Virginia, Showing Battlefields, Fortifications...** Phila 1861 27 x 25 Folding Map HC engraving *Cloth folder* **$850.00**

• Johnson & Browning **Johnson's New Military Map of the United States** NY 1861 17 x 23 Ex-atlas Lithograph after engraving *Johnson's New Illustrated Family Atlas. U.S. in States* Illustrated **$175.00**

Johnson & Ward **Johnson's New Military Map of the United States** NY 1861 17 x 23 Ex-atlas Lithograph after engraving *U.S. in States. Variant Scrollwork border* **$175.00**

Johnson & Ward **Johnson's New Military Map of the United States** NY 1862 17 x 23 Ex-atlas Lithograph after engraving *Variant Scrollwork border. U.S. in Military Depts.* **$175.00**

Asher & Co. **The Historical War Map** Baltimore 1862 24 x 33 Folding Map HC engraving *Imprint of E. F. Hazelton, Baltimore* **$600.00**

Colton, J. W. & G. W. **Colton's... Map of the Seat of War in Virginia, Maryland, &c.** NY 1862 26.5 x 19 Folding Map Lithograph after engraving *Cloth or leather folder* **$1,000.00**

Colton, J. W. & G. W. **Colton's New ...Map of the States of Virginia. Maryland and Delaware...** NY 1862 30.5 x 44.5 Folding Map Lithograph after engraving *Cloth or leather folder* **$750.00**

Asher & Co. **The Historical War Map** Baltimore 1863 24 x 33 Folding Map HC engraving *Imprint of Barnitz, Cincinnati. With 72p text* **$600.00**

Colorado

Colorado became a state in August 1876

Mitchell, S. A. **Map of Kansas, Nebraska and Colorado** Phila 1860 11.5 x 14 Ex-atlas Lithograph after engraving *From A New General Atlas* **$150.00**

• Mitchell, S. A. **Map of Kansas, Nebraska and Colorado** Phila 1861 11 x 13 Ex-atlas Lithograph after engraving *Showing Also Eastern Portion of Idaho. From a New General Atlas* Illustrated **$85.00**

• Johnson & Ward **Johnson's Nebraska, Dakota, Colorado, Montana & Kansas** NY 1862 12 x 15 Ex-atlas Lithograph after engraving *Johnson's New Illustrated Family Atlas* Illustrated **$95.00**

Mitchell, S. A. **Map of Kansas, Nebraska and Colorado** Phila 1867 11 x 14 Ex-atlas Lithograph after engraving *Showing Southern Portion of Dacotah. From a New General Atlas* **$85.00**

Lloyd, H. H. **Map of Utah, Arizona, New Mexico, Kansas, Colorado & Indian Territory** NY 1870 16.5 x 27 Ex-atlas Lithograph after engraving *Issued as a supplement to state and county atlases* **$225.00**

Mitchell, S. A. **County Map of Dakota, Wyoming, Kansas, Nebraska and Colorado** Phila 1870 19.5 x 15 Ex-atlas Lithograph after engraving *From A New General Atlas* **$95.00**

Mitchell, S. A. **County Map of Kansas, Nebraska, Colorado, Dakota, Wyoming** Phila 1872 20 x 14 Ex-atlas Lithograph after engraving *From A New General Atlas* **$125.00**

Colton, J. W. & G. W. **Colton's Utah & Colorado** NY 1872-72 12.5 x 16 Ex-atlas Lithograph after engraving *From Colton's General Atlas* **$125.00**

Colton, J. W. & G. W. **Colorado, Utah, &c.** NY 1873 13 x 16 Ex-atlas Lithograph after engraving *From Colton's General Atlas Phillips (A) 866* **$125.00**

Mitchell, S. A. **County Map of Colorado, Wyoming, Dakota, Montana** Phila 1874-78 19.5 x 14 Ex-atlas Lithograph after engraving *From A New General Atlas* **$95.00**

Gray **Colorado** NY 1878 12 x 15 Ex-atlas Lithograph after engraving **$85.00**

Mitchell, S. A. **Colorado** Phila 1878-87 12 x 15 Ex-atlas Lithograph after engraving *From A New General Atlas* **$85.00**

Rand McNally & Co. **Colorado** Chicago 1883 19 x 13 Ex-atlas Wax engraving *From Indexed Atlas of the World* **$75.00**

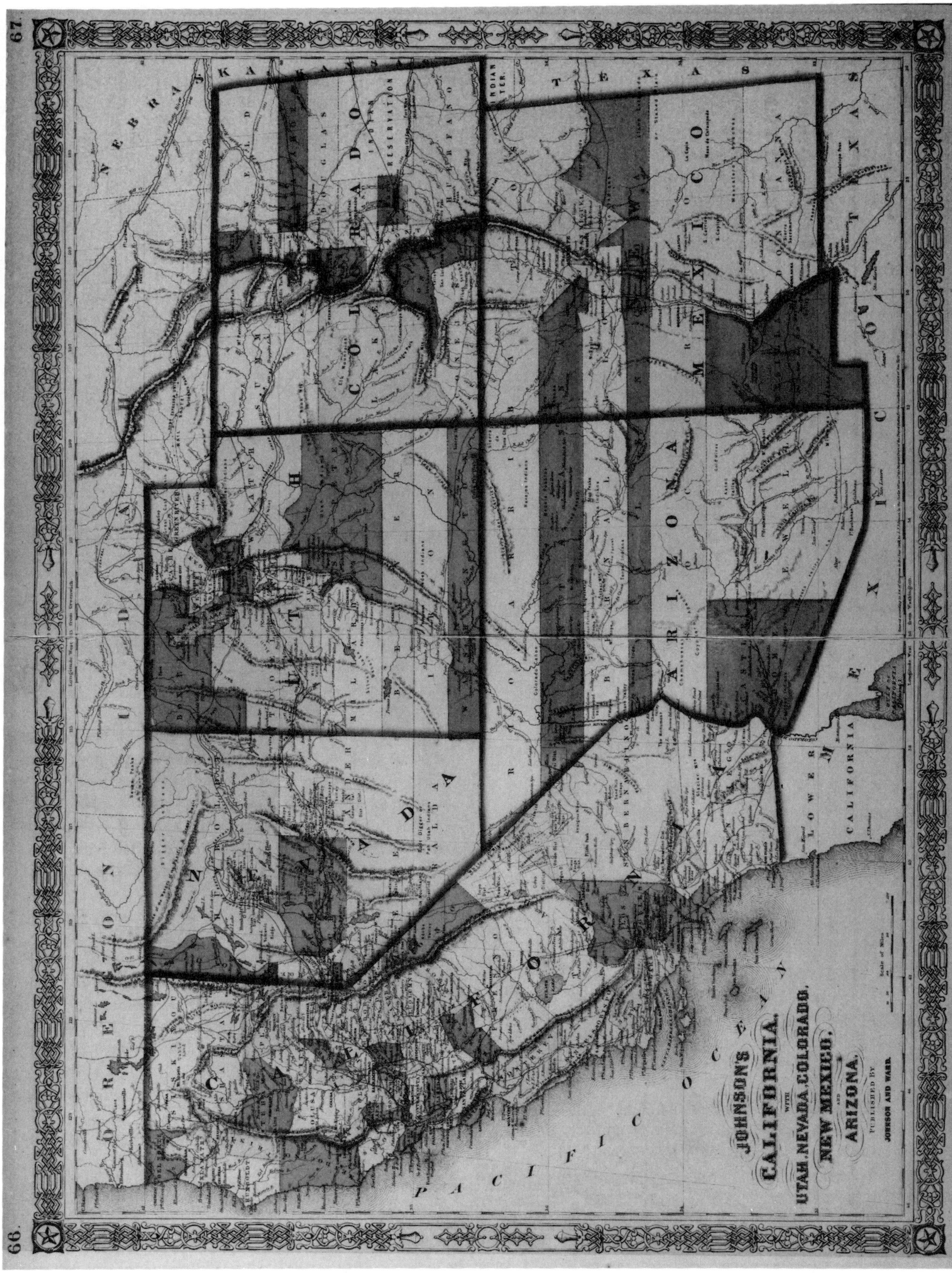

Johnson & Ward ***Johnson's California, Territories of Utah, Nevada, Colorado, New Mexico...*** *NY 1864 18 x 24 Ex-atlas Lithograph after engraving. California became a state in Sept. 1850, Nevada in Oct., 1864, Utah in Jan., 1896, New Mexico in Jan., 1912. Probably the first depiction of Nevada as a state. See Phillips (M) 461*

Bradley **Colorado** Phila 1887 17 x 21 Ex-atlas Lithograph *From New General Atlas See Phillips (A) 920* $100.00

Colton, J. W. & G. W. **Wyoming, Colorado and Utah** NY 1887 17 x 25 Ex-atlas Lithograph after engraving *From Colton's General Atlas* $125.00

Bradley **Colorado** Phila 1889 17 x 21 Ex-atlas Lithograph *From New General Atlas See Phillips (A) 920* $100.00

Rand McNally & Co. **Indexed County and Township Map of Colorado** Chicago 1901 19 x 26 Folding Map Wax engraving $95.00

Connecticut

Connecticut became a state in 1788

Carey, Matthew **Connecticut** Phila 1805 6 x 7.5 Ex-atlas UC engraving *From the Pocket Atlas Phillips (A) 1368 Illustrated* $150.00

Carey & Lea **Geographical, ...Historical Map of Connecticut** Phila 1822-23 17.5 x 22 Ex-atlas HC engraving *Complete Historical, Chronological and Geographical American Atlas Phillips (A) 1373a* $275.00

Lucas, Fielding **Connecticut** Baltimore 1823 11.5 X 14.5 Ex-atlas HC engraving *From A General Atlas Phillips (A) 742* $225.00

Finley, A. **Connecticut** Phila 1831-34 8.5 x 11 Ex-atlas HC engraving $125.00

Tanner, Henry S. **Connecticut** Phila 1836 11 x 14 Ex-atlas HC engraving *One railroad shown Phillips (A) 774* $150.00

Bradford, T. G. **Connecticut** Boston 1838 11.5 x 14.5 Ex-atlas HC engraving *From An Illustrated Atlas* $100.00

Morse & Breese **Connecticut** NY 1846 11 x 14 Ex-atlas Cerographic prtd color *From North American Atlas Phillips (A) 1228,8* $100.00

Mitchell, S. A. **Connecticut** Phila 1848 12.5 x 15 Ex-atlas HC engraving *From A New Universal Atlas* $85.00

Colton, J. W. & G. W. **Connecticut** NY 1855-56 15 x 18 Ex-atlas Lithograph after engraving *From Colton's Atlas of the World Phillips (A) 816* $95.00

Desilver **Map of Connecticut** Phila 1856-57 12.5 x 14.5 Ex-atlas HC Engraving *From A New Universal Atlas Phillips (A) 823* $85.00

Gray **Gray's Atlas Map of Connecticut With Portions of New York & Rhode Island** NY 1874 14 x 17.5 Ex-atlas Lithograph after engraving $75.00

Dakota

North Dakota and South Dakota became states in Nov. 1889

Colton, J. W. & G. W. **Minnesota and Dakota** NY 1860 13 x 16 Ex-atlas Lithograph after engraving *From Colton's General Atlas* $85.00

Mitchell, S. A. **Minnesota and Dacotah** Phila 1860 10.5 x 13.5 Ex-atlas Lithograph after engraving *First edition of this map. From a New General Atlas Phillips (A) 831* $125.00

Johnson & Browning **Johnson's Minnesota & Dakota** NY 1861 13 x 16 Ex-atlas Lithograph after engraving *Johnson's New Illustrated Family Atlas* $75.00

• Johnson & Ward **Johnson's Nebraska, Dakota, Colorado, Montana & Kansas** NY 1862 12 x 15 Ex-atlas Lithograph after engraving *Johnson's New Illustrated Family Atlas* Illustrated $95.00

Johnson & Ward **Johnson's Minnesota & Dakota** NY 1864 12 x 15 Ex-atlas Lithograph after engraving *Johnson's New Illustrated Family Atlas Phillips (A) 843* $75.00

Johnson & Ward **Johnson's Nebraska, Dakota, Idaho, Montana and Wyoming** NY 1865 17 x 23 Ex-atlas Lithograph after engraving *Johnson's New Illustrated Family Atlas* $125.00

Johnson & Ward **Johnson's Nebraska, Dakota, Idaho and Montana** NY 1867 17 x 23 Ex-atlas Lithograph after engraving *Johnson's New Illustrated Family Atlas* $95.00

Colton, J. W. & G. W. **Dakota and Wyoming** NY 1868-72 13.5 x 16.5 Ex-atlas Lithograph after engraving *From Colton's General Atlas Phillips (A) 856* $150.00

Mitchell, S. A. **County Map of Dakota, Wyoming, Kansas, Nebraska and Colorado** Phila 1870 19.5 x 15 Ex-atlas Lithograph after engraving *From A New General Atlas* $95.00

Lloyd, H. H. **Nebraska, and the Territories of Dakota, Idaho, Montana, Wyoming** NY 1872 15.5 x 24.5 Ex-atlas Lithograph after engraving *Issued as a supplement to state and county atlases* $225.00

Mitchell, S. A. **County Map of Kansas, Nebraska, Colorado, Dakota, Wyoming** Phila 1872 20 x 14 Ex-atlas Lithograph after engraving *From A New General Atlas* $125.00

Gray **Dakota** NY 1873 15.5 x 12.5 Ex-atlas Lithograph after engraving $100.00

Colton, J. W. & G. W. **Dakota** NY 1873-1887 16 x 13 Ex-atlas Lithograph after engraving *From Colton's General Atlas Phillips (A) 866* $85.00

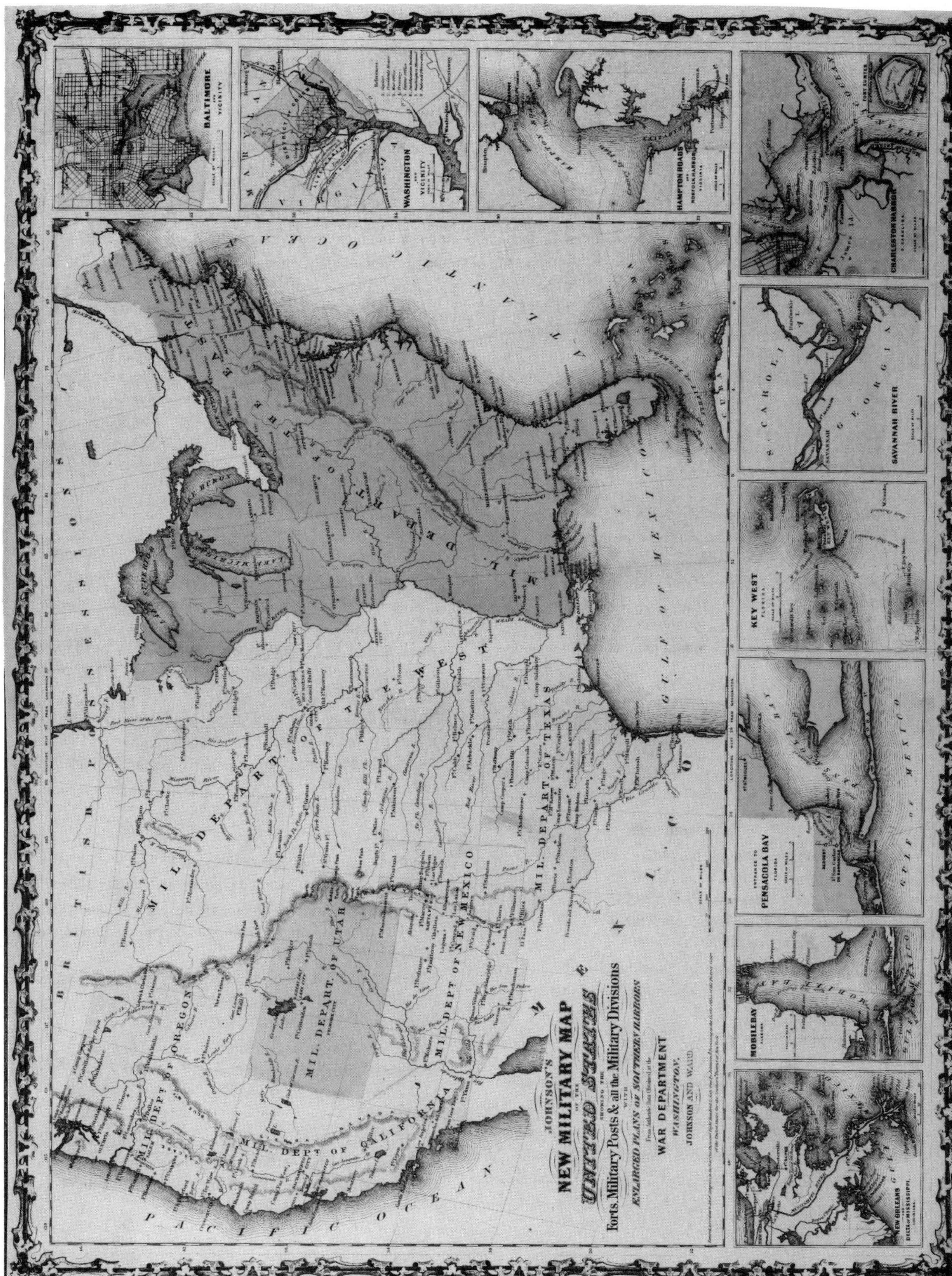

Johnson & Browning ***Johnson's New Military Map of the United States*** *NY 1861 17 x 23 Ex-atlas Lithograph after engravingJohnson's New Illustrated Family Atlas. The United States shown in Military Departments, with inset maps of Southern Harbors. Another version of this map shows the U.S. in states.*

Mitchell, S. A. **County Map of Colorado, Wyoming, Dakota, Montana** Phila 1874-78 19.5 x 14 Ex-atlas Lithograph after engraving *From A New General Atlas* $95.00

Rice, G. J. **Rice's Sectional Map of Dakota** St. Paul 1874-78 32 x 26 Folding Map Lithograph after engraving *Cloth folder* $750.00

Asher & Adams **Asher & Adams Dakota** NY 1875 22.5 x 16.5 Ex-atlas Lithograph *Asher & Adams New Statistical and Topographical Atlas* $85.00

Mitchell, S. A. **Territory of Dakota** Phila 1879 14 x 12 Ex-atlas Lithograph after engraving *From A New General Atlas* $85.00

Rand McNally & Co. **Indexed County and Township Map of Dakota** Chicago 1882 28 x 22 Folding Map Wax engraving $95.00

Bradley **County and Township Map of Dakota** Phila 1887 15 x 12.5 Ex-atlas Lithograph *From New General Atlas See Phillips (A) 920* $85.00

Mitchell, S. A. **County and Township Map of Dakota** Phila 1887 15 x 12 Ex-atlas Lithograph after engraving *From A New General Atlas* $85.00

Delaware

Delaware became the first state in the union in Dec. 1787

• Carey, Matthew **Delaware** Phila 1795 16 x 9 Ex-atlas UC engraving *From Carey's American Edition of Guthrie's Geography... Illustrated* $500.00

Morse, J. **Map of the States of Maryland and Delaware by J. Denison** Phila 1796 7 x 9.5 Ex-atlas Engraving $200.00

Carey, Matthew **Delaware** Phila 1801 8 x 6 Ex-atlas UC engraving *From the Pocket Atlas* $150.00

Arrowsmith & Lewis **Delaware** Phila 1804 10.5 x 8.5 Ex-atlas Engraving *From New and Elegant General Atlas Phillips (A) 702* $150.00

Arrowsmith & Lewis **Delaware** Boston 1805 10.5 x 8.5 Ex-atlas Engraving *From New and Elegant General Atlas Phillips (A) 708* $150.00

Carey, Matthew **Delaware, from the Best Authorities** Phila 1814 16 x 9 Ex-atlas HC engraving *From the General Atlas Phillips (A) 722* $400.00

Arrowsmith & Lewis **Delaware** Boston 1819 10.5 x 8.5 Ex-atlas Engraving *Phila: John Conrad & Co. Phillips (A) 734* $150.00

Tanner, Henry S. **Virginia, Maryland and Delaware** Phila 1820-23 20.5 x 29 Ex-atlas HC engraving *From American Atlas* $750.00

Carey & Lea **Geographical, ... Historical Map of Delaware** Phila 1822-23 17.5 x 22 Ex-atlas HC engraving *Complete Historical, Chronological and Geographical American Atlas Phillips (A) 1373a* $225.00

Lucas, Fielding **Delaware** Baltimore 1823 14.5 X 11.5 Ex-atlas HC engraving *From A General Atlas Phillips (A) 742* $225.00

Finley, A. **Delaware** Phila 1829 11.5 x 8.5 Ex-atlas HC engraving *From New General Atlas Phillips (A) 752* $175.00

Mitchell, S. A. **Map of Pennsylvania, New Jersey and Delaware** Phila 1832 17 x 21 Folding Map HC engraving *Cloth or leather covers* $300.00

Burr, David H. **Delaware & Maryland** NY 1836 12 x 15 Ex-atlas HC engraving *From The Universal Atlas Phillips (A) 1379a* $175.00

Tanner, Henry S. **A New Map of Maryland and Delaware With Their Canals, Roads...** Phila 1836 11 x 14 Ex-atlas HC engraving *From Universal Atlas Phillips (A) 774* $175.00

Bradford, T. G. **Delaware** Boston 1838 14.5 x 11.5 Ex-atlas HC engraving *From An Illustrated Atlas* $125.00

Bradford & Goodrich **Delaware** Boston 1838-46 14.5 x 11.5 Ex-atlas HC engraving *From Universal Illustrated Atlas Phillips (A) 783* $100.00

Mitchell, S. A. **A New Map of Maryland and Delaware** Phila 1850 13 x 16 Ex-atlas HC engraving *From A New Universal Atlas* $75.00

Thomas, Cowperthwait & Co **A New Map of Maryland and Delaware** Phila 1850-54 10 x 13.5 Ex-atlas HC engraving *From A New Universal Atlas Phillips (A) 800* $95.00

Colton, J. W. & G. W. **Delaware and Maryland** NY 1855-56 15 x 18 Ex-atlas Lithograph after engraving *From Colton's Atlas of the World Phillips (A) 816* $95.00

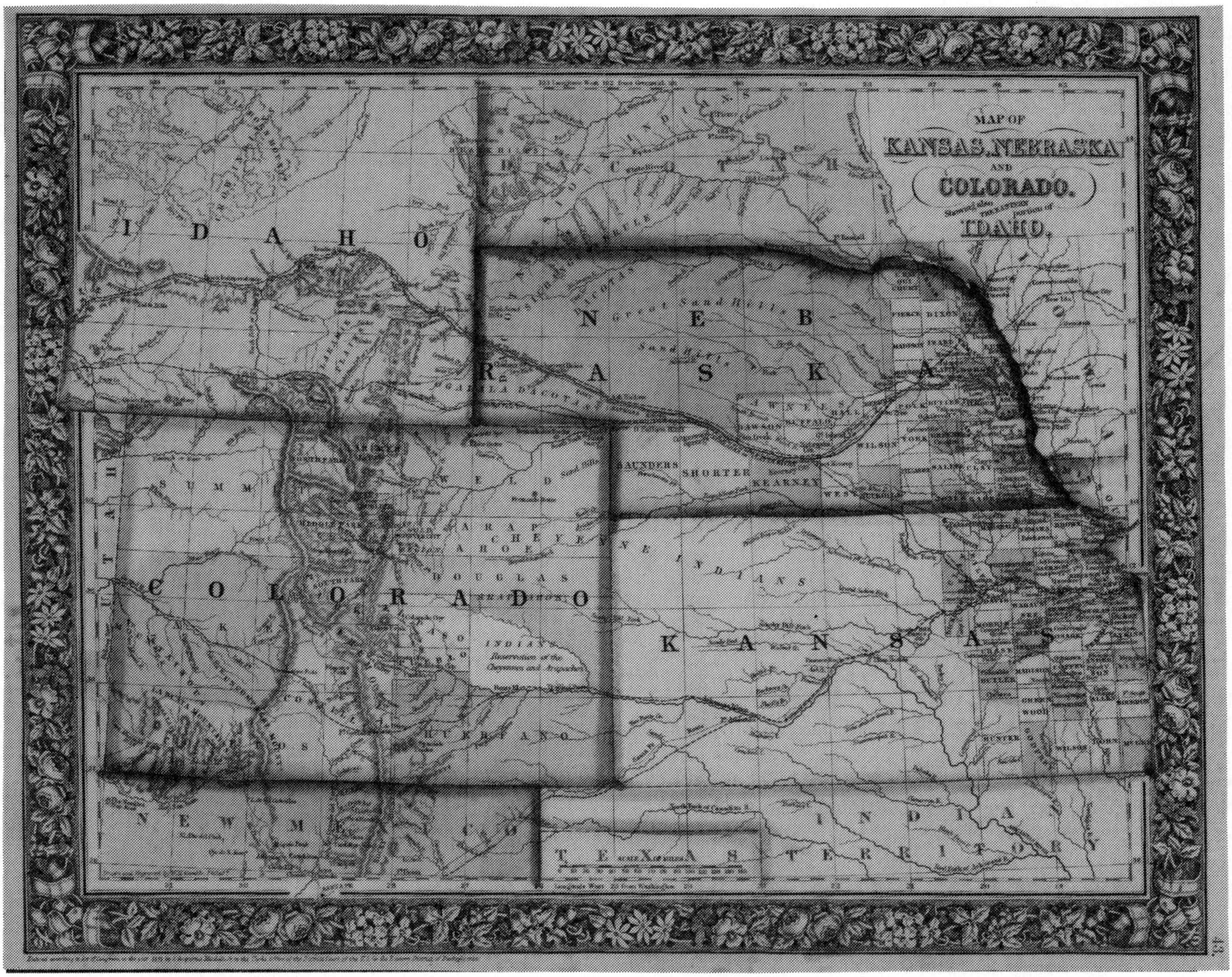

Mitchell, S. A. ***Map of Kansas, Nebraska and Colorado*** *Phila 1861 11 x 13 Ex-atlas Lithograph after engraving Showing Also Eastern Portion of Idaho. From A New General Atlas. Kansas in the first year of statehood*

Colton, J. W. & G. W. **Delaware and Maryland** NY 1855-56 15 x 18 Ex-atlas Lithograph after engraving *From Colton's Atlas of the World Phillips (A) 816* $95.00

Johnson & Browning **Johnson's Delaware and Maryland** NY 1861 12 x 17 Ex-atlas Lithograph after engraving *Johnson's* $65.00

Johnson & Browning **Johnson's Pennsylvania, Virginia, Delaware, Maryland** NY 1861 17 x 23 Ex-atlas Lithograph after engraving *Johnson's New Illustrated Family Atlas* $85.00

Map of ... Virginia. Maryland and Delaware...East Tennessee...Military Sta.. NY 1862 30.5 x 44.5 Folding Map Lithograph after engraving *Cloth or leather folder* $750.00

Colton, J. W. & G. W. **Colton's New Topographical Map of ... Virginia, West Virginia, Maryland & Delaware...** NY 1870 28 x 42 Folding Map Lithograph after engraving *Cloth folder* $450.00

Rand McNally & Co. **Indexed County and Township Map of Maryland and Delaware** Chicago 1890 13 x 19.5 Folding Map Wax engraving $85.00

Detroit

Mitchell, S. A. **Plan of Detroit** Phila 1879 10 x 14 Ex-atlas Lithograph after engraving *From A New General Atlas* $60.00

Florida

Florida became a state in 1845. Ceded by Spain in 1819

Carey & Lea **Geographical, ... Historical Map of Florida** Phila 1822-23 17.5 x 22 Ex-atlas HC engraving *Complete Historical, Chronological and Geographical American Atlas Phillips (A) 1373a* $325.00

Lucas, Fielding **Florida** Baltimore 1823 11.5 X 14.5 Ex-atlas HC engraving *From A General Atlas Phillips (A) 742* $275.00

Tanner, Henry S. **Map of Florida** Phila 1823 27 x 21 Ex-atlas HC engraving *From A New American Atlas* $975.00

Finley, A. **Map of Florida According to the Latest Authorities (with) West Indies** Phila 1827 na Folding Map HC engraving *Leather folder* $1,000.00

• Tanner, Henry S. **Florida** Phila 1833 16 x 13 Ex-atlas HC engraving *From The Universal Atlas Illustrated* $275.00

Burr, David H. **Map of the Territory of Florida** NY 1834-36 13 x 11 Ex-atlas HC engraving *From The Universal Atlas Phillips (A) 1379a* $250.00

Bradford, T. G. **Florida** Boston 1838 14 x 13 Ex-atlas HC engraving *From An Illustrated Atlas* $150.00

Burr, David H. **Map of Florida** Washington 1839 50 x 35 Folding Map HC engraving $1,500.00

Goodrich **Florida** Boston 1841 15 x 13 Ex-atlas HC engraving $275.00

Bradford & Goodrich **Florida** Boston 1846 14.5 x 11.5 Ex-atlas HC engraving *From Universal Illustrated Atlas Phillips (A) 783* $150.00

Mitchell, S. A. **Florida** Phila 1846 14.5 x 11.5 Ex-atlas HC engraving *From A New Universal Atlas* $225.00

Thomas, Cowperthwait & Co **Map of Florida** Phila 1850-55 16 x 13 Ex-atlas HC engraving *From A New Universal Atlas Phillips (A) 807* $100.00

Colton, J. W. & G. W. **Florida** NY 1855-56 15 x 18 Ex-atlas Lithograph after engraving *From Colton's Atlas of the World Phillips (A) 816* $95.00

Johnson & Browning **Johnson's Florida** NY 1861 12 x 16 Ex-atlas Lithograph after engraving *Johnson's New Illustrated Family Atlas* $85.00

Johnson & Ward **Johnson's Florida** NY 1863-64 12 x 16 Ex-atlas Lithograph after engraving *Johnson's New Illustrated Family Atlas Phillips (A) 840* $85.00

Mitchell, S. A. **County Map of Florida** Phila 1867 10.5 x 13.5 Ex-atlas Lithograph after engraving *From A New General Atlas* $75.00

Mitchell, S. A. **County Map of Florida** Phila 1869 10.5 x 13.5 Ex-atlas Lithograph after engraving *From A New General Atlas* $75.00

Asher & Adams **Florida** NY 1872 16.5 x 22.5 Ex-atlas Lithograph *Asher & Adams New Statistical and Topographical Atlas Phillips(A) 1272* $75.00

Mitchell, S. A. **County Map of Florida** Phila 1872 10.5 x 13.5 Ex-atlas Lithograph after engraving *From A New General Atlas* $75.00

Colton, J. W. & G. W. **Florida** NY 1877 17 x 28 Ex-atlas Lithograph after engraving *From Colton's General Atlas* $125.00

Bradley **County Map of Florida** Phila 1887 12 x 15 Ex-atlas Lithograph *From New General Atlas See Phillips (A) 920* $95.00

Rand McNally & Co. **Florida Railroads** Chicago 1895 19 x 27 Ex-atlas Wax engraving $85.00

Rand McNally & Co. **New Business Map of Florida** Chicago 1898 21.5 x 27.5 Folding Map Wax engraving $85.00

Georgia

Carey, Matthew **Georgia** Phila 1795 9 x 15.5 Ex-atlas HC engraving *From Carey's American Edition of Guthrie's Geography...* $650.00

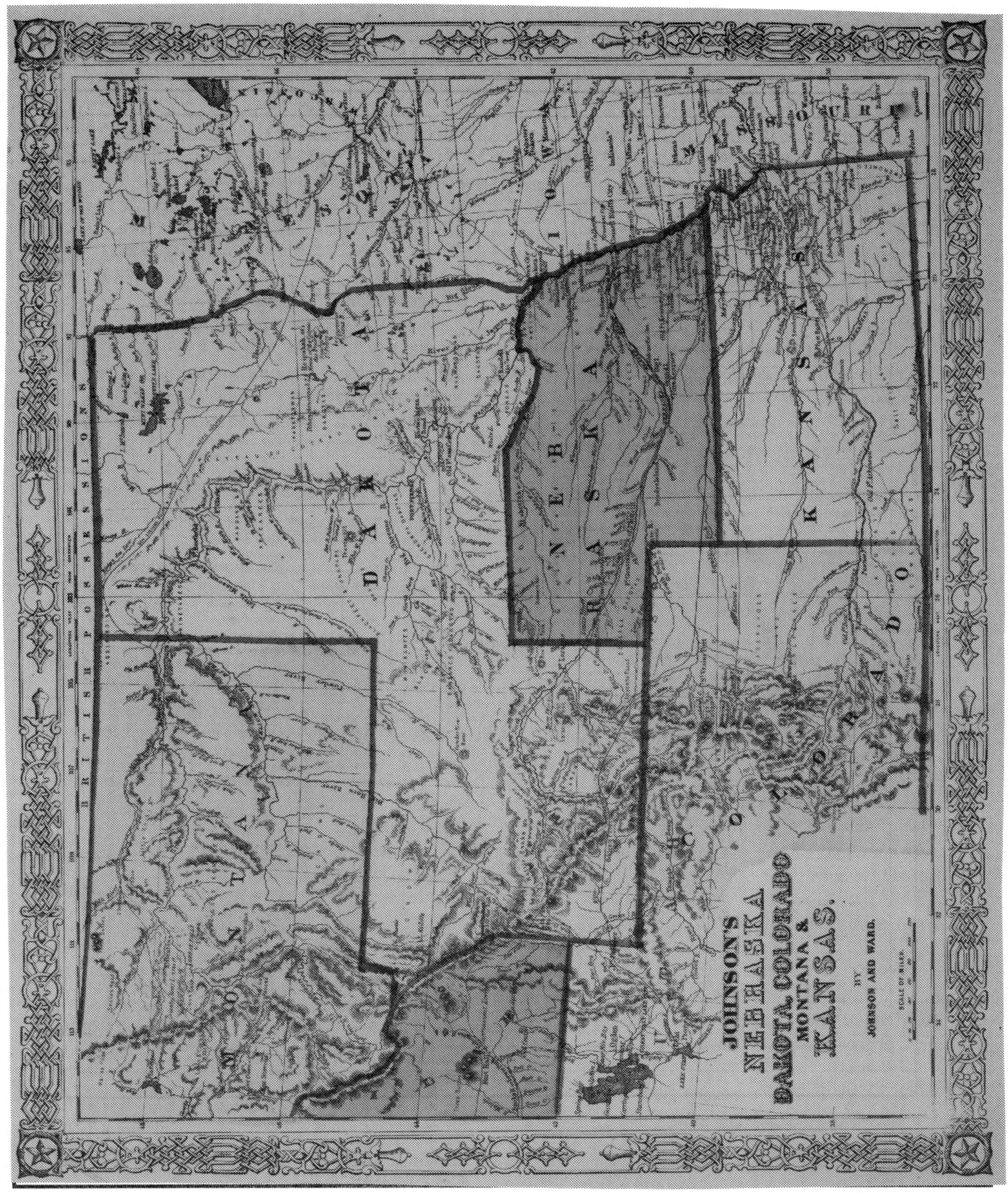

Johnson & Ward ***Johnson's Nebraska, Dakota, Colorado, Montana & Kansas*** *NY 1862 12 x 15 Ex-atlas Lithograph after engraving From Johnson's New Illustrated Atlas. Colorado became a state in August 1876, North Dakota and South Dakota became states in Nov. 1889, Kanas became a state in Jan. 1861, Nebraska became a state in March 1867, Montana became a state in Nov. 1889*

Morse, J. **A Correct Map of the Georgia Western Territory** Phila 1797 7 x 6 Ex-atlas Engraving *Wheat & Brun 618* $250.00

Arrowsmith & Lewis **Georgia** Phila 1804 8.5 x 10.5 Ex-atlas Engraving *From New and Elegant General Atlas Phillips (A) 702* $150.00

Carey, Matthew **Georgia** Phila 1805 8 x 6 Ex-atlas HC engraving *From the Pocket Atlas Phillips (A) 1368* $200.00

Carey, Matthew **Mississippi Territory & Georgia** Phila 1805 6 x 8 Ex-atlas UC engraving *From the Pocket Atlas Phillips (A) 1368* $250.00

Tanner, Henry S. **Georgia and Alabama** Phila 1819-23 20 x 27 Ex-atlas HC Engraving *From American Atlas* $850.00

Carey & Lea **Geographical, ... Historical Map of Georgia** Phila 1822-23 17.5 x 22 Ex-atlas HC engraving *Complete Historical, Chronological and Geographical American Atlas Phillips (A) 1373a* $250.00

Lucas, Fielding **Georgia** Baltimore 1823 14.5 X 11.5 Ex-atlas HC engraving *From A General Atlas Phillips (A) 742* $225.00

Burr, David H. **Georgia** NY 1836 13 x 11 Ex-atlas HC engraving *From The Universal Atlas* $175.00

Tanner, Henry S. **A New Map of Georgia With Its Roads and Distances** Phila 1833-36 13 x 10.5 Ex-atlas HC engraving *From A New Universal Atlas Phillips (A) 774 Illustrated* $175.00

Bradford, T. G. **Georgia** Boston 1838 10 x 8 Ex-atlas HC engraving *From a Comprehensive Atlas* $85.00

Bradford & Goodrich **Georgia** Boston 1841 14.5 x 11.5 Ex-atlas HC engraving *From Universal Illustrated Atlas Phillips (A) 783* $125.00

Mitchell, S. A. **A New Map of Georgia With Its Canals, Roads, Distances** Phila 1847 14 x 12 Ex-atlas HC engraving *From A New Universal Atlas* $95.00

Thomas, Cowperthwait & Co **A New Map of Georgia With Its Roads and Distances** Phila 1850 14 x 11.5 Ex-atlas HC engraving *From A New Universal Atlas Phillips (A) 800* $95.00

Colton, J. W. & G. W. **Georgia** NY 1855-56 15 x 18 Ex-atlas Lithograph after engraving *From Colton's Atlas of the World Phillips (A) 816* $95.00

Desilver **A New Map of the State of Georgia Exhibiting Its Internal Improvements** Phila 1856-57 16 x 13 Ex-atlas HC Engraving *From A New Universal Atlas Phillips (A) 823* $95.00

Mitchell, S. A. **County Map of Georgia and Alabama** Phila 1860 12.5 x 15 Ex-atlas Lithograph after engraving *From A New General Atlas* $50.00

Johnson & Browning **Johnson's Georgia & Alabama** NY 1861 17 x 23 Ex-atlas Lithograph after engraving *Johnson's New Illustrated Family Atlas* $75.00

Mitchell, S. A. **County Map of Georgia and Alabama** Phila 1863 12.5 x 15 Ex-atlas Lithograph after engraving *From A New General Atlas* $50.00

Colton, J. W. & G. W. **Colton's Georgia** NY 1864 14 x 11 Folding Map Lithograph after engraving *Cloth or leather folder* $300.00

Colton, J. W. & G. W. **Colton's Map of the State of Georgia** NY 1866 38 x 24.5 Folding Map Lithograph after engraving *Cloth or leather folder* $850.00

Asher & Adams **Georgia & Alabama** NY 1872 16.5 x 22.5 Ex-atlas Lithograph *Asher & Adams New Statistical and Topographical Atlas* $75.00

Taintor Bros. & Merrill **Map of the State of Georgia** NY 1874 21.5 x 16.5 Ex-atlas Lithograph after engraving $95.00

Mitchell, S. A. **County Map of the States of Georgia and Alabama** Phila 1880 14 x 21.5 Ex-atlas Lithograph after engraving *From A New General Atlas* $60.00

Mitchell, S. A. **County Map of the States of Georgia and Alabama** Phila 1880 14 x 21.5 Ex-atlas Lithograph after engraving *From A New General Atlas* $60.00

Bradley **County Map of Georgia and Alabama** Phila 1887 12.5 x 20 Ex-atlas Lithograph *From New General Atlas* $65.00

Gray **Georgia** NY 1887-81 26 x 16 Ex-atlas Lithograph after engraving $85.00

Hawaii

Hawaii annexed 1898

Colton, J. W. & G. W. **Hawaiian Group or Sandwich Islands** NY 1855 16 x 13 Ex-atlas Lithograph after engraving *From Colton's Atlas of the World Phillips (A) 816* $85.00

Idaho

Idaho became a state in July 1890

Colton, J. W. & G. W. **Oregon, Washington, Idaho, California, Utah and New Mexico** NY 1858 13 x 11 Ex-atlas Lithograph after engraving *From Colton's General Atlas* $175.00

Carey, Matthew **Delaware** *Phila 1795 16 x 9 Ex-atlas UC engraving From Carey's American Edition of Guthrie's Geography Improved, originally issued in London in 1770. The American maps from this book were the basis for Carey's American Atlas, the first atlas of the United States, also issued in 1795. Delaware became the first state in the union in Dec. 1787*

Johnson & Ward**Johnson's Nebraska, Dakota, Idaho, Montana and Wyoming**NY 1865 17 x 23 Ex-atlas Lithograph after engraving *Johnson's New Illustrated Family Atlas* $125.00

Johnson & Ward**Johnson's Nebraska, Dakota, Idaho and Montana**NY 1867 17 x 23 Ex-atlas Lithograph after engraving *Johnson's New Illustrated Family Atlas* $95.00

Lloyd, H. H. **Nebraska, and the Territories of Dakota, Idaho, Montana, Wyoming**NY 1872 15.5 x 24.5 Ex-atlas Lithograph after engraving *Issued as a supplement to state and county atlases* $225.00

Asher & Adams **Asher & Adams Idaho, Montana Western Portion** NY 1875 16.5 x 22.5 Ex-atlas Lithograph *Asher & Adams New Statistical and Topographical Atlas* $125.00

Colton, J. W. & G. W. **Montana, Idaho & Wyoming** NY 1876-77 17.5 x 25 Ex-atlas Lithograph after engraving *From Colton's General Atlas Phillips (A)879* $150.00

Mitchell, S. A. **Territory of Idaho** Phila 1880 14.5 x 10.5 Ex-atlas Lithograph after engraving *From A New General Atlas* $95.00

Mitchell, S. A. **Territory of Idaho** Phila 1885 15 x 12.5 Ex-atlas Lithograph after engraving *12 Counties shown. From A New General Atlas* $85.00

Bradley **County and Township Map of Montana, Idaho and Wyoming** Phila 1887 15.5 x 23.5 Ex-atlas Lithograph *From New General Atlas See Phillips (A)920* $95.00

Colton, J. W. & G. W. **Montana, Idaho & Wyoming** NY 1887 17.5 x 25 Ex-atlas Lithograph after engraving *From Colton's General Atlas* $125.00

Illinois

Illinois became a state in Dec., 1818

• Carey & Lea **Geographical, ... Historical Map of Illinois** Phila 1822-23 17.5 x 22 Ex-atlas HC engraving *Complete Historical, Chronological and Geographical American Atlas Phillips (A) 1373a Illustrated* $295.00

Lucas, Fielding **Illinois** Baltimore 1823 14.5 X 11.5 Ex-atlas HC engraving *From A General Atlas Phillips (A) 742* $295.00

Tanner, Henry S. **Illinois and Missouri** Phila 1823 28 x 22.5 Ex-atlas HC engraving *From A New American Atlas See Phillips (M)327* $975.00

Finley, A. **Illinois** Phila 1824-26 11.5 x 8.5 Ex-atlas HC engraving *From New General Atlas Phillips (A)1378* $175.00

Finley, A. **Illinois** Phila 1834 18.5 x 13 Ex-atlas HC engraving *Inset map of "Lead Mine Region" (Michigan & Wisc.) Phillips (M)327* $275.00

Mitchell, S. A. **Tourist's Pocket Map of the State of Illinois...** Phila 1834 15 x 12.5 Folding Map HC engraving $600.00

• Bradford, T. G. **Missouri, Illinois and Iowa** Boston 1835 10.5 x 8 Ex-atlas HC Engraving *From a Comprhensive Atlas* $150.00

Burr, David H. **Illinois** NY 1836 15 x 12 Ex-atlas HC engraving *From The Universal Atlas Phillips (A) 1379a Phillips (M) 327* $200.00

Bradford, T. G. **Illinois** Boston 1838 14.5 x 11.5 Ex-atlas HC engraving *From An Illustrated Atlas* $100.00

Tanner, Henry S. **A New Map of Illinois With Its Proposed Canals, Roads...** Phila 1841 14 x 11.5 Ex-atlas HC engraving *From A New Universal Atlas* $175.00

Mitchell, S. A. **A New Map of Illinois With Its Proposed Canals, Roads and Distances** Phila 1847 16 x 13 Ex-atlas HC engraving *From A New Universal Atlas* $95.00

Greenleaf **Illinois** Brattleboro 1848 11 x 13 Ex-atlas HC engraving *From A New Universal Atlas* $175.00

Thomas, Cowperthwait & Co **A New Map of the State of Illinois With Its Proposed Canals, Roads...** Phila 1851-54 15.5 x 13.5 Ex-atlas HC engraving *From A New Universal Atlas Phillips (A) 807* $95.00

Colton, J. W. **New Sectional Map of the State of Illinois** NY 1852 30 x 25 Folding Map HC Engraving *Cloth or leather folder* $500.00

Colton, J. W. **Map of Illinois** NY 1854 14 x 11 Folding Map HC Engraving *Cloth folder* $325.00

Peck, J. **A New Sectional Map of the State of Illinois** 1854 35.5 x 26.5 Folding Map HC engraving *Cloth or leather folder* $1,250.00

Colton, J. W. & G. W. **Illinois** NY 1855-56 15 x 18 Ex-atlas Lithograph after engraving *From Colton's Atlas of the World Phillips (A)816* $95.00

Desilver **A New Map of the State of Illinois** Phila 1856-57 15.5 x 13 Ex-atlas HC Engraving *From A New Universal Atlas Phillips (A)823* $100.00

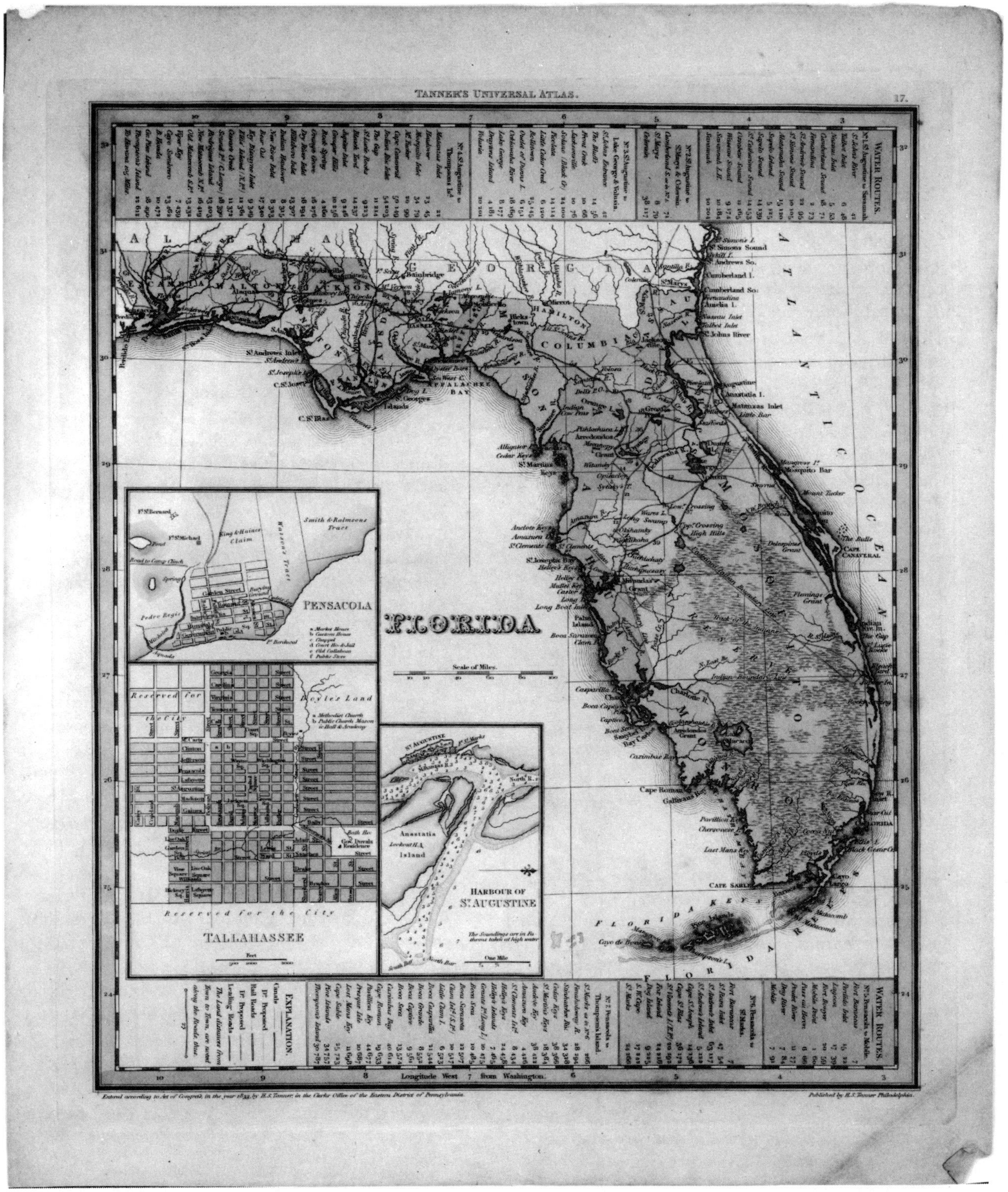

Tanner, Henry S. **Florida** Phila 1833 16 x 13 Ex-atlas HC engraving From The Universal Atlas
Florida became a state in 1845. Ceded by Spain in 1819

Chapman **Chapman's Sectional Map ofIllinois** Milwaukee 1857 38.5 x 23 Folding Map HC engraving *Cloth folder* $750.00

Chapman **Chapman's Township Map ofIllinois** Milwaukee 1857 17 x 13.5 Folding Map HC engraving *Cloth folder* $450.00

Johnson & Browning **Johnson's Illinois** NY 1861 17 x 13 Ex-atlas Lithograph after engraving *Johnson's New Illustrated Family Atlas* $75.00

Mitchell, S. A. **State of Illinois** Phila 1861 13 x 11 Ex-atlas Lithograph after engraving *From A New General Atlas* $60.00

Asher & Adams **Illinois** NY 1872 22.5 x 16.5 Ex-atlas Lithograph *Asher & Adams New Statistical and Topographical Atlas Phillips(A)1272* $75.00

Mitchell, S. A. **County Map of Illinois** Phila 1874 13.5 x 10.5 Ex-atlas Lithograph after engraving *From A New General Atlas* $50.00

Indian Territory

See Oklahoma

Gray **Gray's New Map ofTexas and Indian Territory** NY 1881 17 x 26.5 Ex-atlas Lithograph after engraving *7 Insets* $250.00

Bradley **Indian Territory** Phila 1889 12.5 x 17 Ex-atlas Lithograph *From New General Atlas See Phillips (A)920* $95.00

Colton, J. W. & G. W. **Colton's Indian Territory** NY 1867-68 13 x 16 Ex-atlas Lithograph after engraving *From Colton's General Atlas* $175.00

Lloyd, H. H. **Map ofUtah, Arizona, New Mexico, Kansas, Colorado & Indian Territory** NY 1870 16.5 x 27 Ex-atlas Lithograph after engraving *Issued as a supplement to state and county atlases* $225.00

Colton, J. W. & G. W. **Indian Territory** NY 1872-73 13 x 16 Ex-atlas Lithograph after engraving *From Colton's General Atlas Phillips (A) 866* $125.00

Asher & Adams **Asher & Adams Indian Territory and Texas North West Portion** NY 1875 16.5 x 22.5 Ex-atlas Lithograph *Asher & Adams New Statistical and Topographical Atlas* $95.00

Cram, George F. **Railroad and Twonship Map of Indian Ty.** Chicago 1875 19.5 x 14 Ex-atlas Lithograph *From New Commercial Atlas of the U.S. and Territories* $200.00

Gray **Gray's New Map of Texas and Indian Territory** NY 1875 24 x 16 Ex-atlas Lithograph after engraving *From National Atlas* $225.00

Mitchell, S. A. **Indian Territory** Phila 1879-87 11 x 13.5 Ex-atlas Lithograph after engraving *From A New General Atlas* $75.00

Colton, J. W. & G. W. **Colton's Indian Territory** NY 1887 13 x 16 Ex-atlas Lithograph after engraving *From Colton's General Atlas* $125.00

Indiana

also see Ohio & Michigan

Indiana became a state in Dec. 1816.

Tanner, Henry S. **Ohio and Indiana** Phila 1819-23 21 x 26 Ex-atlas HC engraving *From A New American Atlas* $650.00

Carey & Lea **Geographical, ... Historical Map of Indiana** Phila 1822-23 17.5 x 22 Ex-atlas HC engraving *Complete Historical, Chronological and Geographical American Atlas Phillips (A) 1373a* $295.00

Lucas, Fielding **Indiana** Baltimore 1823 14.5 X 11.5 Ex-atlas HC engraving *From A General Atlas Phillips (A) 742* $295.00

Young, J. H. **The Tourist's Pocket Map ofIndiana** Phila 1833 15.75 x 13.25 Folding Map HC engraving $275.00

Bradford, T. G. **Indiana & Ohio** Boston 1835 8 x 10 Ex-atlas HC engraving *From a Comprehensive Atlas* $85.00

Burr, David H. **Indiana** NY 1836 15 x 12 Ex-atlas HC engraving *From The Universal Atlas Phillips (A) 1379a* $200.00

Tanner, Henry S. **A New Map ofIndiana With Its Roads and Distances** Phila 1836 13 x 10.5 Ex-atlas HC engraving *From A New Universal Atlas Phillips (A)774* $175.00

Bradford, T. G. **Indiana** Boston 1838 14.5 x 11.5 Ex-atlas HC engraving *From An Illustrated Atlas* $125.00

Bradford & Goodrich **Indiana** Boston 1842 14.5 x 11.5 Ex-atlas HC engraving *From Universal Illustrated Atlas Phillips (A) 783* $100.00

• Greenleaf **Indiana** Brattleboro 1842 11 x 13 Ex-atlas HC engraving *From New General Atlas Phillips (A) 784* Illustrated $175.00

• Morse & Breese **Indiana** NY 1842 14 x 11 Ex-atlas Cerograph Illustrated $175.00

Tanner, Henry S. **A New Map ofGeorgia With Its Roads and Distances** *Phila 1833-36 13 x 10.5 Ex-atlas HC engravingFrom A New Universal Atlas Phillips (A)774Georgia became the 4th state in Jan 1788*

Bradford, T. G. ***Missouri, Illinois and Iowa*** *Boston 1835 10.5 x 8 Ex-atlas HC EngravingFrom a Comprehensive Atlas*

Mitchell, S. A.**A New Map ofIndiana With Its Roads and Distances**Phila184714 x 11.5Ex-atlasHC engraving *From A New Universal Atlas* $85.00

Thomas, Cowperthwait & Co**A New Map of Indiana With Its Roads and Distances**Phila185012.5 x 10Ex-atlasHC engraving*From A New Universal AtlasPhillips (A)800*$95.00

Colton, J. W. & G. W. **Indiana**NY1855-5615 x 18Ex-atlasLithograph after engraving*From Colton's Atlas of the WorldPhillips (A)816*$95.00

Desilver**A New Map ofIndiana With Its Roads and Distances...**Phila185616 x 13.5Ex-atlasHC Engraving *From A New Universal AtlasPhillips (A)823*$100.00

Desilver**A New Map ofIndiana Exhibiting Its Internal Improvements...**Phila185716 x 13.5Ex-atlasHC Engraving*From A New Universal AtlasPhillips (A)823* $100.00

Mitchell, S. A.**County Map of Ohio and Indiana**Phila 1860-6711 x 13Ex-atlasLithograph after engraving*From A New General AtlasPhillips (A)850*$50.00

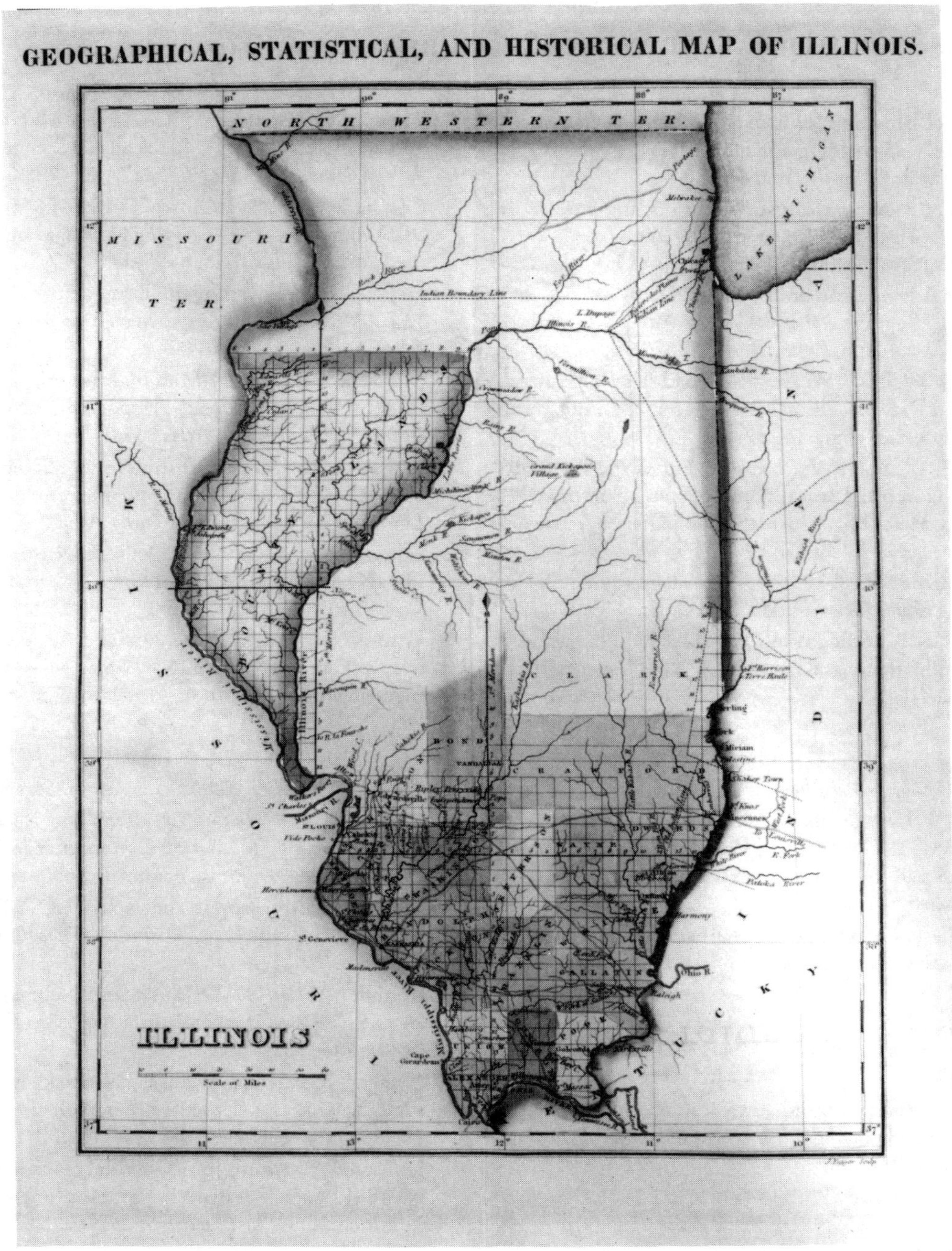

Carey & Lea **Geographical, ... Historical Map of Illinois** *Phila 1822-23 17.5 x 22 Ex-atlas HC engraving Complete Historical, Chronological and Geographical American Atlas Phillips (A) 1373a. Illinois became a state in Dec., 1818. The first separate map of the state. Phillips (M) 327. A typical Carey & Lea map shown without the surrounding text.*

Johnson & Browning **Johnson's Michigan & Indiana** NY 1861 Ex-atlas Lithograph after engraving *Johnson's New Illustrated Family Atlas* $85.00

Johnson & Browning **Johnson's Ohio & Indiana** NY 1861 17 x 23 Ex-atlas Lithograph after engraving *Johnson's New Illustrated Family Atlas* $85.00

Asher & Adams **Ohio and Indiana** NY 1872 16.5 x 22.5 Ex-atlas Lithograph *Asher & Adams New Statistical and Topographical Atlas Phillips(A)1272* $75.00

Colton, J. W. & G. W. **New Railroad Map of Indiana, Ohio and Part of Illinois** NY 1875 16 x 28 Folding Map Lithograph after engraving $75.00

Colton, J. W. & G. W. **Colton's Map of the State of Indiana Compiled from...United States Surveys...** NY 1877 40 x 26 Folding Map Lithograph after engraving *Cloth or leather folder* $500.00

Gray **Indiana** NY 1877 25 x 15.5 Ex-atlas Lithograph after engraving *Frank Gray: O. W. Gray & Son* $75.00

Mitchell, S. A. **Indiana** Phila 1884 14 x 11 Ex-atlas Lithograph after engraving *From A New General Atlas* $50.00

Iowa

also see Nebraska, Missouri

Iowa became a state in Dec. 1846

• Bradford, T. G. **Missouri, Illinois and Iowa** Boston 1835 10.5 x 8 Ex-atlas HC Engraving *From A Comprhensive Atlas* $150.00

Bradford, T. G. **Iowa and Wisconsin** Boston 1838 14.5 x 11.5 Ex-atlas HC engraving *From An Illustrated Atlas* $175.00

• Tanner, H. S. **Iowa** Phila 1841 16 x 13 Ex-atlas HC engraving *From A New Universal Atlas Illustrated* $175.00

Greenleaf **Wisconsin and Iowa** Brattleboro 1842 11 x 13 Ex-atlas HC engraving *From New General Atlas Phillips (A) 784* $275.00

Mitchell, S. A. **Iowa** Phila 1845 16 x 13 Ex-atlas HC engraving *From A New Universal Atlas* $225.00

Mitchell, S. A. **Iowa** Phila 1847 16 x 13 Ex-atlas HC engraving *From A New Universal Atlas* $125.00

Mitchell, S. A. **Iowa** Phila 1848 16 x 13 Ex-atlas HC engraving *31 Counties. From a New Universal Atlas* $125.00

Colton, J. W. **Map of Iowa** NY 1854 12.5 x 14.5 Folding Map HC Engraving *Cloth or leather folder* $325.00

Thomas, Cowperthwait & Co **A New Map of the State of Iowa** Phila 1854 13.5 x 16 Ex-atlas HC engraving *From A New Universal Atlas Phillips (A)814* $85.00

Colton, J. W. & G. W. **Iowa** NY 1855-56 15 x 18 Ex-atlas Lithograph after engraving *From Colton's Atlas of the World Phillips (A)816* $95.00

Desilver **A New Map of the State of Iowa** Phila 1856-57 13.5 x 16 Ex-atlas HC Engraving *From A New Universal Atlas Phillips (A)823* $100.00

Mitchell, S. A. **County Map of Iowa and Missouri** Phila 1860 12.5 x 15 Ex-atlas Lithograph after engraving *From A New General Atlas* $65.00

Johnson & Browning **Johnson's Iowa & Nebraska** NY 1861 16 x 13 Ex-atlas Lithograph after engraving *Johnson's New Illustrated Family Atlas* $65.00

Colton, J. W. & G. W. **Colton's Township Map of ... Iowa** NY 1863-66 16 x 22 Folding Map Lithograph after engraving *Cloth folder* $275.00

Watson **New Railroad and Distance Map of Minnesota & Iowa** Chicago 1877-83 16 x 12.5 Ex-atlas Wax engraving *From New Indexed Family Atlas* $75.00

Kansas

also see Nebraska, Western States

Kanas became a state in Jan. 1861

Whitman and Searl **Map of Eastern Kansas** Boston 1856 27 x 21 Folding Map HC engraving $650.00

Morse & Gaston **Kansas and Nebraska** NY 1857 6 x 5 Ex-atlas Cerograph *From Diamond Atlas Phillips (A)824* $60.00

Colton, J. W. & G. W. **Kansas and Nebraska** NY 1860 24 x 15 Ex-atlas Lithograph after engraving *From Colton's General Atlas* $75.00

Mitchell, S. A. **Map of Kansas, Nebraska and Colorado** Phila 1860 11.5 x 14 Ex-atlas Lithograph after engraving *From A New General Atlas* $150.00

Johnson & Browning **Johnson's Nebraska and Kansas** NY 1861 13 x 16 Ex-atlas Lithograph after engraving *Johnson's New Illustrated Family Atlas* $175.00

Johnson & Browning **Johnson's Missouri & Kansas** NY 1861 17 x 23 Ex-atlas Lithograph after engraving *3 vignettes Illustrated* $95.00

Mitchell, S. A. **Map of Kansas, Nebraska and Colorado** Phila 1861 11 x 13 Ex-atlas Lithograph after engraving *Showing Also Eastern Portion of Idaho. From a New General Atlas* $85.00

Greenleaf, J. **Indiana** Brattleboro 1842 11 x 13 Ex-atlas HC engraving From New General Atlas Phillips (A) 784 Indiana became a state in Dec. 1816. A typical map from this atlas, one of many "New General Atlases" to appear in the 1840's.

Colton, J. W. & G. W. **Kansas** NY 1866-72 16.5 x 24 Ex-atlas Lithograph after engraving *From Colton's General Atlas See Phillips (A)856* $85.00

Mitchell, S. A. **Map of Kansas, Nebraska and Colorado** Phila 1867 11 x 14 Ex-atlas Lithograph after engraving *Showing Southern Portion of Dacotah. From a New General Atlas* $85.00

Colton, J. W. & G. W. **Colton's New Sectional Map of ... Kansas** NY 1869 29 x 56 Folding Map Lithograph after engraving *Cloth folder* $650.00

Lloyd, H. H. **Map of Utah, Arizona, New Mexico, Kansas, Colorado & Indian Territory** NY 1870 16.5 x 27 Ex-atlas Lithograph after engraving *Issued as a supplement to state and county atlases* $225.00

Mitchell, S. A. **County Map of Dakota, Wyoming, Kansas, Nebraska and Colorado** Phila 1870 19.5 x 15 Ex-atlas Lithograph after engraving *From A New General Atlas* $95.00

Mitchell, S. A. **County Map of Kansas, Nebraska, Colorado, Dakota, Wyoming** Phila 1872 20 x 14 Ex-atlas Lithograph after engraving *From A New General Atlas* $125.00

Ross, E. H. **New Railroad and Sectional Map of Kansas** St. Louis 1872 23.5 x 38 Folding Map Lithograph $1,000.00

Mitchell, S. A. **County and Township Map of ... Kansas and Nebraska** Phila 1878 15 x 23 Ex-atlas Lithograph after engraving *From A New General Atlas* $85.00

Bradley **Kansas** Phila 1885 16 x 22 Ex-atlas Lithograph *From New General Atlas See Phillips (A)920* $75.00

Kentuckey

Kentucky became a state in June 1792

• Carey, Matthew **Kentuckey** Phila 1805 8 x 6 Ex-atlas HC engraving *From the Pocket Atlas Phillips (A) 1368 Illustrated* $200.00

Arrowsmith & Lewis **Kentucky** Phila 1804 8.5 x 10.5 Ex-atlas Engraving *From New and Elegant General Atlas Phillips (A)702* $175.00

Melish, J. **Kentucky** Phila 1812 8 x 14 Ex-atlas HC engraving *From Travels Through the United States Howes M496* $450.00

Carey, Matthew **Kentucky** Phila 1814 10 x 18.5 Ex-atlas HC engraving *From the General Atlas Phillips (A) 722* $400.00

Carey & Lea **Geographical, ... Historical Map of Kentucky** Phila 1822-23 17.5 x 22 Ex-atlas HC engraving *Complete Historical, Chronological and Geographical American Atlas Phillips (A) 1373a* $295.00

Lucas, Fielding **Kentucky** Baltimore 1823 14.5 X 20.5 Ex-atlas HC engraving *From A General Atlas Phillips (A) 742* $295.00

Finley, A. **Kentucky** Phila 1825 11.5 x 8.5 Ex-atlas HC engraving *From New General Atlas* $175.00

Burr, David H. **Kentucky & Tennessee** NY 1836 12 x 15 Ex-atlas HC engraving *From The Universal Atlas Phillips (A) 1379a* $150.00

Bradford, T. G. **Kentucky** Boston 1838-42 10.5 x 14 Ex-atlas HC engraving *From An Illustrated Atlas* $100.00

Burr, David H. **Map of Kentucky and Tennessee** Washington 1839 36 x 50 Folding Map HC engraving $1,500.00

Mitchell, S. A. **A New Map of Kentucky With Its Roads and Distances** Phila 1843 11.5 x 13.5 Folding Map HC engraving *Cloth or leather covers* $400.00

Mitchell, S. A. **A New Map of Kentucky With Its Roads and Distances** Phila 1846 11.5 x 14 Ex-atlas HC engraving *From A New Universal Atlas* $125.00

Tanner, Henry S. **A New Map of Kentucky With Its Roads and Distances** Phila 1846 13.5 x 16 Ex-atlas HC engraving *From A New Universal Atlas* $175.00

Colton, J. W. & G. W. **Kentucky & Tennessee** NY 1855-56 15 x 18 Ex-atlas Lithograph after engraving *From Colton's Atlas of the World Phillips (A)816* $95.00

Desilver **A New Map of Kentucky With Its Roads and Distances** Phila 1856-59 11.5 x 14 Ex-atlas HC Engraving *Baltimore: Cushing & Bailey Phillips-A-6135,28* $95.00

Johnson & Browning **Johnson's Kentucky & Tennessee** NY 1861 17 x 23 Ex-atlas Lithograph after engraving *3 vignettes* $85.00

Asher & Adams **Kentucky & Tennessee** NY 1872 16.5 x 22.5 Ex-atlas Lithograph *Asher & Adams New Statistical and Topographical Atlas Phillips(A)1272* $75.00

Mitchell, S. A. **County Map of Kentucky & Tennessee** Phila 1873 13 x 20 Ex-atlas Lithograph after engraving *From A New General Atlas Phillips (A) 870* $60.00

Bradley **Kentucky and Tennessee** Phila 1888 14 x 21 Ex-atlas Lithograph *From New General Atlas See Phillips (A)920* $65.00

Morse & Breese ***Indiana*** *NY 1842 14 x 11 Ex-atlas From the Cerographic Atlas, issued in parts 1842-1845 Cerograph, or wax engraving, from the first cerographic atlas. Wax engraving became, and continued to be, the the most widely used method for producing maps after 1870 until the mid 20th century.*

Lake Ontario

Melish, J. **East End of Lake Ontario and River St. Lawrence** Phila 1815 18 x 22 Ex-atlas HC engraving *From Military and Topographical Atlas of the United States* **$275.00**

Louisiana

Louisiana became a state in 1812

Carey, Matthew **Louisiana** Phila 1805 8 x 6 Ex-atlas UC engraving *From the Pocket Atlas Phillips (A) 1368* **$275.00**

• Carey, Matthew **Louisiana** Phila 1814 15.5 x 17.5 Ex-atlas HC engraving *From the General Atlas Phillips (A) 722 Illustrated* **$500.00**

Melish, J. **A Map of the State of Louisiana With Part of Mississippi Territory...** Phila 1816 46 x 33 Folding Map HC engraving **$2,500.00**

Carey & Lea **Geographical, ... Historical Map of Louisiana** Phila 1822-23 17.5 x 22 Ex-atlas HC engraving *Complete Historical, Chronological and Geographical American Atlas Phillips (A) 1373a* **$275.00**

Lucas, Fielding **Louisiana** Baltimore 1823 14.5 X 20.5 Ex-atlas HC engraving *From A General Atlas Phillips (A) 742* **$400.00**

Tanner, Henry S. **Louisiana and Mississippi** Phila 1825 29 x 23 Ex-atlas HC engraving *From A New American Atlas Phillips (A) 774* **$850.00**

Finley, A. **Map of Louisiana, Mississippi, and Alabama...** Phila 1827 17 x 20 Folding Map HC engraving **$850.00**

Mitchell, S. A. **Map of the States of Louisiana, Mississippi and Alabama** Phila 1835 17.5 x 21.5 Folding Map HC engraving *Cloth or leather covers* **$600.00**

Burr, David H. **Louisiana** NY 1836 12 x 15 Ex-atlas HC engraving *From The Universal Atlas Phillips (A) 1379a* **$175.00**

Bradford, T. G. **Louisiana and Part of Arkansas** Boston 1838 10 x 8 Ex-atlas HC engraving *From a Comprehensive Atlas* **$75.00**

Greenleaf **Louisiana** Brattleboro 1842 11 x 13 Ex-atlas HC engraving *From New General Atlas Phillips (A) 784* **$125.00**

Tanner, Henry S. **A New Map of Louisiana With Its Canals, Roads...** Phila 1842 11.5 x 14.5 Ex-atlas HC engraving *From A New Universal Atlas* **$150.00**

Mitchell, S. A. **A New Map of Louisiana** Phila 1850 13 x 16 Ex-atlas HC engraving *From A New Universal Atlas* **$95.00**

Thomas, Cowperthwait & Co **A New Map of Louisiana With Its Canals, Roads and Distances...** Phila 1853 11.5 x 14.5 Ex-atlas HC engraving *From A New Universal Atlas Phillips (A) 809* **$85.00**

Colton, J. W. & G. W. **Louisiana** NY 1855-56 15 x 18 Ex-atlas Lithograph after engraving *From Colton's Atlas of the World Phillips (A) 816* **$95.00**

Desilver **A New Map of Louisiana With Its Canals, Roads & Distances...** Phila 1856-57 11.5 x 14 Ex-atlas HC Engraving *From A New Universal Atlas Phillips (A) 823* **$125.00**

Mitchell, S. A. **County Map of Louisiana, Mississippi and Arkansas** Phila 1860 13.5 x 10.5 Ex-atlas Lithograph after engraving *From A New General Atlas Phillips (A) 831* **$65.00**

Johnson & Browning **Johnson's Arkansas, Mississippi, Louisiana** NY 1861 23 x 17 Ex-atlas Lithograph after engraving *Johnson's New Illustrated Family Atlas* **$75.00**

Mitchell, S. A. **Map of Louisiana, Mississippi and Arkansas** Phila 1861 15 x 12.5 Ex-atlas Lithograph after engraving *From A New General Atlas* **$50.00**

Colton, J. W. & G. W. **Colton's Map of the State of Louisiana and Eastern Part of Texas** NY 1871 30 x 39.5 Folding Map Lithograph after engraving *Cloth folder* **$650.00**

Asher & Adams **Louisiana & Mississippi** NY 1872 16.5 x 22.5 Ex-atlas Lithograph *Asher & Adams New Statistical and Topographical Atlas Phillips (A) 1272* **$75.00**

Mitchell, S. A. **County Map of Arkansas, Mississippi and Louisiana** Phila 1874 21 x 13.5 Ex-atlas Lithograph after engraving *From A New General Atlas* **$50.00**

Gray **Gray's Atlas Map of Louisiana** NY 1875 14 x 17 Ex-atlas Lithograph after engraving **$75.00**

Gray **Louisiana** NY 1878-81 16 x 26 Ex-atlas Lithograph after engraving **$75.00**

Louisville

Colton, J. W. & G. W. **Louisville & New Orleans** NY 1855-56 15 x 18 Ex-atlas Lithograph after engraving *From Colton's Atlas of the World Phillips (A) 816* **$95.00**

Gray **City of Louisville** NY 1876 12 x 14.5 Ex-atlas Lithograph after engraving **$75.00**

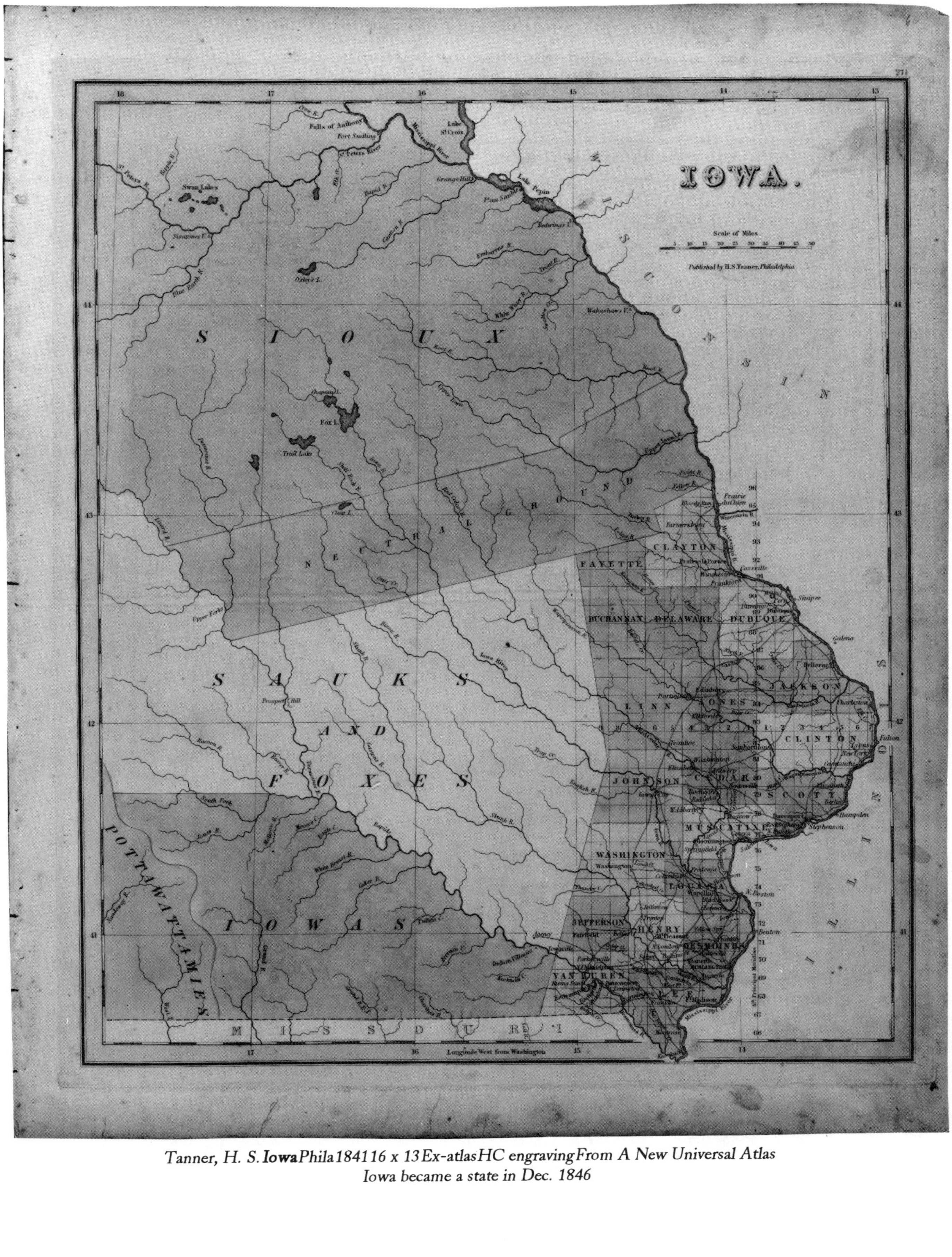

Tanner, H. S. **Iowa** Phila 1841 16 x 13 Ex-atlas HC engraving From A New Universal Atlas
Iowa became a state in Dec. 1846

Maine

Maine became a state in 1820

• Carey, Matthew **The District of Maine** Phila 1814 15.5 x 11 Ex-atlas HC engraving *From the General Atlas Phillips (A) 722 Illustrated* $375.00

Arrowsmith & Lewis **Maine** Phila 1804 8.5 x 10.5 Ex-atlas Engraving *From New and Elegant General Atlas Phillips (A) 702* $125.00

Carey, Matthew **Maine** Phila 1805 8 x 6 Ex-atlas UC engraving *From the Pocket Atlas Phillips (A) 1368* $150.00

Carey & Lea **Geographical, ... Historical Map of Maine** Phila 1822-23 17.5 x 22 Ex-atlas HC engraving *Complete Historical, Chronological and Geographical American Atlas Phillips (A) 1373a* $225.00

Lucas, Fielding **Maine** Baltimore 1823 14.5 X 11.5 Ex-atlas HC engraving *From A General Atlas Phillips (A) 742* $225.00

Tanner, Henry S. **Map of the States of Maine, New Hampshire, Vermont, Massachusetts...** Phila 1823 27 x 22 Ex-atlas HC engraving *From A New American Atlas* $750.00

Finley, A. **Map of Maine, New Hampshire and Vermont** Phila 1826 17 x 21.5 Ex-atlas HC engraving *From New American Atlas Phillips (A) 1378* $350.00

Finley, A. **Maine** Phila 1828 11.5 x 8.5 Folding Map HC engraving $225.00

Tanner, Henry S. **A New Map of Maine** Phila 1833-39 14 x 11 Ex-atlas HC engraving *From A New Universal Atlas Phillips-A-6086, 5* $150.00

Bradford, T. G. **Maine** Boston 1835 10 x 8 Ex-atlas HC engraving *From a Comprehensive Atlas* $75.00

Burr, David H. **Maine** NY 1836 15 x 12 Ex-atlas HC engraving *From The Universal Atlas Phillips (A) 1379a* $145.00

Greenleaf **Maine** Brattleboro 1842 11 x 13 Ex-atlas HC engraving *From New General Atlas Phillips (A) 784* $150.00

Greenleaf **Map of the State of Maine with the Province of New Brunswick** Brattleboro 1844 50 x 42 Wall Map HC engraving $2,000.00

Mitchell, S. A. **A New Map of Maine** Phila 1850 16 x 13 Ex-atlas HC engraving *From A New Universal Atlas* $75.00

Colton, J. W. & G. W. **Maine** NY 1855-56 15 x 18 Ex-atlas Lithograph after engraving *From Colton's Atlas of the World Phillips (A) 816* $95.00

Desilver **A New Map of Maine** Phila 1856-59 15.5 x 12.5 Ex-atlas HC Engraving *From A New Universal Atlas Phillips (A) 823* $85.00

Mitchell, S. A. **County Map of the State of Maine** Phila 1860 10.5 x 13.5 Ex-atlas Lithograph after engraving *From A New General Atlas Phillips (A) 831* $60.00

Johnson & Browning **Johnson's Maine** NY 1861 17 x 13 Ex-atlas Lithograph after engraving *Johnson's New Illustrated Family Atlas* $60.00

Walling **Map of the State of Maine** Portland 1862 61 x 63 Wall Map HC Engraving $600.00

Colton, J. W. & G. W. **Colton's Maine** NY 1877 17 x 13 Folding Map Lithograph after engraving *Cloth or leather folder* $150.00

Colby **Map of the State of Maine** Houlton 1889 33.5 x 25 Folding Map Lithograph *Cloth folder* $325.00

Maryland

Maryland became a state in 1788

Carey, Matthew **The State of Maryland, From the Best Authorities** Phila 1795 17 x 21 Ex-atlas UC engraving *From Carey's American Edition of Guthrie's Geography...* $700.00

Morse, J. **Map of the States of Maryland and Delaware by J. Denison** Phila 1796 7 x 9.5 Ex-atlas Engraving $200.00

Carey, Matthew **Maryland** Phila 1801 6 x 8 Ex-atlas UC engraving *From the Pocket Atlas* $200.00

Arrowsmith & Lewis **Maryland** Phila 1804 8.5 x 10.5 Ex-atlas Engraving *From New and Elegant General Atlas Phillips (A) 702* $150.00

Arrowsmith & Lewis **Maryland** Boston 1805 8.5 x 10.5 Ex-atlas Engraving *From New and Elegant General Atlas Phillips (A) 708* $150.00

Arrowsmith & Lewis **Maryland** Boston 1819 8.5 x 10.5 Ex-atlas Engraving *From New and Elegant General Atlas Phillips (A) 734* $150.00

Tanner, Henry S. **Virginia, Maryland and Delaware** Phila 1820-23 20.5 x 29 Ex-atlas HC engraving *From American Atlas* $750.00

Carey & Lea **Geographical, ... Historical Map of Maryland** Phila 1822-23 17.5 x 22 Ex-atlas HC engraving *Complete Historical, Chronological and Geographical American Atlas Phillips (A) 1373a* $295.00

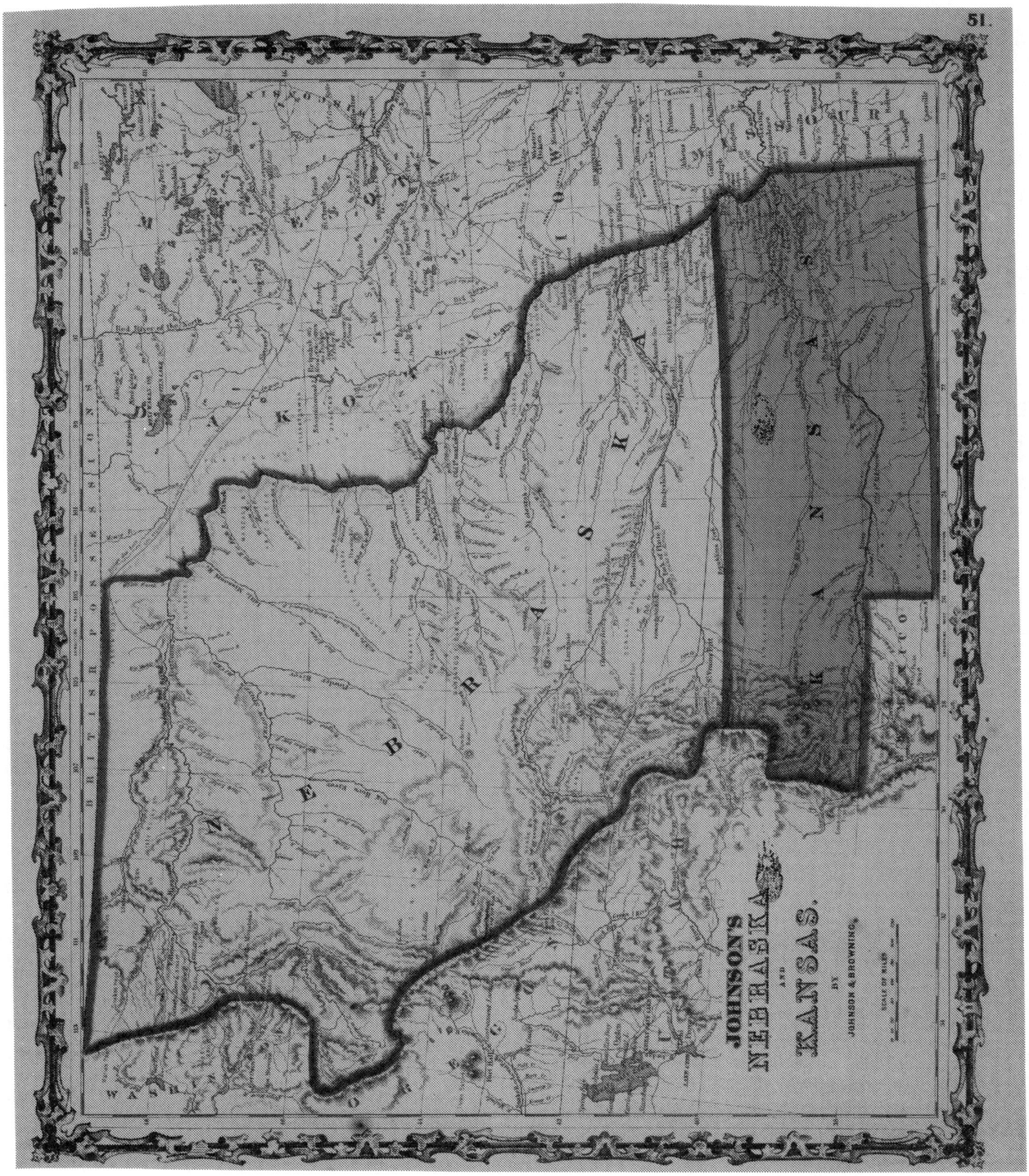

Johnson & Browning ***Johnson's Nebraska and Kansas*** *NY1861 13 x 16 Ex-atlas Lithograph after engraving From Johnson's New Illustrated Family Atlas. Kanas became a state in Jan. 1861, Nebraska became a state in March 1867*

Lucas, Fielding **Maryland-City of Baltimore** Baltimore 1823 14.5 X 20.5 Ex-atlas HC engraving *From A General Atlas Phillips (A) 742* $375.00

Finley, A. **Maryland** Phila 1825 8.5 x 11 Ex-atlas HC engraving *From New General Atlas Phillips (A)1378* $200.00

Tanner, Henry S. **A New Map of Maryland and Delaware With Their Canals, Roads...** Phila 1836 11 x 14 Ex-atlas HC engraving *From Universal Atlas* $175.00

Bradford, T. G. **Maryland** Boston 1838-41 11.5 x 14.5 Ex-atlas HC engraving *From An Illustrated Atlas* $100.00

Mitchell, S. A. **A New Map of Maryland and Delaware** Phila 1850 13 x 16 Ex-atlas HC engraving *From A New Universal Atlas* $75.00

Thomas, Cowperthwait & Co **A New Map of Maryland and Delaware** Phila 1850-54 10 x 13.5 Ex-atlas HC engraving *From A New Universal Atlas* $95.00

Colton, J. W. & G. W. **Delaware and Maryland** NY 1855-56 15 x 18 Ex-atlas Lithograph after engraving *From Colton's Atlas of the World* $95.00

Desilver **A New Map of Maryland and Delaware...** Phila 1856 11.5 x 15 Ex-atlas HC Engraving *From A New Universal Atlas Phillips (A)823* $95.00

Johnson & Browning **Johnson's Delaware & Maryland** NY 1861 12 x 17 Ex-atlas Lithograph after engraving *Johnson's New Illustrated Family Atlas* $65.00

Johnson & Browning **Johnson's Pennsylvania, Virginia, Delaware, Maryland** NY 1861 17 x 23 Ex-atlas Lithograph after engraving *Johnson's New Illustrated Family Atlas* $85.00

Colton, J. W. & G. W. **Colton's New Topographical Map of ... Virginia. Maryland and Delaware...East Tennessee...Military Sta..** NY 1862 30.5 x 44.5 Folding Map Lithograph after engraving *Cloth or leather folder* $750.00

Colton, J. W. & G. W. **Colton's New Topographical Map of ... Virginia, West Virginia, Maryland & Delaware...** NY 1870 28 x 42 Folding Map Lithograph after engraving *Cloth folder* $450.00

Rand McNally & Co. **Maryland and D. C. Delaware** Chicago 1888 12 x 18.5 Ex-atlas Wax engraving *From Indexed Atlas of the World* $75.00

Rand McNally & Co. **Indexed County and Township Map of Maryland and Delaware** Chicago 1890 13 x 19.5 Folding Map Wax engraving $85.00

Massachusets

Massachusetts became a state in 1788

Scott **Massachusetts** Phila 1795 6 x 7 Ex-atlas Engraving *From the United States Gazeteer. Wheat & Brun 216* $125.00

Arrowsmith & Lewis **Massachusetts** Phila 1804 8.5 x 10.5 Ex-atlas Engraving *From New and Elegant General Atlas Phillips (A)702* $125.00

• Carey, Matthew **Massachusetts** Phila 1805 6 x 8 Ex-atlas UC engraving *From the Pocket Atlas Phillips (A) 1368 Illustrated* $150.00

Carey & Lea **Geographical, ...Historical Map of Massachusets** Phila 1822-23 17.5 x 22 Ex-atlas HC engraving *Complete Historical, Chronological and Geographical American Atlas Phillips (A) 1373a* $275.00

Lucas, Fielding **Massachusetts** Baltimore 1823 14.5 X 20.5 Ex-atlas HC engraving *From A General Atlas Phillips (A) 742* $295.00

Finley, A. **Massachusetts** Phila 1826 9 x 11 Folding Map HC engraving *Leather folder* $375.00

Carleton, Osgood **Map of Massachusetts Proper** Boston 1832 32 x 47 Folding Map HC engraving $2,250.00

Burr, David H. **Massachusetts, Rhose Island & Connecticut** NY 1836 12 x 15 Ex-atlas HC engraving *From The Universal Atlas Phillips (A) 1379a* $175.00

Bradford, T. G. **Massachusetts** Boston 1842 11.5 x 14.5 Ex-atlas HC engraving *From An Illustrated Atlas* $125.00

Mitchell, S. A. **Massachusetts and Rhode Island** Phila 1850 13 x 16 Ex-atlas HC engraving *From A New Universal Atlas* $75.00

Colton, J. W. **Massachusetts & Rhode Island** NY 1854 12 x 16 Folding Map HC Engraving *Cloth folder* $175.00

Colton, J. W. & G. W. **Massachusetts and Rhode Island** NY 1855-56 15 x 18 Ex-atlas Lithograph after engraving *From Colton's Atlas of the World Phillips (A)816* $95.00

Mitchell, S. A. **County Map of Massachusetts, Connecticut and Rhode Island** Phila 1860 11.5 x 13.5 Ex-atlas Lithograph after engraving *From A New General Atlas Phillips (A)831* $65.00

Johnson & Browning **Johnson's Massachusetts, Connecticut, Rhode Island** NY 1861 Ex-atlas Lithograph after engraving *Johnson's New Illustrated Family Atlas* $85.00

Carey, Matthew **Kentuckey** Phila 1805 8 x 6 Ex-atlas HC engraving From The Pocket Atlas Phillips (A) 1368
Kentucky became a state in June, 1792

Colton, J. W. & G. W. **Colton's Massachusetts & Rhode Island** NY 1867 15 x 15 Folding Map Lithograph after engraving *Cloth or leather folder* $150.00

Tanner, Henry S. **Map of the States of Maine, New Hampshire, Vermont, Massachusetts...** Phila 1823 27 x 22 Ex-atlas HC engraving *From A New American Atlas* $750.00

Mexico

Carey & Lea **Geographical, ...Historical Map of Mexico (California)** Phila 1822-23 17.5 x 22 Ex-atlas HC engraving *Complete Historical, Chronological and Geographical American Atlas Phillips (A) 1373a* $675.00

Lucas, Fielding **Mexico** Baltimore 1823 11.5 X 14.5 Ex-atlas HC engraving *From A General Atlas Phillips (A) 742* $325.00

Tanner, Henry S. **Mexico and Guatemala** Phila 1834 12 x 15 Ex-atlas HC engraving *Texas not part of Mexico* $250.00

Tanner, Henry S. **Mexico and Guatemala** Phila 1835-45 11.5 x 14.5 Ex-atlas HC engraving *Carey & Hart Publishers Phillips (A) 774* $400.00

Bradford, T. G. **Mexico, Guatemala and the West Indies** Boston 1835 8 x 11 Ex-atlas HC engraving *From A Comprehensive Atlas* $125.00

Burr, David H. **United States of Mexico** NY 1836 15 x 12 Ex-atlas HC engraving *From The Universal Atlas Phillips (A) 1379a* $425.00

Morse & Breese **Mexico** NY 1842 12 x 16 Ex-atlas Cerographic prtd color *From Cerographic Atlas* $250.00

Colton, J. W. & G. W. **Mexico** NY 1855-56 15 x 18 Ex-atlas Lithograph after engraving *From Colton's Atlas of the World Phillips (A) 816* $95.00

Colton, J. W. & G. W. **Colton's Mexico** NY 1861 11 x 14 Folding Map Lithograph after engraving *Cloth folder* $450.00

Johnson & Browning **Johnson's Mexico** NY 1861 12 x 15 Ex-atlas Lithograph after engraving *Johnson's New Illustrated Family Atlas* $75.00

Mitchell, S. A. **Map of Mexico, Central America and the West Indies** Phila 1870 15 x 23.5 Ex-atlas Lithograph after engraving *From A New General Atlas Phillips (A) 859* $95.00

Michigan

Michigan became a state in Jan. 1837

• Carey & Lea **Geographical, ...Historical Map of Michigan Territory** Phila 1822-23 17.5 x 22 Ex-atlas HC engraving *Complete Historical, Chronological and Geographical American Atlas Phillips (A) 1373a Illustrated* $675.00

Lucas, Fielding **Michigan Territory** Baltimore 1823 11.5 X 14.5 Ex-atlas HC engraving *From A General Atlas Phillips (A) 742* $425.00

Farmer **Map of the Surveyed Part ...Territory of Michigan on a Scale of 8 miles...** Detroit 1826 20 x 21 Folding Map HC engraving *Phillips (M) 424* $1,250.00

Farmer **Map of the Territories of Michigan and Ouisconsin** Detroit 1830 40 x 34 Folding Map HC engraving *Phillips (M) 424* $1,250.00

Burr, David H. **Michigan** NY 1831-36 15 x 12 Ex-atlas HC engraving *From The Universal Atlas Phillips (A) 1379a Phillips (M) 424* $325.00

Tanner, Henry S. **The Traveller's Pocket Map of Michigan With Its Canals, Roads and Distances** Phila 1832 10.5 x 13 Folding Map HC engraving *Phillips (M) 424* $375.00

Finley, A. **Map of Ohio and the Settled Parts of Michigan** Phila 1834 19 x 13 Folding Map HC engraving *Leather folder* $750.00

Bradford, T. G. **Michigan and the Great Lakes** Boston 1835 7.5 x 10 Ex-atlas HC engraving *From a Comprehensive Atlas* $175.00

Farmer **An Improved ... Map of the Surveyed Part of...Michigan** NY 1835 21 x 31 Folding Map HC engraving *Cloth or leather folder. Second Issue Phillips (M) 425* $1,500.00

Farmer **Improved Map of the Territories of Michigan and Ouisconsin** Albany 1835 20 x 34 Folding Map HC engraving *Phillips (M) 424* $1,000.00

Mitchell, S. A. **The Tourist's Pocket Map of Michigan** Phila 1835 12 x 15 Folding Map HC engraving *Phillips (M) 425* $375.00

Farmer **An Improved ... Map of the Surveyed Part of...Michigan** NY 1836 21 x 31 Folding Map HC engraving *Cloth or leather folder. Second Issue* $1,500.00

Tanner, Henry S. **A New Map of Michigan With Its Canals, Roads and Distances** Phila 1841 15 x 12 Ex-atlas HC engraving *From A New Universal Atlas* $185.00

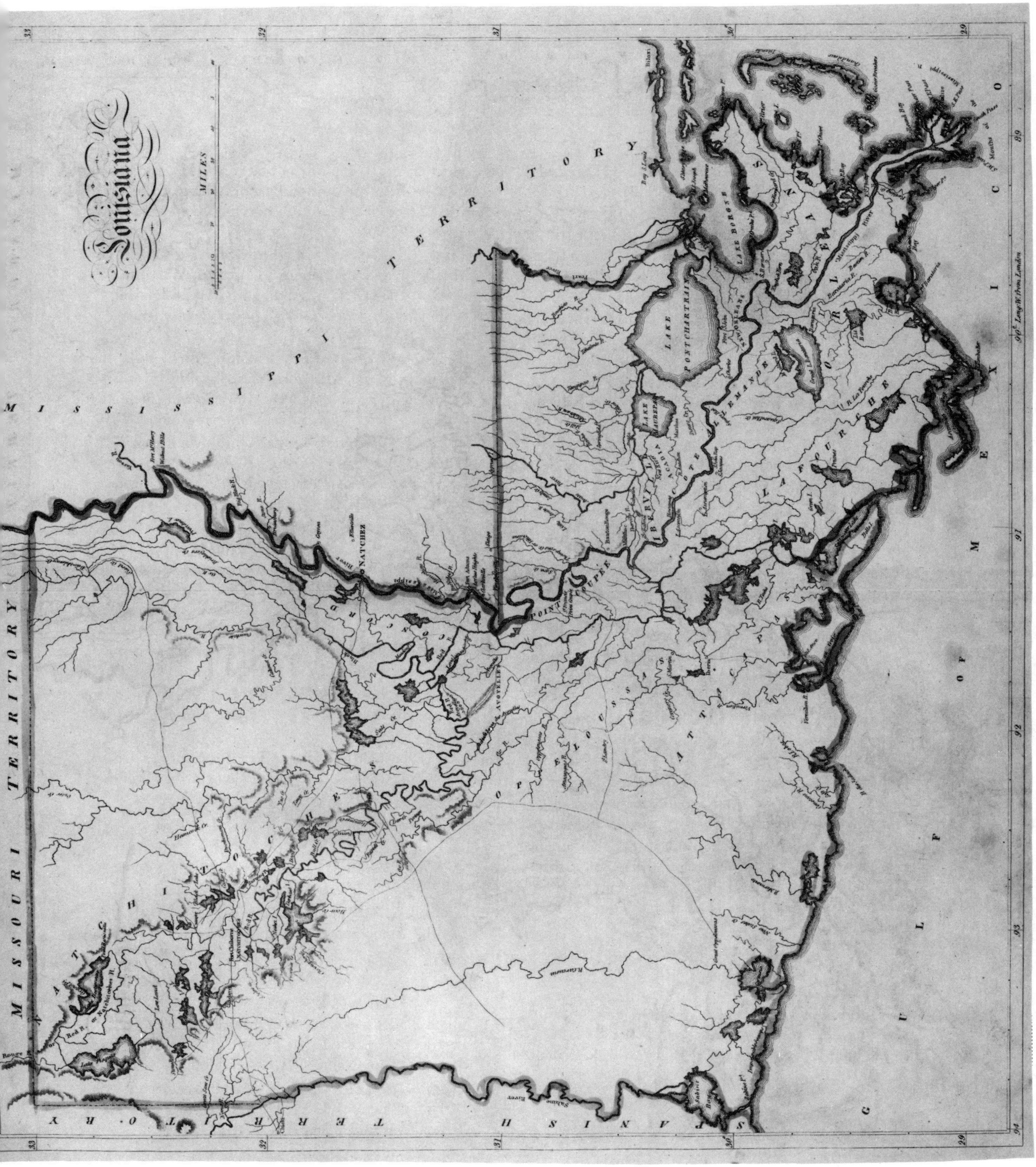

Carey, Matthew **Louisiana** Phila 1814 15.5 x 17.5 Ex-atlas HC engraving From the General Atlas Phillips (A) 722
Louisiana became a state in 1812

Greenleaf**Michigan**Brattleboro184214 x 12Ex-atlasHC engraving*From New General Atlas Phillips (A) 784* **$375.00**

Mitchell, S. A.**A New Map ofMichigan With Its Canals, Roads and Distances**Phila184614.5 x 11.5Ex-atlasHC engraving*From A New Universal Atlas* **$150.00**

Thomas, Cowperthwait & Co**A New Map of Michigan With Its Canals, Roads and Distances**Phila 185015 x 11.5Ex-atlasHC engraving*Also 1854Phillips (A)800***$125.00**

Colton, J. W. & G. W. **Lake Superior and the Northern Part of Michigan**NY185413 x 16Ex-atlas Lithograph after engraving **$85.00**

Colton, J. W. & G. W. **Lake Superior and the Northern Part of Michigan**NY185413 x 16Folding Map Lithograph after engraving*Cloth folder* **$350.00**

Colton, J. W. & G. W. **Michigan**NY1855-5615 x 18 Ex-atlas Lithograph after engraving*From Colton's Atlas of the World Phillips (A)816***$125.00**

Colton, J. W. & G. W. **Michigan**NY1855-5615 x 18 Ex-atlas Lithograph after engraving*From Colton's Atlas of the World Phillips (A)816***$125.00**

Desilver**A New Map ofMichigan With Its Canals, Roads...**Phila1856-5714.5 x 11.5Ex-atlasHC Engraving *From A New Universal Atlas Phillips (A)823***$125.00**

Mitchell, S. A. **County Map of Michigan and Wisconsin**Phila186011 x 13.5Ex-atlas Lithograph after engraving*From A New General Atlas Phillips (A)831* **$65.00**

Johnson & Browning**Johnson's Michigan & Indiana** NY186117 x 23Ex-atlas Lithograph after engraving *Johnson's New Illustrated Family Atlas* **$85.00**

Colton, J. W. & G. W. **Colton's Map ofLake Superior and Upper Peninsula of Michigan...**NY186816.5 x 24.5Folding Map Lithograph after engraving*Cloth folder. "Showing...Portage Lake...Canal...Iron Lands...Separate issue"* **$350.00**

Rand McNally & Co. **Indexed Map of Michigan** Chicago187712.5 x 9Folding Map Wax engraving*On two sheets. Wraps* **$175.00**

Page**Indexed Township Map ofMichigan Showing...Railroad Stations, Post Offices** 188125 x 16.5Folding Map Lithograph after engraving*Stiff wraps* **$325.00**

Mitchell, S. A.**Map of the States ofOhio, Indiana and Illinois With the Settled Part of Michigan**Phila1835 18 x 22.5Folding Map HC engraving*Cloth or leather covers* **$675.00**

Smith, J. C. **Guide Through the States ofOhio, Michigan, Indiana, Illinois, Missouri, Wisconsin & Iowa**NY185417.5 x 22Folding Map HC Engraving *From Colton, The Western Tourist and Emigrant's Guide...* **$175.00**

Colton, J. W. **Guide Through Ohio, Michigan, Indiana, Illinois, Missouri, Wisconsin & Iowa**NY 185520.5 x 25.5Folding Map HC Engraving*Bound with Colton's Western Tourist and Emigrant's Guide* **$450.00**

Colton, J. W. **Guide Through Ohio, Michigan, Indiana, Illinois**NY185720 x 27Folding Map HC Engraving*Cloth folder stamped "Map of the Western States"* **$400.00**

Midwestern States

Northwest Territory

The Northwest Territory was created by the Ordinance of 1787 which outlined the states of Ohio, Indiana, Illinois, Michigan, Wisconsin

Scott**N. W. Territory**Phila17957.5 x 6Ex-atlas Engraving*From the United States Gazeteer* **$350.00**

Carey, Matthew**N.W. Territory**Phila18056 x 8Ex-atlas UC engraving*From the Pocket Atlas Phillips (A) 1368* **$250.00**

Carey, Matthew**The Upper Territories of the United States**Phila18148 x 6Ex-atlasUC engraving*From the Pocket Atlas Phillips (A) 1370***$175.00**

Milwaukee

Sherman & Smith**Map ofMilwaukee**Milw185740 x 27.5Folding Map Engraving **$350.00**

Mitchell, S. A. **Plan ofMilwaukee**Phila187414 x 10.5 Ex-atlas Lithograph after engraving*From A New General Atlas* **$60.00**

Minnesota

Minnesota became a state in May, 1858

Thomas, Cowperthwait & Co**Map ofMinnesota Territory**Phila185013 x16 Ex-atlasHC engraving*9 Counties shown Phillips (A)800***$175.00**

Thomas, Cowperthwait & Co**Map ofMinnesota Territory**Phila185413 x16 Ex-atlasHC engraving*From A New Universal Atlas Phillips (A)813***$125.00**

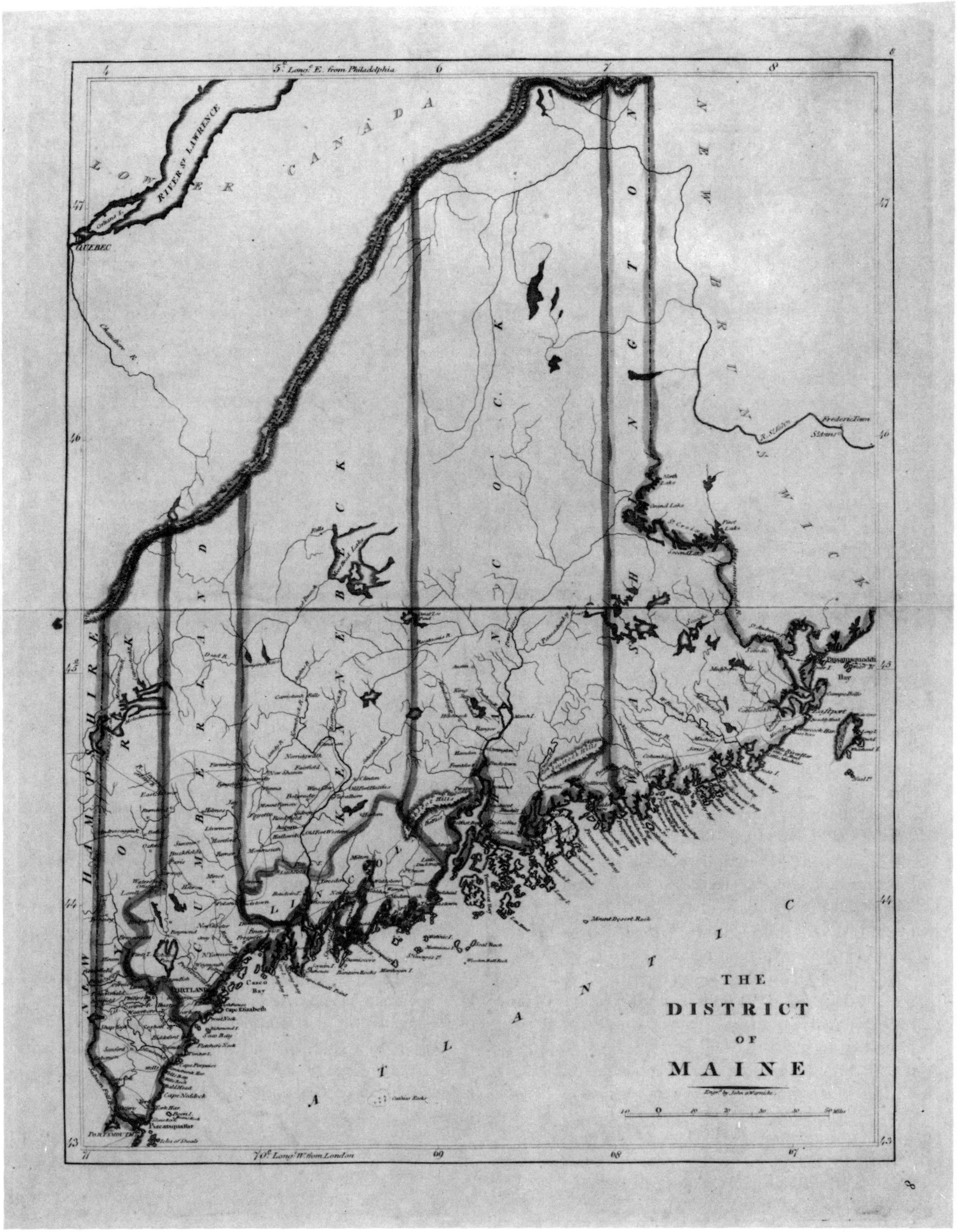

Carey, Matthew **The District of Maine** Phila 1814 15.5 x 11 Ex-atlas HC engraving From the General Atlas
Phillips (A) 722. Maine , formerly a district of the Commonwealth of Massachusetts, became a state in 1820

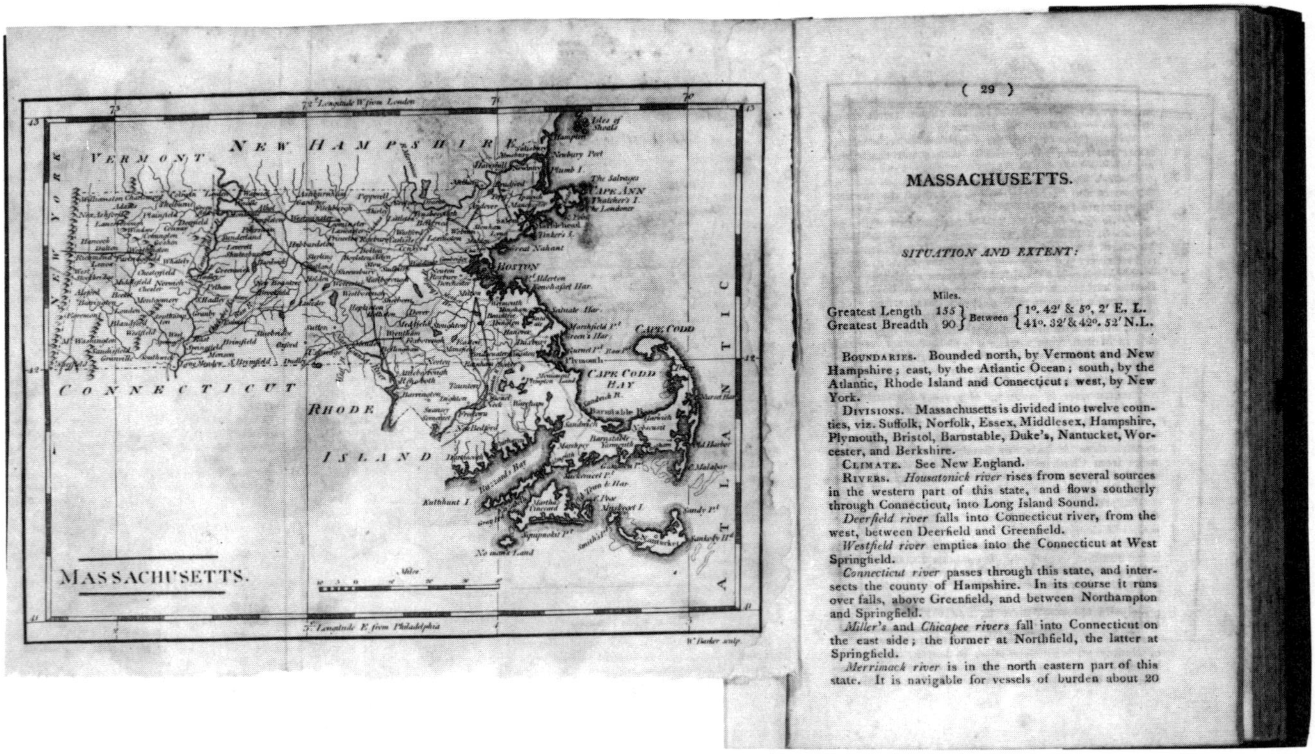

Carey, Matthew **Massachusetts** *Phila 1805 6 x 8 Ex-atlas UC engraving From the Pocket Atlas Phillips (A) 1368*

Colton, J. W. & G. W. **Minnesota** NY 1855-56 15 x 18 Ex-atlas Lithograph after engraving *From Colton's Atlas of the World Phillips (A) 816* **$125.00**

Colton, J. W. & G. W. **Minnesota** NY 1857 13 x 16 Ex-atlas Lithograph after engraving *Last year as territory Phillips (A) 827* **$175.00**

Colton, J. W. & G. W. **Minnesota** NY 1858 13 x 16 Ex-atlas Lithograph after engraving *First Year of Statehood Phillips (A) 827* **$175.00**

Colton, J. W. & G. W. **Minnesota and Dakota** NY 1860 11 x 14 Ex-atlas Lithograph after engraving *From Colton's General Atlas* **$85.00**

Mitchell, S. A. **Minnesota and Dacotah** Phila 1860 10.5 x 13.5 Ex-atlas Lithograph after engraving *First edition of this map. From a New General Atlas* **$125.00**

Johnson & Browning **Johnson's Minnesota & Dakota** NY 1861 12 x 15 Ex-atlas Lithograph after engraving *Johnson's New Illustrated Family Atlas* **$75.00**

Johnson & Ward **Johnson's Minnesota & Dakota** NY 1864 12 x 15 Ex-atlas Lithograph after engraving *Johnson's New Illustrated Family Atlas* **$75.00**

Mitchell, S. A. **County Map of Minnesota** Phila 1864 11 x 14 Ex-atlas Lithograph after engraving **$75.00**

Colton, J. W. & G. W. **Colton's New Sectional Map of the State of Minnesota** NY 1873 20 x 25 Folding Map Lithograph after engraving *Cloth folder. 2 maps* **$400.00**

Asher & Adams **Minnesota** NY 1874 16.5 x 22.5 Ex-atlas Lithograph *Asher & Adams New Statistical and Topographical Atlas* **$75.00**

Watson **New Railroad and Distance Map of Minnesota & Iowa** Chicago 1877-83 16 x 12.5 Ex-atlas Wax engraving *From New Indexed Family Atlas* **$75.00**

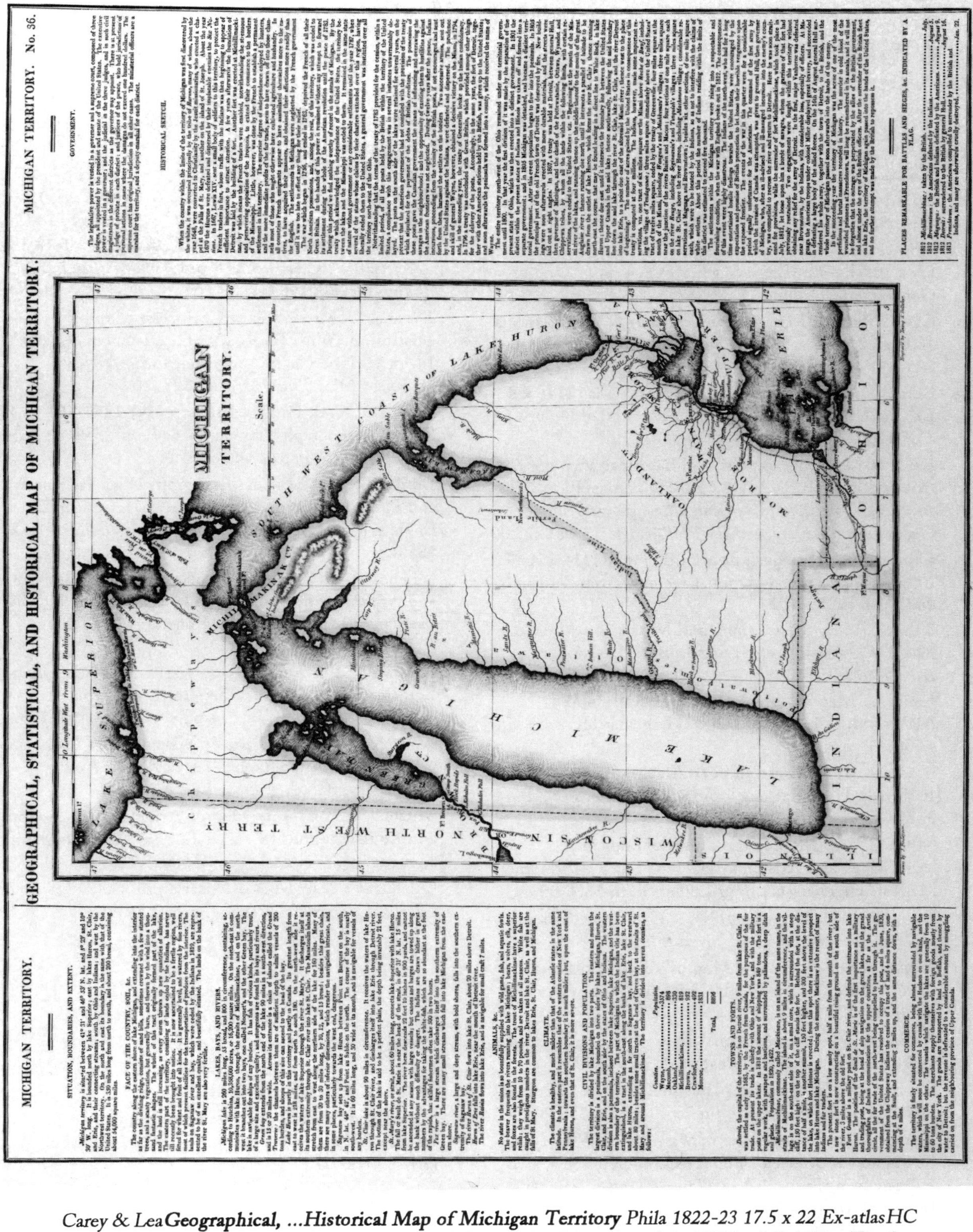

Carey & Lea **Geographical, ...Historical Map of Michigan Territory** *Phila 1822-23 17.5 x 22 Ex-atlas HC engraving Complete Historical, Chronological and Geographical American Atlas Phillips (A) 1373a. The first separate map of Michigan. Michigan became a state in 1837. Phillips (M)424.*

Mississippi

also see Alabama, Georgia

Mississippi became a state in 1817

Arrowsmith & Lewis **Mississippi Territory** Phila 1804 8.5 x 10.5 Ex-atlas Engraving *From New and Elegant General Atlas Phillips (A) 702* $275.00

Arrowsmith & Lewis **Mississippi Territory** Boston 1805 8.5 x 10.5 Ex-atlas Engraving *From New and Elegant General Atlas Phillips (A) 708* $250.00

Carey, Matthew **Mississippi Territory & Georgia** Phila 1805 6 x 8 Ex-atlas UC engraving *From the Pocket Atlas* $250.00

Carey, Matthew **Mississippi Territory** Phila 1814 6 x 8 Ex-atlas UC engraving *From the Pocket Atlas Phillips (A) 1370* $200.00

Carey & Lea **Geographical, ... Historical Map of Mississippi** Phila 1822-23 17.5 x 22 Ex-atlas HC engraving *Complete Historical, Chronological and Geographical American Atlas Phillips (A) 1373a* $225.00

• Lucas, Fielding **Mississippi** Baltimore 1823 14.5 X 11.5 Ex-atlas HC engraving *From A General Atlas Phillips (A) 742 Illustrated* $250.00

Tanner, Henry S. **Louisiana and Mississippi** Phila 1825 29 x 23 Ex-atlas HC engraving *From A New American Atlas* $850.00

Finley, A. **Map of Louisiana, Mississippi, and Alabama...** Phila 1827 17 x 20 Folding Map HC engraving $850.00

Bradford, T. G. **Mississippi & Alabama** Boston 1835 8 x 10 Ex-atlas HC engraving *From a Comprehensive Atlas* $125.00

Mitchell, S. A. **Map of the States of Louisiana, Mississippi and Alabama** Phila 1835 17.5 x 21.5 Folding Map HC engraving *Cloth or leather covers* $600.00

Burr, David H. **Mississippi** NY 1835-36 14 x 11 Ex-atlas HC engraving *From The Universal Atlas* $185.00

Tanner, Henry S. **A New Map of Mississippi** Phila 1836-45 14 x 11.5 Ex-atlas HC engraving *Carey & Hart Publishers* $175.00

Bradford, T. G. **Mississippi** Boston 1838 14 x 11 Ex-atlas HC engraving *From An Illustrated Atlas* $150.00

Bradford, T. G. **Mississippi** Boston 1839 10 x 8 Ex-atlas HC engraving *From a Comprehensive Atlas* $95.00

Tanner, H. S. **A New Map of Mississippi With Its Roads and Distances...** Phila 1841 14.5 X 11.5 Ex-atlas HC engraving *From A New Universal Atlas (Tanner's Universal Atlas)* $175.00

Bradford & Goodrich **Mississippi** Boston 1842 14.5 x 11.5 Ex-atlas HC engraving *From Universal Illustrated Atlas Phillips (A) 783* $100.00

Greenleaf **Mississippi** Brattleboro 1842 13 x 11 Ex-atlas HC engraving *From New General Atlas Phillips (A) 784* $150.00

Mitchell, S. A. **A New Map of Mississippi** Phila 1850 16 x 13 Ex-atlas HC engraving *From A New Universal Atlas Phillips (A) 800* $95.00

Thomas, Cowperthwait & Co **A New Map of Mississippi With Its Roads and Distances** Phila 1850 14.5 x 11.5 Ex-atlas HC engraving *From A New Universal Atlas Phillips (A) 800* $95.00

Colton, J. W. & G. W. **Mississippi** NY 1855-56 15 x 18 Ex-atlas Lithograph after engraving *From Colton's Atlas of the World Phillips (A) 816* $95.00

Desilver **A New Map of Mississippi With Its Roads and Distances...** Phila 1856 14.5 x 11.5 Ex-atlas HC Engraving *From A New Universal Atlas Phillips (A) 823* $85.00

Mitchell, S. A. **County Map of Louisiana, Mississippi and Arkansas** Phila 1860 13.5 x 10.5 Ex-atlas Lithograph after engraving *From A New General Atlas Phillips (A) 831* $65.00

Johnson & Browning **Johnson's Arkansas, Mississippi, Louisiana** NY 1861 23 x 17 Ex-atlas Lithograph after engraving *Johnson's New Illustrated Family Atlas* $75.00

Asher & Adams **Louisiana & Mississippi** NY 1872 16.5 x 22.5 Ex-atlas Lithograph *Asher & Adams New Statistical and Topographical Atlas* $75.00

Mitchell, S. A. **County Map of Arkansas, Mississippi and Louisiana** Phila 1874 21 x 13.5 Ex-atlas Lithograph after engraving *From A New General Atlas* $50.00

Gray **Gray's New Map of Mississippi** NY 1878 28 x 17.5 Ex-atlas Lithograph after engraving $75.00

Missouri

Missouri became a state in Aug. 1821

Carey, Matthew **Missouri Territory** Phila 1814 12 x 14 Ex-atlas UC engraving *From the General Atlas Phillips (A) 722* $675.00

Carey, Matthew **Missouri Territory** Phila 1818 12 x 14 Ex-atlas UC engraving *From the General Atlas Phillips (A) 732* $650.00

Lucas, Fielding ***Mississippi*** *Baltimore 1823 14.5 X 11.5 Ex-atlas HC engraving From A General Atlas Phillips (A) 742. Mississippi became a state in 1817. An early map of the state, this also appeared in the Carey & Lea Complete Historical, Chronological and Geographical American Atlas Phillips (A) 1373. A General Atlas was Lucas' finest work, and one of the best early American atlases. Fielding also drew 20 of the 46 maps in the Carey & Lea atlas.*

Carey & Lea **Geographical, ... Historical Map of Missouri** Phila 1822-23 17.5 x 22 Ex-atlas HC engraving *Complete Historical, Chronological and Geographical American Atlas Phillips (A) 1373a* $295.00

Lucas, Fielding **Missouri** Baltimore 1823 14.5 X 11.5 Ex-atlas HC engraving *From A General Atlas Phillips (A) 742* $300.00

Tanner, Henry S. **Illinois and Missouri** Phila 1823 28 x 22.5 Ex-atlas HC engraving *From A New American Atlas* $975.00

• Finley, A. **Missouri** Phila 1832 12 x 9.5 Ex-atlas HC engraving *From New General Atlas* Illustrated $175.00

Burr, David H. **Missouri** NY 1834-36 11 x 12.5 Ex-atlas HC engraving *From The Universal Atlas Phillips (A) 1379a* $275.00

• Bradford, T. G. **Missouri, Illinois and Iowa** Boston 1835 10.5 x 8 Ex-atlas HC Engraving *From A Comprhensive Atlas* Illustrated $150.00

Bradford, T. G. **Missouri** Boston 1838 11 x 14 Ex-atlas HC engraving *From An Illustrated Atlas* $150.00

• Tanner, H. S. **A New Map of Missouri...** Phila 1841 16 x 13 Ex-atlas HC engraving *From A New Universal Atlas Illustrated* $150.00

Greenleaf **Missouri** Brattleboro 1842 13 x 11 Ex-atlas HC engraving *From New General Atlas Phillips (A) 784* $175.00

Morse & Breese **Missouri** NY 1844-46 12.5 x 15 Ex-atlas Cerographic prtd color *From North American Atlas Phillips (A) 1228,32* $125.00

• Mitchell, S. A. **Map of Missouri** Phila 1847 16 x 13 Ex-atlas HC engraving *From A New Universal Atlas* Illustrated $125.00

Mitchell, S. A. **Map of Missouri** Phila 1850 16 x 13 Ex-atlas HC engraving *From A New Universal Atlas Phillips (A) 800* $95.00

Thomas, Cowperthwait & Co **A New Map of the State of Missouri** Phila 1854 13.5 x 16 Ex-atlas HC engraving *From A New Universal Atlas Phillips (A)813* $85.00

• Colton, J. W. & G. W. **Missouri** NY 1855-56 15 x 18 Ex-atlas Lithograph after engraving *From Colton's Atlas of the World Phillips (A)816* Illustrated $95.00

Desilver **A New Map of the State of Missouri** Phila 1856-57 13 x 16 Ex-atlas HC Engraving *From A New Universal Atlas Phillips (A)823* $125.00

Mitchell, S. A. **County Map of Iowa and Missouri** Phila 1860 12.5 x 15 Ex-atlas Lithograph after engraving *From A New General Atlas* $65.00

Johnson & Browning **Johnson's Missouri & Kansas** NY 1861 17 x 26 Ex-atlas Lithograph after engraving *3 vignettes* $95.00

Colton, J. W. & G. W. **Colton's New Map of Missouri** NY 1869 21 x 27 Folding Map Lithograph after engraving *Cloth folder* $250.00

Taintor Bros. & Merrill **Map of the State of Missouri** 1874 17 x 21.5 Ex-atlas Lithograph after engraving $95.00

Gray **Gray's Atlas Map of Missouri** NY 1875 12.5 x 15 Ex-atlas Lithograph after engraving $75.00

Montana

also see Western States

Montana became a state in Nov. 1889

Johnson & Ward **Johnson's Nebraska, Dakota, Idaho, Montana and Wyoming** NY 1865 17 x 23 Ex-atlas Lithograph after engraving *Johnson's New Illustrated Family Atlas* $125.00

Colton, J. W. & G. W. **Oregon, Washington, Idaho, Montana & British Columbia** NY 1868 16.5 x 27 Ex-atlas Lithograph after engraving *From Colton's General Atlas* $175.00

Lloyd, H. H. **Nebraska, and the Territories of Dakota, Idaho, Montana, Wyoming** NY 1872 15.5 x 24.5 Ex-atlas Lithograph after engraving *Issued as a supplement to state and county atlases* $225.00

Asher & Adams **Asher & Adams Idaho, Montana Western Portion** NY 1875 16.5 x 22.5 Ex-atlas Lithograph *Asher & Adams New Statistical and Topographical Atlas* $125.00

Asher & Adams **Asher & Adams Montana Eastern Portion** NY 1875 16.5 x 22.5 Ex-atlas Lithograph *Asher & Adams New Statistical and Topographical Atlas* $125.00

Colton, J. W. & G. W. **Montana, Idaho & Wyoming** NY 1876-77 17.5 x 25 Ex-atlas Lithograph after engraving *From Colton's General Atlas* $150.00

Mitchell, S. A. **Territory of Montana** Phila 1879 11 x 14.5 Ex-atlas Lithograph after engraving *From A New General Atlas Phillips (A)890* $85.00

Rand McNally & Co. **Montana** Chicago 1882 12.5 x 19.5 Ex-atlas Wax engraving *From Indexed Atlas of the World* $85.00

Page **Page's Indexed Township Map of Montana Showing ...Railroad Stations, Post offices...** 1883 16 x 24 Folding Map Lithograph after engraving *Stiff wraps* $675.00

Finley, A. ***Missouri*** *Phila 1832 12 x 9.5 Ex-atlas HC engraving*
From A New General Atlas

Bradley **Montana, Idaho and Wyoming** Phila 1884 15 x 22 Ex-atlas Lithograph *From New General Atlas* $85.00

Bradley **County and Township Map of Montana, Idaho and Wyoming** Phila 1887 15.5 x 23.5 Ex-atlas Lithograph *From New General Atlas* $95.00

Colton, J. W. & G. W. **Montana, Idaho & Wyoming** NY 1887 17.5 x 25 Ex-atlas Lithograph after engraving *From Colton's General Atlas* $125.00

Ide **Ide's Map of Montana** Helena 1891 21 x 38 Folding Map Lithograph $800.00

National Road

Melish, J. **Map of the National Road Between Cumberland and Wheeling** Phila 1816-22 6 x 11 Ex-atlas HC engraving $150.00

Nebraska

also see Western States

Nebraska became a state in March 1867

Colton, J. W. & G. W. **Nebraska & Kanzas** NY 1855-56 15 x 18 Ex-atlas Lithograph after engraving *From Colton's Atlas of the World. 1st state of this map "Kanzas"* $175.00

Colton, J. W. & G. W. **Nebraska & Kanzas** NY 1855-56 15 x 18 Ex-atlas Lithograph after engraving *From Colton's Atlas of the World. 1st state of this map "Kanzas" Phillips (A)816* $175.00

Morse & Gaston **Kansas and Nebraska** NY 1857 6 x 5 Ex-atlas Cerograph *From Diamond Atlas* $60.00

Colton, J. W. & G. W. **Kansas and Nebraska** NY 1860 24 x 15 Ex-atlas Lithograph after engraving *From Colton's General Atlas* $75.00

Mitchell, S. A. **Map of Kansas, Nebraska and Colorado** Phila 1860 11.5 x 14 Ex-atlas Lithograph after engraving *From A New General Atlas Phillips (A)831 Phillips (M)241* $150.00

Johnson & Browning **Johnson's Iowa & Nebraska** NY 1861 13 x 16 Ex-atlas Lithograph after engraving *Johnson's New Illustrated Family Atlas* $65.00

Johnson & Browning **Johnson's Nebraska and Kansas** NY 1861 13 x 16 Ex-atlas Lithograph after engraving *Johnson's New Illustrated Family Atlas* $175.00

Mitchell, S. A. **Map of Kansas, Nebraska and Colorado** Phila 1861 11 x 13 Ex-atlas Lithograph after engraving *Showing Also Eastern Portion of Idaho. From a New General Atlas* $85.00

• Johnson & Ward **Johnson's Nebraska, Dakota, Colorado, Montana & Kansas** NY 1862 12 x 15 Ex-atlas Lithograph after engraving *Johnson's New Illustrated Family Atlas Illustrated* $95.00

Johnson & Ward **Johnson's Nebraska, Dakota, Idaho, Montana and Wyoming** NY 1865 17 x 23 Ex-atlas Lithograph after engraving *Johnson's New Illustrated Family Atlas* $125.00

Johnson & Ward **Johnson's Nebraska, Dakota, Idaho and Montana** NY 1867 17 x 23 Ex-atlas Lithograph after engraving *Johnson's New Illustrated Family Atlas* $95.00

Mitchell, S. A. **Map of Kansas, Nebraska and Colorado** Phila 1867 11 x 14 Ex-atlas Lithograph after engraving *Showing Southern Portion of Dacotah. From a New General Atlas Phillips (A)850* $85.00

Colton, J. H. **Colton's New Sectional Map of Nebraska and Part of Dakota** NY 1870 28 x 37 Folding Map Lithograph $300.00

Colton, J. W. & G. W. **Sectional Map of Nebraska and Part of Dakota** NY 1872 33 x 40 Folding Map Lithograph after engraving *Cloth or leather folder* $400.00

Colton, J. W. & G. W. **Sectional Map of Nebraska and Part of Dakota** NY 1872 33 x 40 Folding Map Lithograph after engraving *Cloth or leather folder* $400.00

Lloyd, H. H. **Nebraska, and the Territories of Dakota, Idaho, Montana, Wyoming** NY 1872 15.5 x 24.5 Ex-atlas Lithograph after engraving *Issued as a supplement to state and county atlases* $225.00

Mitchell, S. A. **County Map of Kansas, Nebraska, Colorado, Dakota, Wyoming** Phila 1872 20 x 14 Ex-atlas Lithograph after engraving *From A New General Atlas* $125.00

Asher & Adams **Nebraska** NY 1873 16.5 x 22.5 Ex-atlas Lithograph *Asher & Adams New Statistical and Topographical Atlas* $75.00

Rand McNally & Co. **Nebraska** Chicago 1882 12.5 x 20 Ex-atlas Wax engraving *From Indexed Atlas of the World* $85.00

Nevada

Nevada became a state in Oct. 1864

Mitchell, S. A. **County Map of Utah and Nevada** Phila 1865 11.5 x 14 Ex-atlas Lithograph after engraving *Also 1867 and 1869. From a New General Atlas* $125.00

Frey, A. C. **Topographical Railroad & County Map of ... California and Nevada** NY 1868 38.5 x 30.5 Folding Map Lithograph after engraving $850.00

Asher & Adams **California & Nevada. North (and) South** NY 1872 16.5 x 22.5 Ex-atlas Lithograph *Asher & Adams New Statistical and Topographical Atlas. 2 sheets. Phillips(A)1272* $175.00

Lloyd, H. H. **California and Nevada** NY 1872 15.5 x 12 Ex-atlas Lithograph after engraving *Issued as a supplement to state and county atlases* $150.00

Colton, J. W. & G. W. **Colton's California & Nevada** NY 1873 25 x 17 Folding Map Lithograph after engraving *Cloth or leather folder* $500.00

Colton, J. W. & G. W. **Colton's California and Nevada** NY 1873 29 x 17 Ex-atlas Lithograph after engraving *From Colton's General Atlas Phillips (A) 866* $125.00

Gray **Gray's California and Nevada** NY 1874 27 x 17 Ex-atlas Lithograph after engraving $100.00

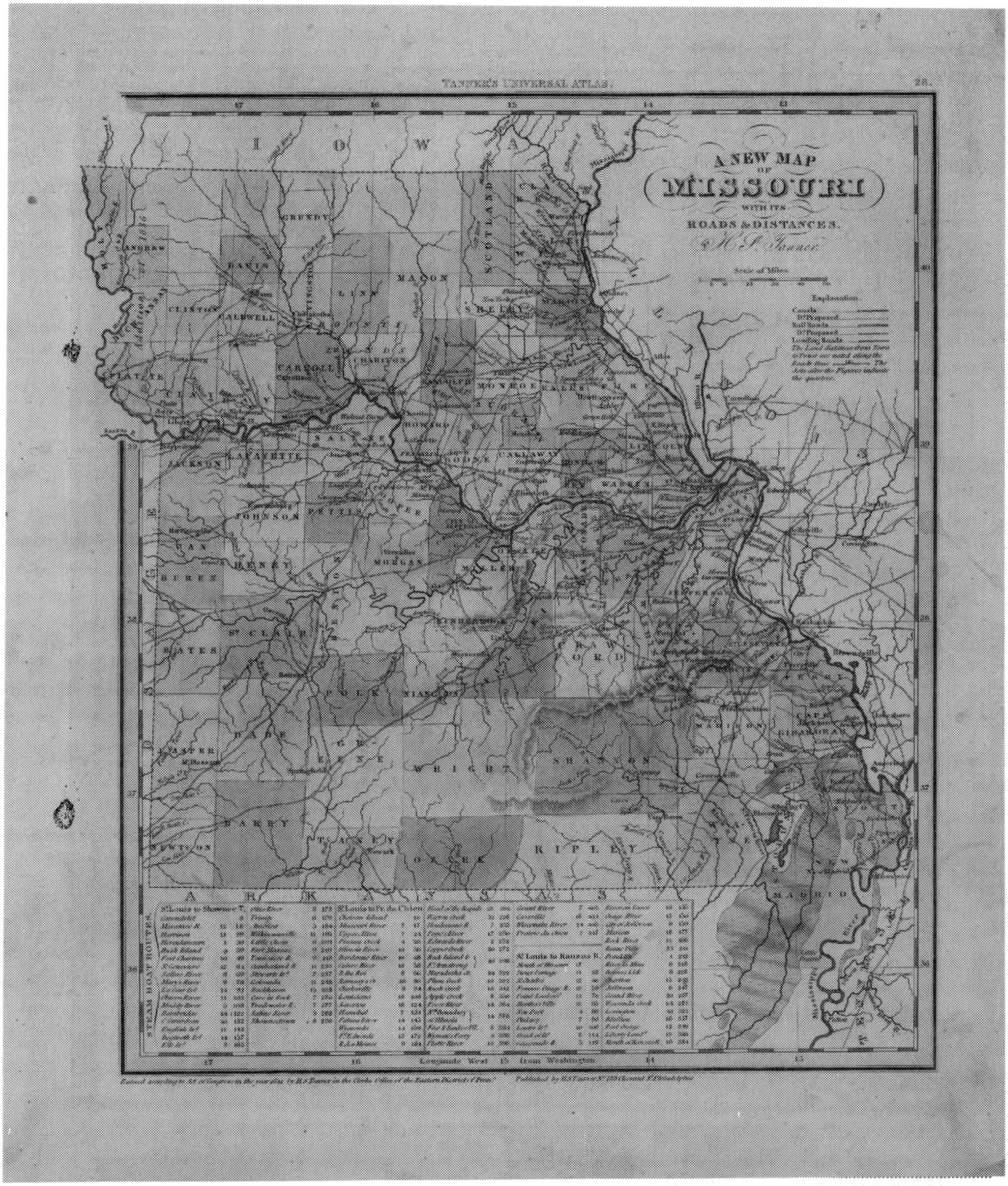

Tanner, H. S. **A New Map of Missouri...** *Phila 1841 16 x 13 Ex-atlas HC engraving From A New Universal Atlas*

Missouri became a state in Aug. 1821. Editions of The Universal Atlas were published from 1833-1843. S. A. Mitchell acquired Tanner's copyright from Carey & Hart, who published the 1843 and 1844 editions, and began publishing A New Universal Atlas in 1846. It is likely that the maps in the 1846 and later editions were lithographs, transferred from the original engraved plates. These maps have a distinctive hand colored scrollwork border. See next illustration.

Mitchell, S. A. **County and Township Map of Utah and Nevada** Phila 1881 15 x23 Ex-atlas Lithograph after engraving *From A New General Atlas* $75.00

Rand McNally & Co. **Nevada** Chicago 1882 19.5 x 13 Ex-atlas Wax engraving *From Indexed Atlas of the World* $85.00

Colton, J. W. & G. W. **Colton's California and Nevada** NY 1887 25 x 17 Ex-atlas Lithograph after engraving *From Colton's General Atlas* $100.00

New England

Tanner, Henry S. **Map of the States of Maine, New Hampshire, Vermont, Massachusetts...** Phila 1823 27 x 22 Ex-atlas HC engraving *From A New American Atlas* $750.00

Snow & Co. **Map of the Railways in New England and Part of New York** NY 1849 8.5 x 7 Folding Map Engraving *From Pathfinder Railway Guide for the New England States* $100.00

Mitchell, S. A. **County Map of the States of New York, New Hampshire, Vermont, Massachusetts** Phila 1860 13.5 x 21 Ex-atlas Lithograph after engraving *Rhode Island and Connecticut. From a New General Atlas Phillips (A)831* $50.00

Johnson & Browning **Johnson's New England** NY 1861 17 x 23 Ex-atlas Lithograph after engraving *Johnson's New Illustrated Family Atlas* $95.00

New Hampshire

also see Vermont

New Hampshire became a state in 1788

• Carey, Matthew **The State of New Hampshire** Phila 1794 17.5 x 11 Ex-atlas UC engraving *From the General Atlas Illustrated* $400.00

Arrowsmith & Lewis **New Hampshire** Phila 1804 10.5 x 8.5 Ex-atlas Engraving *From New and Elegant General Atlas Phillips (A)702* $100.00

Carey, Matthew **New Hampshire** Phila 1805 8 x 6 Ex-atlas UC engraving *From the Pocket Atlas Phillips (A) 1368* $150.00

Carey & Lea **Geographical, ... Historical Map of New Hampshire** Phila 1822-23 17.5 x 22 Ex-atlas HC engraving *Complete Historical, Chronological and Geographical American Atlas Phillips (A) 1373a* $225.00

Lucas, Fielding **New Hampshire** Baltimore 1823 14.5 X 11.5 Ex-atlas HC engraving *From A General Atlas Phillips (A) 742* $225.00

Tanner, Henry S. **Map of the States of Maine, New Hampshire, Vermont, Massachusetts...** Phila 1823 27 x 22 Ex-atlas HC engraving *From A New American Atlas* $750.00

Finley, A. **Map of Maine, New Hampshire and Vermont** Phila 1826 17 x 21.5 Ex-atlas HC engraving *From New American Atlas* $350.00

Finley, A. **New Hampshire** Phila 1832 11 x 9 Ex-atlas HC engraving *From New General Atlas Phillips (A)1378* $200.00

Tanner, Henry S. **New Hampshire and Vermont** Phila 1833-36 14 x 11 Ex-atlas HC engraving *From A New Universal Atlas Phillips-A-774, 6* $125.00

Bradford, T. G. **New Hampshire & Vermont** Boston 1835 10 x 7.5 Ex-atlas HC engraving *From a Comprehensive Atlas* $95.00

Bradford, T. G. **New Hampshire & Vermont** Boston 1835 10 x 7.5 Ex-atlas HC engraving *From a Comprehensive Atlas* $95.00

Burr, David H. **Vermont & New Hampshire** NY 1836 15 x 12 Ex-atlas HC engraving *From The Universal Atlas* $145.00

Bradford, T. G. **New Hampshire** Boston 1838 14.5 x 11.5 Ex-atlas HC engraving *From An Illustrated Atlas* $100.00

Greenleaf **Vermont and New Hampshire** Brattleboro 1842 11 x 13 Ex-atlas HC engraving *From New General Atlas* $175.00

Colton, J. W. & G. W. **New Hampshire** NY 1855-56 15 x 18 Ex-atlas Lithograph after engraving *From Colton's Atlas of the World Phillips (A)816* $95.00

Johnson & Browning **Johnson's New Hampshire and Vermont** NY 1861 17 x 23 Ex-atlas Lithograph after engraving *Johnson's New Illustrated Family Atlas* $95.00

Mitchell, S. A. **New Hampshire and Vermont** Phila 1862 13 x 11 Ex-atlas Lithograph after engraving *From A New General Atlas* $60.00

Mitchell, S. A. **County and Township Map of ... New Hampshire and Vermont** Phila 1879 19 x 12 Ex-atlas Lithograph after engraving *From A New General Atlas Phillips (A)890* $50.00

Mitchell, S. A. **Map of Missouri** Phila 1847 16 x 13 Ex-atlas HC engraving From A New Universal Atlas. Several editions of this atlas, from various publishers, appeared between 1845 and 1857. The engraved, hand colored border was a regular feature of maps from this atlas. The map is a combination of lithography and engraving. See previous illustration.

New Jersey

New Jersey became a state in 1787

Carey, Matthew **The State of New Jersey** Phila 1795 18.5 x 12 Ex-atlas UC engraving *From the General Atlas* $400.00

Carey, Matthew **New Jersey** Phila 1796 8 x 6 Ex-atlas UC engraving *From the Pocket Atlas Phillips (A) 1364* $175.00

• Arrowsmith & Lewis **New Jersey** Phila 1804 10.5 x 8.5 Ex-atlas Engraving *From New and Elegant General Atlas Phillips (A) 702 Illustrated* $125.00

Carey, Matthew **New Jersey** Phila 1805 8 x 6 Ex-atlas UC engraving *From the Pocket Atlas Phillips (A) 1368* $150.00

Arrowsmith & Lewis **New Jersey** Boston 1819 10.5 x 8.5 Ex-atlas Engraving *From New and Elegant General Atlas Phillips (A) 734* $125.00

Carey & Lea **Geographical, ... Historical Map of New Jersey** Phila 1822-23 17.5 x 22 Ex-atlas HC engraving *Complete Historical, Chronological and Geographical American Atlas Phillips (A) 1373a* $225.00

Lucas, Fielding **New Jersey** Baltimore 1823 14.5 X 11.5 Ex-atlas HC engraving *From A General Atlas Phillips (A) 742* $225.00

Tanner, Henry S. **Map of Pennsylvania and New Jersey** Phila 1823 21 x 28 Ex-atlas HC engraving *From American Atlas* $750.00

Finley, A. **New Jersey** Phila 1826 11.5 x 8.5 Ex-atlas HC engraving *From New General Atlas Phillips (A) 1378* $125.00

Mitchell, S. A. **Map of Pennsylvania, New Jersey and Delaware** Phila 1832 17 x 21 Folding Map HC engraving *Cloth or leather covers* $300.00

Bradford, T. G. **Pennsylvania & New Jersey** Boston 1835 8 x 10 Ex-atlas HC engraving *From a Comprehensive Atlas* $75.00

Burr, David H. **New Jersey** NY 1836 12 x 15 Ex-atlas HC engraving *From The Universal Atlas Phillips (A) 1379a* $150.00

Bradford, T. G. **New Jersey** Boston 1838 14 x 11 Ex-atlas HC engraving *From An Illustrated Atlas* $125.00

Burr, David **Map of New Jersey and Pennsylvania** Washington 1839 37.5 x 50.5 Folding Map HC engraving *2 sheets* $800.00

Burr, David H. **Map of New Jersey & Pennsylvania** Washington 1839 36 x 50 Folding Map HC engraving $1,500.00

Greenleaf **New Jersey** Brattleboro 1842 12.5 x 10.5 Ex-atlas HC engraving *From New General Atlas Phillips (A) 784* $125.00

Tanner, Henry S. **A Map of the Canals and Railroads of Pennsylvania and New Jersey** Phila 1850 21 x 27.5 Sep. issue HC engraving *Separately issued* $650.00

Thomas, Cowperthwait & Co **Map of New Jersey Reduced from...Gordon's Map** Phila 1850 15 x 12.5 Ex-atlas HC engraving *20 Counties shown Phillips (A) 800* $95.00

Colton, J. W. & G. W. **New Jersey** NY 1855-56 15 x 18 Ex-atlas Lithograph after engraving *From Colton's Atlas of the World Phillips (A) 816* $95.00

Desilver **Map of New Jersey Compiled From the Latest Authorities** Phila 1856 15.5 x 12.5 Ex-atlas HC Engraving *20 Counties Phillips (A) 823* $95.00

Desilver **A New Map of the State of Pennsylvania Including New Jersey** Phila 1860 16 x 26.5 Ex-atlas HC Engraving *Phillips (A) 823* $100.00

Mitchell, S. A. **County Map of New Jersey Maryland and Delaware** Phila 1860 11 x 13 Ex-atlas Lithograph after engraving *Three maps on one sheet. From A New General Atlas* $50.00

Johnson & Browning **Johnson's New Jersey** NY 1861 16 x 13 Ex-atlas Lithograph after engraving *Johnson's New Illustrated Family Atlas* $50.00

Gray **New Jersey** NY 1873 15 x 12 Ex-atlas Lithograph after engraving *Phillips (A) 1390* $75.00

New Mexico

New Mexico became a state in Jan. 1912

Thomas, Cowperthwait & Co **A New Map of California...Oregon, Washington, Utah & New Mexico** Phila 1850-52 15.5 x 12.5 Ex-atlas HC engraving *The Chief Part of New Mexico"* $375.00

Colton, J. W. & G. W. **Territories of New Mexico and Utah** NY 1855-56 15 x 18 Ex-atlas Lithograph after engraving *From Colton's Atlas of the World Phillips (A) 816* $175.00

Morse & Gaston **Utah & New Mexico** NY 1857 5 x 6 Ex-atlas Cerograph *From Diamond Atlas Phillips (A) 824* $75.00

Colton, J. W. & G. W. **Colton's Territories of New Mexico and Utah** NY 1861 13 x 15.5 Ex-atlas Lithograph after engraving *Shows Confederate Arizona territory* $200.00

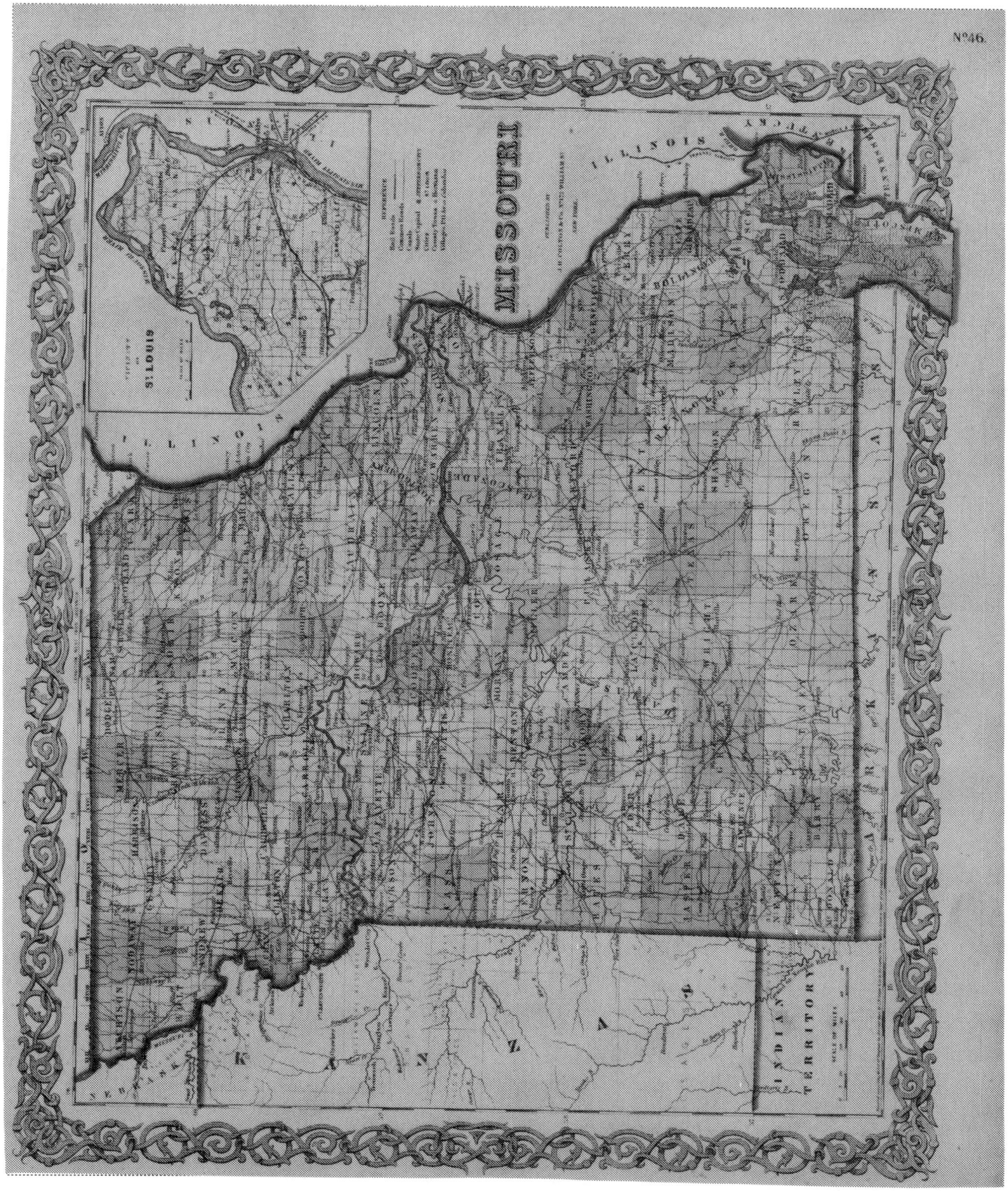

Colton, J. W. & G. W. **Missouri** *NY 1855-56 15 x 18 Ex-atlas Lithograph after engraving From Colton's Atlas of the World Phillips (A)816. A typical state map from this atlas, often considered the last of the elegant American atlases. A page, or more, of descriptive text accompanied each of the maps.*

Johnson & Browning **Johnson's California, Territories of New Mexico and Utah** NY 1861 18 x 24 Ex-atlas Lithograph after engraving *Johnson's New Illustrated Family Atlas* $125.00

Mitchell, S. A. **Arizona and New Mexico** Phila 1867 11.5 x 14.5 Ex-atlas Lithograph after engraving *From A New General Atlas Phillips (A) 850* $75.00

Lloyd, H. H. **Map of Utah, Arizona, New Mexico, Kansas, Colorado & Indian Territory** NY 1870 16.5 x 27 Ex-atlas Lithograph after engraving *Issued as a supplement to state and county atlases* $225.00

Asher & Adams **Asher & Adams New Mexico** NY 1873 16.5 x 22.5 Ex-atlas Lithograph *Asher & Adams New Statistical and Topographical Atlas* $150.00

Colton, J. W. & G. W. **New Mexico and Arizona** NY 1873 17 x 25 Ex-atlas Lithograph after engraving *From Colton's General Atlas* $150.00

Mitchell, S. A. **New Mexico and Arizona** Phila 1874 13 x 11 Ex-atlas Lithograph after engraving *From A New General Atlas* $75.00

Colton, J. W. & G. W. **Colton's Map of New Mexico and Arizona** NY 1877 20 x 24 Folding Map Lithograph after engraving *Cloth or leather folder* $450.00

Mitchell, S. A. **County and Township Map of Arizona and New Mexico** Phila 1881 15 x 22 Ex-atlas Lithograph after engraving *From a New General Atlas Phillips (A) 895* $85.00

Rand McNally & Co. **New Mexico** Chicago 1882 19.5 x 13 Ex-atlas Wax engraving *From Indexed Atlas of the World.* $85.00

Bradley **Arizona and New Mexico** Phila 1886 14.5 x 22 Ex-atlas Lithograph *From New General Atlas See Phillips (A) 920* $75.00

Bradley **County and Township Map of Arizona and New Mexico** Phila 1887 14 x 22 Ex-atlas Lithograph *From New General Atlas See Phillips (A) 920* $85.00

New Orleans

Melish, J. **New Orleans and Adjacent Countrry** Phila 1816 7 x 4 Ex-atlas HC engraving $85.00

Colton, J. W. & G. W. **Louisville & New Orleans** NY 1855-56 15 x 18 Ex-atlas Lithograph after engraving *From Colton's Atlas of the World Phillips (A) 816* $95.00

Mitchell, S. A. **Plan of New Orleans** Phila 1860-71 9 x 11 Ex-atlas Lithograph after engraving *From A New General Atlas* $60.00

Duncan & Co. **Plan of the City and Environs of New Orleans...** Phila 1865 15.5 x 18.5 Folding Map HC engraving $700.00

New York

New York became a state in 1788

• Arrowsmith & Lewis **New York** Phila 1804 8.5 x 10.5 Ex-atlas Engraving *From New and Elegant General Atlas Phillips (A) 702* Illustrated $125.00

Carey, Matthew **New York** Phila 1805 6 x 8 Ex-atlas UC engraving *From the Pocket Atlas Phillips (A) 1368* $150.00

Melish, J. **View of the Country Round the Falls of Niagara** Phila 1816 7 x 4 Ex-atlas HC engraving $85.00

Tanner, Henry S. **New York** Phila 1819-23 22 x 26 Ex-atlas HC engraving *From A New American Atlas* $750.00

Goodrich **Map of the Hudson Between Sandy Hook & Sandy Hill...** NY 1820 47 x 9 Folding Map Engraving *Half leather folder* $1,500.00

Melish, J. **Ballston & Saratoga Springs...Albany and Adjacent country** Phila 1822 6.5 x 4 Ex-atlas Engraving *from Description of the United States* $75.00

Carey & Lea **Geographical, ... Historical Map of New York** Phila 1822-23 17.5 x 22 Ex-atlas HC engraving *Complete Historical, Chronological and Geographical American Atlas Phillips (A) 1373a* $295.00

Lucas, Fielding **New York** Baltimore 1823 14.5 X 20.5 Ex-atlas HC engraving *From A General Atlas Phillips (A) 742* $295.00

Finley, A. **New York** Phila 1824 8.5 x 11 Ex-atlas HC engraving *From New General Atlas* $125.00

Mitchell, S. A. **Map of the State of New York Compiled from the Latest Authorities** Phila 1832 17 x 22 Folding Map HC engraving *Cloth or leather covers* $350.00

Colton, J. W. **New York** NY 1833 17 x 21 Folding Map HC Engraving *Cloth folder. First Colton publication* $600.00

Burr, David H. **Map of the State of New York** NY 1836 12 x 15 Ex-atlas HC engraving *From The Universal Atlas Phillips (A) 1379a* $175.00

Bradford, T. G. **New York** Boston 1838 14 x 11 Ex-atlas HC engraving *From An Illustrated Atlas* $125.00

Bradford & Goodrich **New York** Boston 1838-46 11 x 14 Ex-atlas Lithograph after engraving *From Universal Illustrated Atlas Phillips (A) 783* $85.00

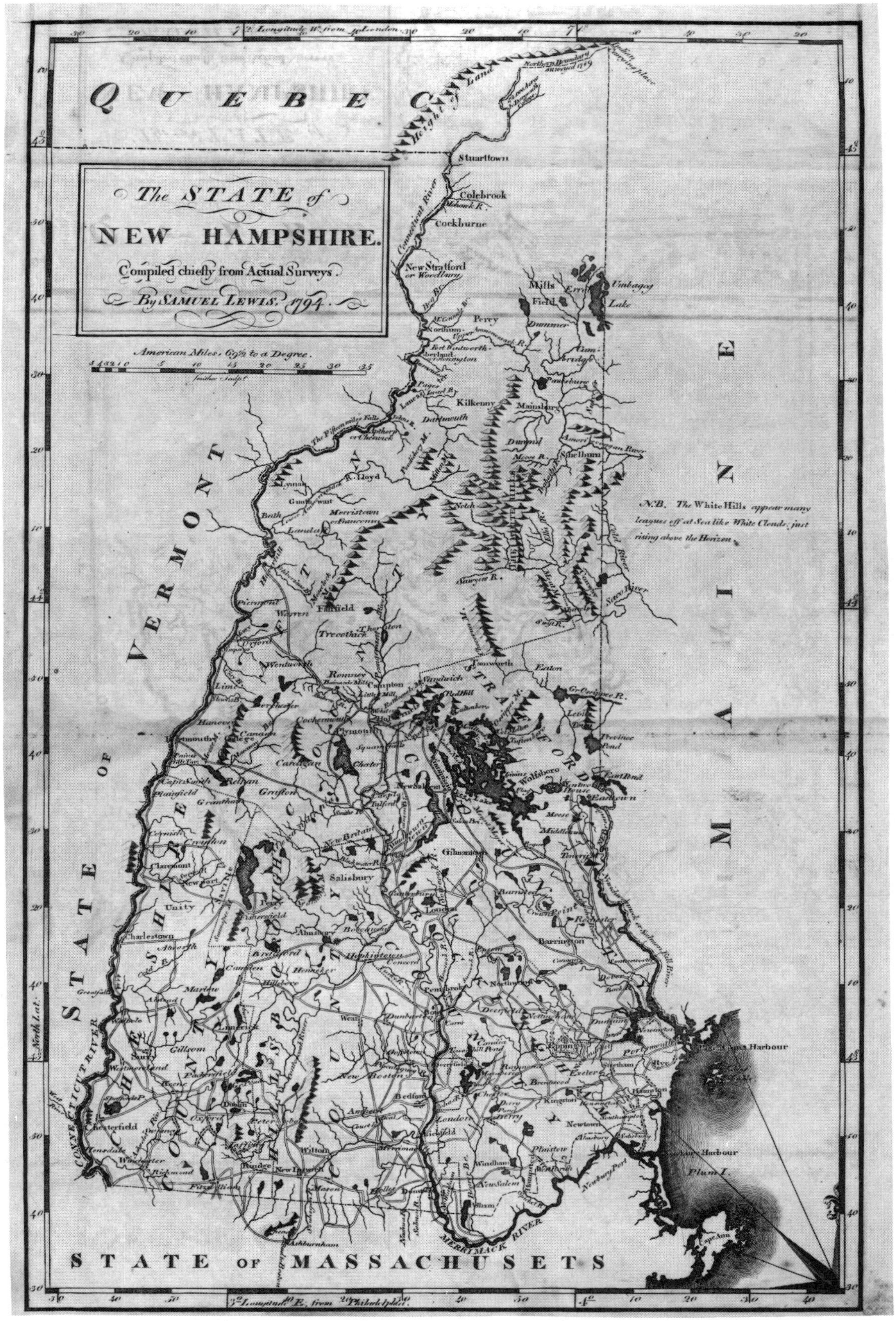

Carey, Matthew **The State of New Hampshire** Phila 1794 17.5 x 11 Ex-atlas UC engraving From the General Atlas. New Hampshire became a state in 1788. This map was included in Carey's American Atlas, the first American atlas, published in 1795. Phillips(M) 478.

Burr, David H. **Map of the State of New York** Ithaca 1839 19 x 24 Folding Map HC engraving *Leather covers* $350.00

Greenleaf **New York** Brattleboro 1842 12.5 x 10.5 Ex-atlas HC engraving *From New General Atlas Phillips (A) 784* $125.00

Morse & Breese **City of New York** NY 1842 14 x 11 Ex-atlas Cerographic prtd color *From Cerographic Atlas* $175.00

Sidney **Sidney's Map of Twelve Miles Around New York, With Names of Property Owners** Phila 1849 33 diam 2 Sheets Engraving $700.00

Colton, J. W. **Colton's Map of New York** NY 1850 20 x 20 Folding Map HC Engraving $275.00

Thomas, Cowperthwait & Co **A New Map of New York With Its Canals, Roads and Distances** Phila 1850 12 x 14.5 Ex-atlas HC engraving *From A New Universal Atlas Phillips (A)800* $85.00

Colton, J. W. & G. W. **Colton's Railroad and Township Map of ... New York** NY 1853-60 28 x 24 Folding Map Lithograph after engraving *Cloth folder* $275.00

Colton, J. W. & G. W. **New York** NY 1854 11 x 14 Folding Map Lithograph after engraving *Cloth folder* $250.00

Smith, J. C. **Map of Long Island With the Environs of New York and...Connecticut** NY 1854 37 x 55.5 Wall Map HC Engraving $750.00

Colton, J. W. & G. W. **New York** NY 1855-56 15 x 18 Ex-atlas Lithograph after engraving *From Colton's Atlas of the World Phillips (A)816* $95.00

Desilver **Map of the State of New York Compiled From the Latest Authorities** Phila 1857 16 x 26 Ex-atlas HC Engraving *Five insets, two columns of data Phillips (A)823* $150.00

Gray **Map of Cayuga and Seneca Counties, New York...by O. W. Gray** NY 1859 58 x 58 Wall Map HC engraving $375.00

Gray **Map of Orleans & Niagara Counties, New York...by O. W. Gray** Phila 1860 60 x 60 Wall Map HC engraving *Phila: A. R. Z. Dawson* $375.00

Mitchell, S. A. **County Map of the State of New York** Phila 1860 14 x 21.5 Ex-atlas Lithograph after engraving *With five inset maps. From a New General Atlas Phillips (A)831* $60.00

Johnson & Browning **Johnson's New York** NY 1861 17 x 23 Ex-atlas Lithograph after engraving *Johnson's New Illustrated Family Atlas* $85.00

Mitchell, S. A. **The Empire State of New York With Its Counties, Towns, Villages** Phila 1864 39 x 48.5 Folding Map Lithograph after engraving *Cloth or leather covers Phillips (M) 512* $600.00

Gray **Map of the Railroads of New York and Part of New England** NY 1874 16.5 x 25.5 Ex-atlas Lithograph after engraving *With Colton copyright* $95.00

Railroad Map **NY Central & Hudson River RR Hudson River Map** NY 1876 90.5 x 4.5 Folding Map Lithograph *Binder* $200.00

Gray **New York** NY 1878 17.5 x 27.5 Ex-atlas Lithograph after engraving $75.00

Rand McNally & Co. **Pocket Map and Shipper's Guide of New York** Chicago 1892 19 x 25.5 Folding Map Wax engraving $75.00

Melish, J. **New York and Adjacent Country** Phila 1822 7 x 4 Ex-atlas HC engraving $85.00

Colton, J. W. **Map of the State of New York....Embracing Plans of the Cities...by David A. Burr** NY 1834 46 x 56 Wall Map HC Engraving $800.00

New York City

Taylor, Benjamin **A New & Accurate Plan of the City of New York** NY 1797 24.5 x 38 Wall Map HC engraving $18,000.00

Randel, John **The City of New York** NY 1821 26 x 37 Folding Map HC engraving $2,000.00

Burr, David H. **Map of the City and County of New York With the Adjacent Country** NY 1829 20 x 49.5 Ex-atlas HC engraving *From Atlas of the State of New York Phillips (A) 1379a* $900.00

Burr, David H. **Map of the Country ...Round New York City** NY 1836 15 x 12 Ex-atlas HC engraving *From The Universal Atlas. Circular Map Phillips (A) 1379a* $250.00

Disturnell **Routes Between New York and Washington** Phila 1837 23.4 x 4.5 Folding Map HC engraving *Cloth folder* $800.00

- Tanner, T. R. **Strangers' New York City Guide** NY 1842 18 x 24 Folding Map HC engraving *Illustrated* $500.00
-

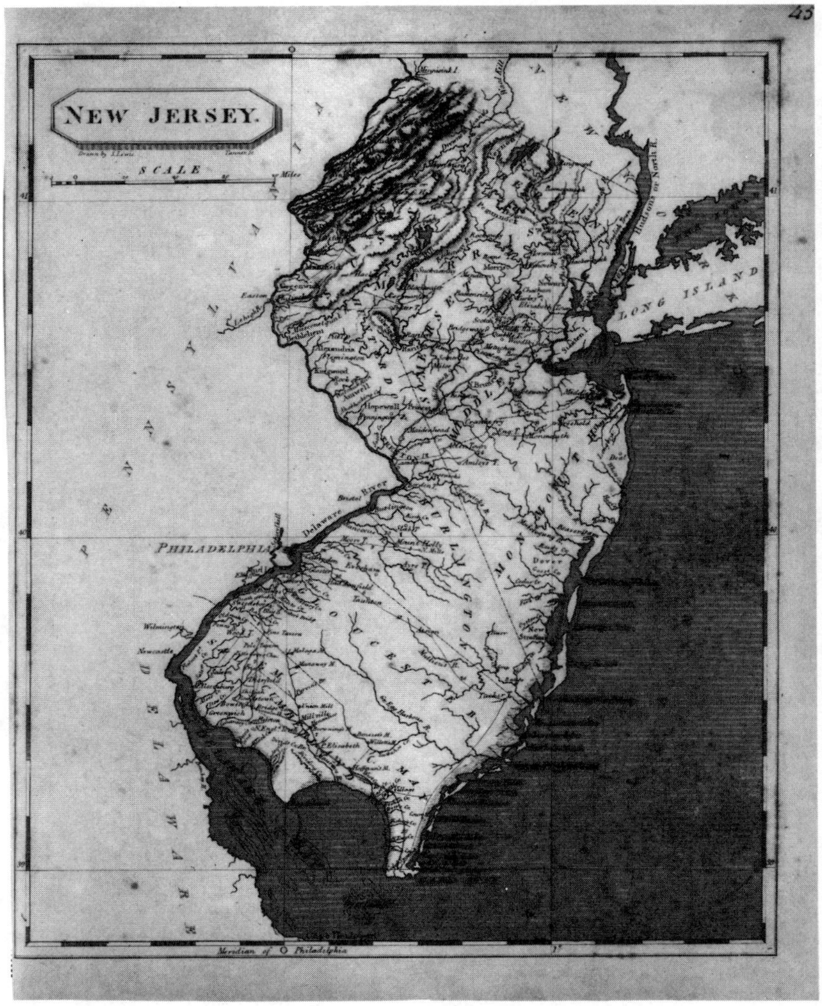

Arrowsmith & Lewis ***New Jersey*** *Phila 1804 10.5 x 8.5 Ex-atlas Engraving From New and Elegant General Atlas Phillips (A)702*
New Jersey became a state in 1787

Mitchell, S. A. **City of New York** Phila 1850 16 x 13 Ex-atlas HC engraving *From A New Universal Atlas* $95.00

Colton, J. W. **New York, Brooklyn, Williamsburgh, Jersey City & the Adjacent..** NY 1853 25 x 51 Wall Map HC Engraving $650.00

Colton, J. W. **Map of the City of Brooklyn...City of Williamsburgh...Part of the City of New York** NY 1855 32.5 x 46 Wall Map HC engraving $425.00

Colton, J. W. **Map ... Thirty Three Miles Around New York City** NY 1855 24.5 x 23 Folding Map HC Engraving *Cloth folder* $500.00

Colton, J. W. & G. W. **Map of New York City** NY 1855-56 18 x 28 Ex-atlas Lithograph after engraving *From Colton's Atlas of the World Phillips (A)816* $175.00

Mitchell, S. A. **Plan of New York** Phila 1860 13 x 11 Ex-atlas Lithograph after engraving *From A New General Atlas Phillips (A)831* $75.00

Colton, J. W. & G. W. **Colton's New York City, Brooklyn, Jersey City, Hoboken..** NY 1873 22.5 x 15 Folding Map Lithograph after engraving *Cloth folder* $375.00

Arrowsmith & Lewis ***New York*** *Phila 18048.5 x 10.5Ex-atlas Engraving From New and Elegant General Atlas Phillips (A)702 New York became a state in 1788*

Gray **Gray's Atlas Map of New York City** NY 187317 x 14Ex-atlas Lithograph after engraving *Phillips (A)1390* $95.00

Colton, J. W. & G. W. **Map ... Thirty Three Miles Around City of New York** NY 187924.5 x 23.5 Circular Map Lithograph after engraving $600.00

Mitchell, S. A. **New York and Brooklyn** Phila 188113.5 x 21 Ex-atlas Lithograph after engraving *From A New General Atlas Phillips (A) 895*$75.00

North America

Morse, J. **A General Map of North America from the Best Authorities** Phila 17967 x 9 Ex-atlas Engraving *From American Universal Geography Wheat & Brun 55* $250.00

Morse, J. **A Map of North America from the latest Discoveries 1806** Phila 18076 x 7 Ex-atlas Engraving *From Geography Made Easy Phillips (M) 597*$200.00

Melish, J. **Map of the Seat of War in North America** Phila 181715. x 21.5 Ex-atlas HC engraving $650.00

Tanner, Henry S. **A Map of North America** Phila 1822 42.5 x 57.5 Wall Map HC engraving $4,750.00

Carey & Lea **Geographical, ... Historical Map of North America** Phila 1822-23 17.5 x 22 Ex-atlas HC engraving *Complete Historical, Chronological and Geographical American Atlas Phillips (A) 1373a*$295.00

• Lucas, Fielding **North America** Baltimore 182314.5 X 11.5 Ex-atlas HC engraving *From A General Atlas Phillips (A) 742*$225.00

Burr, David H. **North America** NY 183615 x 12 Ex-atlas HC engraving *From The Universal Atlas Phillips (A) 1379a*$175.00

Tanner, Henry S. **North America** Phila 1836-4214.5 x 12 Ex-atlas HC engraving *From A New Universal Atlas Phillips-A-788,2*$225.00

Tanner, T. R. ***Strangers' New York City Guide*** *NY 1842 18 x 24 Folding Map HC engraving*

Greenleaf **North America** Brattleboro 1848 13 x 11 Ex-atlas HC engraving *From A New Universal Atlas* $175.00

Monk **Monk's New American Map Exhibiting North America, United States and Territories** NY 1855 57.5 x 61 Wall Map HC engraving *Hoen & Co.* $450.00

Colton, J. W. & G. W. **North America** NY 1855-56 15 x 18 Ex-atlas Lithograph after engraving *From Colton's Atlas of the World Phillips (A)816* $95.00

Mitchell, S. A. **Map of North America** Phila 1860 13 x 11 Ex-atlas Lithograph after engraving *From A New General Atlas Phillips (A)831* $75.00

Johnson & Browning **Johnson's North America** NY 1861 17 x 22 Ex-atlas Lithograph after engraving *Johnson's New Illustrated Family Atlas* $95.00

North & South America

See North America

Aspin **North and South America** Phila 1823 13.5 x 17 Sep. Issue HC engraving *From Abbe Gaultiers Geographical Game. Shows Franklinia in eastern TN* $275.00

North Carolina

North Carolina became a state in 1789

Arrowsmith & Lewis **North Carolina** Phila 1804 8.5 x 10.5 Ex-atlas Engraving *From New and Elegant General Atlas Phillips (A)702* $150.00

Carey, Matthew **North Carolina** Phila 1805 6 x 8 Ex-atlas UC engraving *From the Pocket Atlas Phillips (A) 1368* $175.00

• Carey, Matthew **North Carolina** Phila 1814 11 x 18 Ex-atlas HC engraving *From the General Atlas Illustrated* $475.00

Carey, Matthew **North Carolina, From the Latest Surveys, By Samuel Lewis** Phila 1818 11 x 18.5 Ex-atlas HC engraving *From the General Atlas Phillips (A)732* $475.00

Carey & Lea **Geographical, ... Historical Map of North Carolina** Phila 1822-23 17.5 x 22 Ex-atlas HC engraving *Complete Historical, Chronological and Geographical American Atlas Phillips (A) 1373a* $225.00

Lucas, Fielding **North Carolina** Baltimore 1823 14.5 X 20.5 Ex-atlas HC engraving *From A General Atlas Phillips (A) 742* $250.00

Tanner, Henry S. **Map of North Carolina and South Carolina by H. S. Tanner** Phila 1825 23 x 29 Ex-atlas HC engraving *From American Atlas 2d Edition* $850.00

Mitchell, S. A. **A New Map of North Carolina** Phila 1850 13 x 16 Ex-atlas HC engraving *From A New Universal Atlas Phillips (A) 800* $85.00

Thomas, Cowperthwait & Co **A New Map of Nth Carolina With Its Canals, Roads and Distances...** Phila 1850-55 15 x 12.5 Ex-atlas HC engraving *From A New Universal Atlas Phillips (A)800* $95.00

Colton, J. W. & G. W. **North Carolina** NY 1855-56 15 x 18 Ex-atlas Lithograph after engraving *From Colton's Atlas of the World Phillips (A)816* $95.00

Desilver **A New Map of Nth. Carolina With Its Canals, Roads...** Phila 1856 12 x 14.5 Ex-atlas HC Engraving *From A New Universal Atlas Phillips (A)823* $95.00

Mitchell, S. A. **North Carolina (and) South Carolina (and) Florida** Phila 1860 13 x 11 Ex-atlas Lithograph after engraving *From A New General Atlas Phillips (A)831* $50.00

Mitchell, S. A. **County Map of Virginia and North Carolina** Phila 1860 10 x 12 Ex-atlas Lithograph after engraving *From A New General Atlas Phillips (A)831* $60.00

Colton, J. W. & G. W. **Colton's North Carolina** NY 1869-71 14 x 16 Folding Map Lithograph after engraving *Cloth folder* $350.00

Asher & Adams **North Carolina & South Carolina** NY 1872 16.5 x 22.5 Ex-atlas Lithograph *Asher & Adams New Statistical and Topographical Atlas Phillips(A)1272* $75.00

Gray **Gray's Atlas Map of North Carolina** NY 1873 14.5 x 17 Ex-atlas Lithograph after engraving *Phillips (A)1390* $75.00

North & South Carolina

See North Carolina, South Carolina

Burr, David H. **North and South Carolina** NY 1836 12 x 15 Ex-atlas HC engraving *From The Universal Atlas Phillips (A) 1379a* $145.00

Burr, David H. **North and South Carolina** NY 1836 12 x 15 Ex-atlas HC engraving *From The Universal Atlas Phillips (A) 1379a* $145.00

Johnson & Browning **Johnson's North and South Carolina** NY 1861 17 x 22 Ex-atlas Lithograph after engraving *Johnson's New Illustrated Family Atlas* $75.00

Carey, Matthew **North Carolina** *Phila 1814 11 x 18 Ex-atlas HC engraving From the General Atlas*

Lucas, Fielding ***North America*** *Baltimore 1823 14.5 X 11.5 Ex-atlas HC engraving From A General Atlas Phillips (A) 742*

North & South Dakota

See Dakotas

Bradley **North and South Dakota** Phila 1889 21 x 17 Ex-atlas Lithograph *From New General Atlas See Phillips (A)920 See Dakota* $85.00

Ohio

Ohio became a state in March 1803

• Arrowsmith & Lewis **Ohio** Phila 1804 10.5 x 8.5 Ex-atlas Engraving *First separate map of the new state. From New and Elegant General Atlas Phillips (A)702* Illustrated $325.00

Carey, Matthew **Ohio** Phila 1814 6 x 8 Ex-atlas UC engraving *From the Pocket Atlas Phillips (A) 1370* $150.00

Carey, Matthew **The State of Ohio With Part of Upper Canada** Phila 1814 14.5 x 14 Ex-atlas HC engraving *From the General Atlas Phillips (A) 722* $500.00

Carey, Matthew **Plat of the Seven Ranges of Townships** Phila 1814 24 x 13 Ex-atlas UC engraving *From the General Atlas Phillips (A) 722* $450.00

Melish, J. **Falls of Ohio** Phila 1815 6 x 4 Ex-atlas Engraving $125.00

Tanner, Henry S. **Ohio and Indiana** Phila 1819-23 21 x 26 Ex-atlas HC engraving *From A New American Atlas* $650.00

Carey & Lea **Geographical, ... Historical Map of Ohio** Phila 1822-23 17.5 x 22 Ex-atlas HC engraving *Complete Historical, Chronological and Geographical American Atlas Phillips (A) 1373a* $295.00

Lucas, Fielding **Ohio** Baltimore 1823 14.5 X 11.5 Ex-atlas HC engraving *From A General Atlas Phillips (A) 742* $250.00

• Tanner, Henry S. **A New Map of Ohio...** Phila 1833 15 x 11 Ex-atlas HC engraving *From The Universal Atlas Illustrated* $175.00

Finley, A. **Map of Ohio and the Settled Parts of Michigan** Phila 1834 19 x 13 Folding Map HC engraving *Leather folder* $750.00

Bradford, T. G. **Indiana & Ohio** Boston 1835 8 x 10 Ex-atlas HC engraving *From a Comprehensive Atlas* $85.00

Mitchell, S. A. **Map of the States of Ohio, Indiana and Illinois With the Settled Part of Michigan** Phila 1835 18 x 22.5 Folding Map HC engraving *Cloth or leather covers* $675.00

Burr, David H. **Ohio** NY 1836 12 x 15 Ex-atlas HC engraving *From The Universal Atlas Phillips (A) 1379a* $145.00

Bradford, T. G. **Ohio** Boston 1838 13.5 x 11 Ex-atlas HC engraving *From An Illustrated Atlas* $125.00

Robinson, L. **Map of Ohio Compiled from the Latest Authorities** Akron 1840 26 x 22.5 Wall Map HC Engraving $2,000.00

Greenleaf **Ohio** Brattleboro 1842 13 x 11 Ex-atlas HC engraving *From New General Atlas Phillips (A) 784* $175.00

Smith, J. C. **Guide Through the States of Ohio, Michigan, Indiana, Illinois, Missouri, Wisconsin & Iowa** NY 1854 17.5 x 22 Folding Map HC Engraving *From Colton, The Western Tourist and Emigrant's Guide...* $175.00

Thomas, Cowperthwait & Co **A New Map of the State of Ohio** Phila 1854 16 x 13.5 Ex-atlas HC engraving *From A New Universal Atlas Phillips (A)813* $85.00

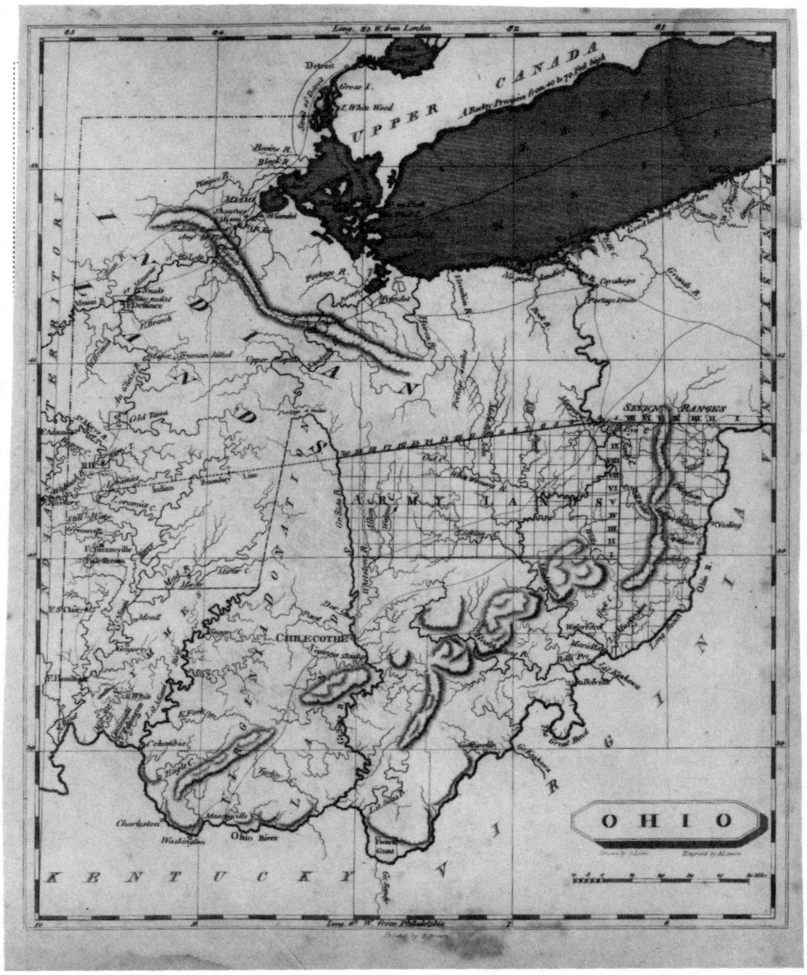

Arrowsmith & Lewis **Ohio** *Phila 1804 10.5 x 8.5 Ex-atlas Engraving First separate map of the new state. From New and Elegant General Atlas. Phillips (A)70. Ohio became a state in March 1803*

Colton, J. W. **Guide Through Ohio, Michigan, Indiana, Illinois, Missouri, Wisconsin & Iowa** NY 1855 20.5 x 25.5 Folding Map HC Engraving *Bound with Colton's Western Tourist and Emigrant's Guide* $450.00

Colton, J. W. & G. W. **Ohio** NY 1855-56 15 x 18 Ex-atlas Lithograph after engraving *From Colton's Atlas of the World Phillips (A)816* $95.00

Desilver **A New Map of the State of Ohio** Phila 1856-57 16 x 13 Ex-atlas HC Engraving *From A New Universal Atlas Phillips (A)823* $100.00

Colton, J. W. **Guide Through Ohio, Michigan, Indiana, Illinois** NY 1857 20 x 27 Folding Map HC Engraving *Cloth folder stamped "Map of the Western States"* $400.00

Mitchell, S. A. **County Map of Ohio and Indiana** Phila 1860-67 11 x 13 Ex-atlas Lithograph after engraving *From A New General Atlas* $50.00

Johnson & Browning **Johnson's Ohio & Indiana** NY 1861 17 x 23 Ex-atlas Lithograph after engraving *Johnson's New Illustrated Family Atlas* $85.00

Colton, J. W. & G. W. **Colton's Railroad and Township Map of Ohio** NY 1867 20 x 24 Folding Map Lithograph after engraving $250.00

Asher & Adams **Ohio and Indiana** NY 1872 16.5 x 22.5 Ex-atlas Lithograph *Asher & Adams New Statistical and Topographical Atlas* $75.00

Colton, J. W. & G. W. **New Railroad Map of Indiana, Ohio and Part of Illinois** NY 1875 16 x 28 Folding Map Lithograph after engraving $75.00

Oil Districts

Barnes, R. L.**Map ofVenango County, Pennsylvania** Phila186524 x 32.5Folding MapHC engraving*Cloth folder*$750.00

Barnes, R. L.**Map ofVenango County, Pennsylvania** Phila186524 x 32.5Folding MapHC engraving*Cloth folderPhillips (A) 783*$750.00

Colton, J. W. & G. W.**Colton's Map of the Oil District ofVenango, Crawford, and Warren Counties, Pennsylvania**NY186531 x 37Folding MapLithograph after engraving*Cloth or leather folder*$600.00

Oklahoma & Indian Territory

See Indian Territory

Oklahoma became a state in Nov. 1907

Mitchell, S. A.**Oklahoma and Indian Territory**Phila 189011.5 x 14.5Ex-atlasLithograph after engraving*From A New General Atlas*$125.00

Rand McNally & Co.**Oklahoma and Indian Territory** Chicago189413 x 20Ex-atlasWax engraving*From Indexed Atlas of the World. 2 sheets*$85.00

Oregon

Oregon became a state in Feb. 1859.

Boundaries settled 1846

Burr, David H.**Oregon Territory**NY1833-3610.5 x 12.5Ex-atlasHC engraving*From The Universal Atlas Phillips (A) 1379a*$300.00

Greenleaf**Oregon Territory**Brattleboro184211 x 13Ex-atlasHC engraving*From New General AtlasPhillips (A) 784*$325.00

Mitchell, S. A.**Oregon and Upper California**Phila 1845-4916 x 13Ex-atlasHC engraving*From A New Universal Atlas*$375.00

Mitchell, S. A.**Map of the State of California...Territories of Oregon and Utah...New Mexico**Phila1845-5016 x 13Ex-atlasHC engraving *From A New Universal Atlas*$375.00

Mitchell, S. A.**Oregon, Upper California and New Mexico**Phila1849-5016 x 13Ex-atlasHC engraving *From A New Universal Atlas*$375.00

Thomas, Cowperthwait & Co**A New Map of California...Oregon, Washington, Utah & New Mexico**Phila1850-5215.5 x 12.5Ex-atlasHC engraving *The Chief Part of New Mexico"Phillips (A) 807*$375.00

Colton, J. W. & G. W.**Washington and Oregon**NY 1855-5615 x 18Ex-atlasLithograph after engraving*From Colton's Atlas of the WorldPhillips (A)816*$125.00

Colton, J. W. & G. W.**The Territories ofWashington and Oregon**NY185612.5 x 16Ex-atlasLithograph after engraving*From Colton's Atlas of the World*$125.00

Morse & Gaston**Washington & Oregon Territories** NY18575 x 6Ex-atlasCerograph*From Diamond Atlas Phillips (A)824*$75.00

Colton, J. W. & G. W.**Oregon, Washington, Idaho, California, Utah and New Mexico**NY185813 x 11Ex-atlasLithograph after engraving*From Colton's General Atlas*$175.00

Mitchell, S. A.**Map ofOregon, Washington and Part of British Columbia**Phila1860-6210.5 x 13.5Ex-atlas Lithograph after engraving*From A New General Atlas* $125.00

Johnson & Browning**Johnson'sWashington & Oregon** NY186111 x 14Ex-atlasLithograph after engraving *Johnson's New Illustrated Family Atlas*$75.00

Mitchell, S. A.**Map ofOregon, Washington, Idaho and Part of Montana**Phila1866-7711 x 13.5Ex-atlas Lithograph after engraving*From A New General Atlas* $75.00

Colton, J. W. & G. W.**Oregon, Washington, Idaho, Montana & British Columbia**NY186816.5 x 27Ex-atlasLithograph after engraving*From Colton's General Atlas*$175.00

Asher & Adams**Asher & Adams Oregon**NY187516.5 x 22.5Ex-atlasLithograph*Asher & Adams New Statistical and Topographical Atlas*$85.00

Colton, J. W. & G. W.**Oregon, Washington and Idaho**NY1876-7717 x 25Ex-atlasLithograph after engraving*From Colton's General AtlasPhillips (A) 879* $125.00

Mitchell, S. A.**County and Township Map ofOregon and Washington**Phila188320 x 14.5Ex-atlasLithograph after engraving*From A New General Atlas*$60.00

Bradley**County and Township Map ofOregon and Washington**Phila188721.5 x 15Ex-atlasLithograph *From New General AtlasSee Phillips (A)920*$95.00

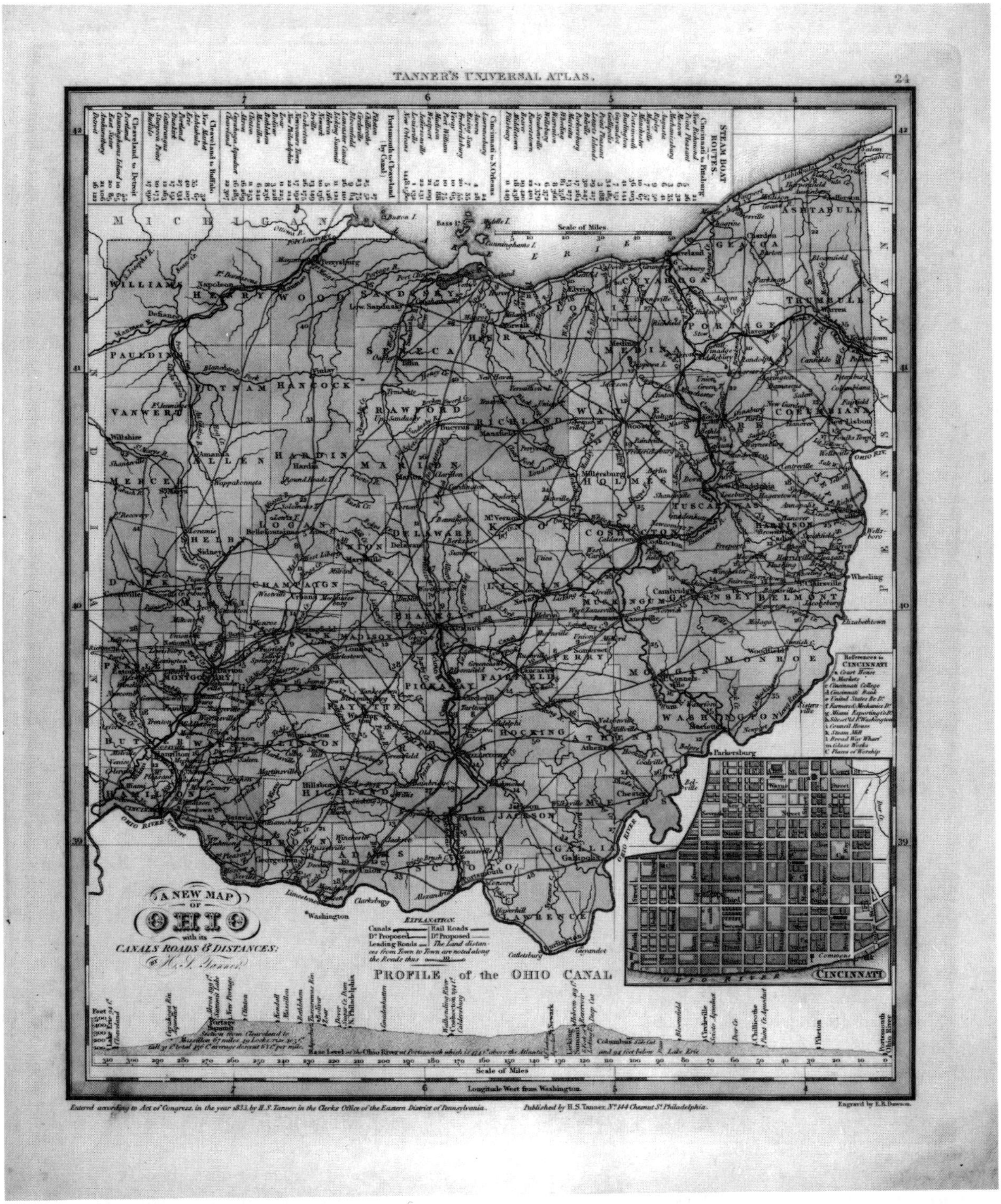

Tanner, Henry S. ***A New Map of Ohio...*** *Phila 1833 15 x 11 Ex-atlas HC engraving From The Universal Atlas. Note the rapid development of the state in less that 30 years.* *See the map on p. 75*

Pennsylvania

Pennsylvania became a state in 1787 as 2d state

• Scott **Pennsylvania** Phila 1795 6 x 7.5 Ex-atlas Engraving *From the United States Gazeteer Illustrated* $125.00

Morse, J. **Pennsylvania Drawn from the Best Authorities** Phila 1796 7.5 x 13 Ex-atlas Engraving *From American Universal Geography Wheat & Brun 446* $175.00

Arrowsmith & Lewis **Pennsylvania** Phila 1804 8.5 x 10.5 Ex-atlas Engraving *From New and Elegant General Atlas Phillips (A) 702* $125.00

Carey, Matthew **Pennsylvania** Phila 1805 6 x 8 Ex-atlas UC engraving *From the Pocket Atlas Phillips (A) 1368* $150.00

Carey, Matthew **Pennsylvaina** Phila 1818 11.5 x 18.5 Ex-atlas HC engraving *From the General Atlas Phillips (A) 732* $475.00

Melish, J. **Map of Dauphin and Lebanon Counties...Pennsylvania** Phila 1818 17 x 23 Folding Map HC engraving $275.00

Tanner, H. S. **A Map of the Roads Leading to ... Britania...Susquehanna County Penn'a.** Phila 1819 Sep. issue Engraving *From The Portfolio* $225.00

Carey & Lea **Geographical, ... Historical Map of Pennsylvania** Phila 1822-23 17.5 x 22 Ex-atlas HC engraving *Complete Historical, Chronological and Geographical American Atlas Phillips (A) 1373a* $295.00

Lucas, Fielding **Pennsylvania** Baltimore 1823 14.5 X 20.5 Ex-atlas HC engraving *From A General Atlas Phillips (A) 742* $275.00

Tanner, Henry S. **Map of Pennsylvania and New Jersey** Phila 1823 21 x 28 Ex-atlas HC engraving *From American Atlas* $750.00

Finley, A. **Pennsylvania** Phila 1824 8.5 x 11 Ex-atlas HC engraving *From New General Atlas* $125.00

Melish, J. **Map of Pennsylvania...** Phila 1826 63 x 77 Folding Map HC engraving $1,500.00

Mitchell, S. A. **Map of Pennsylvania, New Jersey and Delaware** Phila 1832 17 x 21 Folding Map HC engraving *Cloth or leather covers* $300.00

Bradford, T. G. **Pennsylvania & New Jersey** Boston 1835 8 x 10 Ex-atlas HC engraving *From a Comprehensive Atlas* $75.00

Burr, David H. **Pennsylvania** NY 1836 12 x 15 Ex-atlas HC engraving *From The Universal Atlas Phillips (A) 1379a* $175.00

Bradford, T. G. **Pennsylvania** Boston 1838 11.5 x 14.5 Ex-atlas HC engraving *From An Illustrated Atlas* $100.00

Tanner, Henry S. **A New Map of Pennsylvania With It Canals, Railroads...** Phila 1840 11 x 13.5 Ex-atlas HC engraving *Shows 58 counties* $175.00

Mitchell, S. A. **A New Map of Pennsylvania** Phila 1848 11.5 x 14.5 Ex-atlas HC engraving *From A New Universal Atlas* $85.00

Tanner, Henry S. **A Map of the Canals and Railroads of Pennsylvania and New Jersey** Phila 1850 21 x 27.5 Sep. issue HC engraving *Separately issued* $650.00

Thomas, Cowperthwait & Co **A New Map of Pennsylvania** Phila 1851 12 x 14.5 Ex-atlas HC engraving *From A New Universal Atlas Phillips (A) 805* $85.00

Colton, J. W. & G. W. **Pennsylvania** NY 1855-56 15 x 18 Ex-atlas Lithograph after engraving *From Colton's Atlas of the World Phillips (A) 816* $95.00

Barnes, R. L. **County, Township and Railroad Map of ...Pennsylvania** Phila 1857 32.5 x 49 Wall Map HC engraving $500.00

Desilver **A New Map of the State of Pennsylvania Including New Jersey** Phila 1860 16 x 26.5 Ex-atlas HC Engraving *Phillips (A) 823* $100.00

Mitchell, S. A. **County Map of Pennsylvania, New Jersey, Maryland and Delaware** Phila 1860 11x 13 Ex-atlas Lithograph after engraving *From A New General Atlas* $60.00

Johnson & Browning **Johnson's Pennsylvania, Virginia, Delaware, Maryland** NY 1861 17 x 23 Ex-atlas Lithograph after engraving *Johnson's New Illustrated Family Atlas* $85.00

Colton, J. W. & G. W. **Colton's New Township Map of ... Pennsylvania** NY 1866 17 x 27 Folding Map Lithograph after engraving *Cloth folder* $175.00

Colton, J. W. & G. W. **Colton's Map of Pennsylvania** NY 1871 14 x 18 Folding Map Lithograph after engraving $225.00

Philadelphia

Melish, J. **Philadelphia and Adjacent Country** Phila 1822 7 x 4 Ex-atlas HC engraving $85.00

Tanner, Henry S. **Plan of the City of Philadelphia** Phila 1836 16 x 13 Folding Map HC engraving $250.00

Mitchell, S. A. **Philadelphia** Phila 1848 16 x 13 Ex-atlas HC engraving *From A New Universal Atlas* $95.00

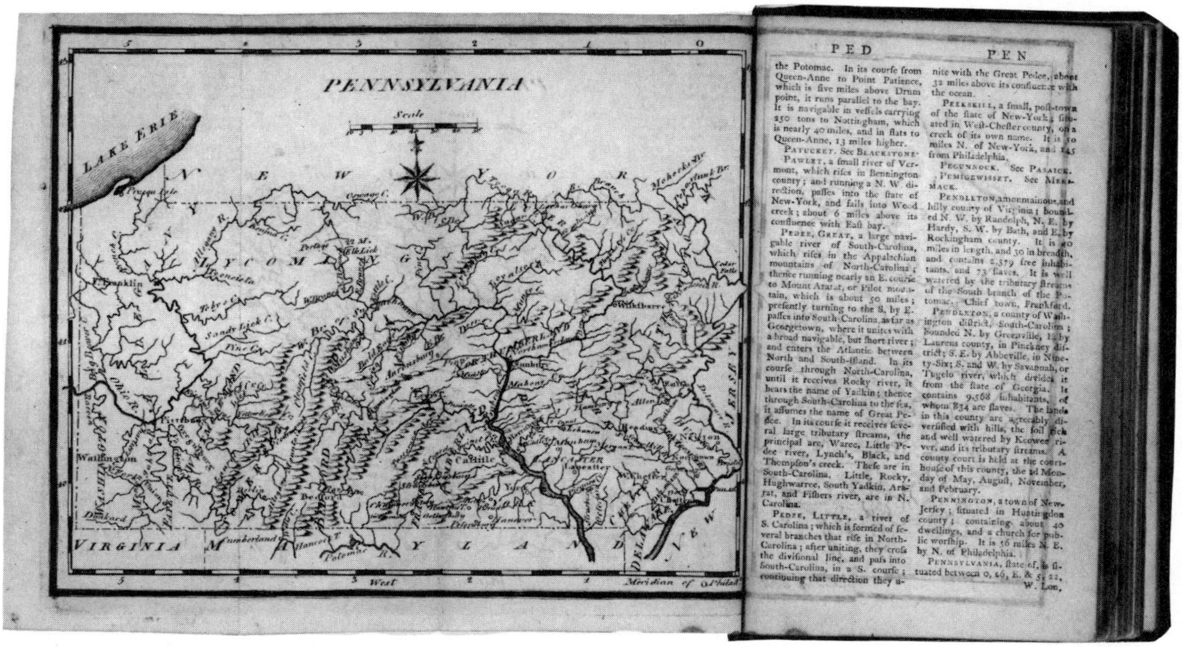

Scott ***Pennsylvania*** *Phila 1795 6 x 7.5 Ex-atlas Engraving From the United States Gazeteer. Ristow 154 Pennsylvania became the 2d state in 1787.*

Thomas, Cowperthwait & Co **Philadelphia** Phila 1851 15.5 x 12.5 Ex-atlas HC engraving *From A New Universal Atlas Phillips (A)805* $85.00

Colton, J. W. & G. W. **Philadelphia** NY 1855-56 15 x 18 Ex-atlas Lithograph after engraving *From Colton's Atlas of the World Phillips (A)816* $125.00

Barnes, R. L. **12 Miles Around Philadelphia** Phila 1858 21 x 21 Folding Map HC engraving *Cloth folder* $400.00

Mitchell, S. A. **Plan of Philadelphia** Phila 1860 13 x 11 Ex-atlas Lithograph after engraving *From A New General Atlas* $75.00

Barnes, R. L. **Barnes Driving Map of Phildelphia and Surroundings** Phila 1874 24.5 x 28.5 Folding Map HC engraving *Cloth folder* $250.00

Pittsburgh

Colton, J. W. & G. W. **Pittsburgh & Cincinnati** NY 1855-56 15 x 18 Ex-atlas Lithograph after engraving *From Colton's Atlas of the World Phillips (A)816* $95.00

Portsmouth on the Ohio River

Colton, J. W. **Portsmouth on the Ohio River** NY 1836 21 x 30 Folding Map HC Engraving *Cloth or leather folder. Bound with Burr's map of Ohio* $1,250.00

Railroad Maps

Colton, J. W. & G. W. **Map of Georgia Central RR and Connections** NY 1859 10 x 14.5 Folding Map Lithograph after engraving *Lang & Lang imprint* $200.00

Rand McNally & Co. **A Geographically Correct County Map of ... Traversed by St. Louis, Iron Mountain & Southern RR** Chicago 1876 16.5 x 15.5 Folding Map Wax engraving *On Broadside with ads* $450.00

Rand McNally & Co. **Map of the Chicago & Northwest'n Railway...** Chicago 1880 9 x 12 Folding Map Wax engraving $75.00

Colton, J. W. & G. W. **Map of the Virginia, Kentucky and Ohio Railroad....** NY 1881 28.5 x 41.5 Wall Map Lithograph after engraving $275.00

Colton, J. W. & G. W. **Map of the Richmond and Louisville RR Connecting... Virginia... Kentucky...** NY 1882 30 x 40 Folding Map Lithograph after engraving *Cloth folder* $350.00

Rand McNally & Co. **A Correct Map of the Chicago, Burlington & Quincy RR...** Chicago 1883 26 x 44.5 Folding Map Wax engraving $300.00

Rand McNally & Co. **Map of the Atchison, Topeka & Santa Fe Railroad System** Chicago 1884 16 x 33 Folding Map Wax engraving *Schedules and ads on verso* $350.00

Rand McNally & Co. **Denver and Rio Grande Railroad System** Chicago 1887 14.5 x 17.5 Folding Map Wax engraving *From Tourist's Handbook issued by the RR* $125.00

Railroad Map **Map of Michigan, S. & N... Indiana Railroad With Their ...** NY 1851 16.5 x 56.5 Folding Map HC engraving *Connections from Council Bluffs to New York* $175.00

Rhode Island

Rhode Island became a state in 1790

Scott **Rhode Island** Phila 1795 7 x 6.5 Ex-atlas Engraving *From the United States Gazeteer. Wheat & Brun 252* $125.00

Arrowsmith & Lewis **Rhode Island** Phila 1804 10.5 x 8.5 Ex-atlas Engraving *From New and Elegant General Atlas Phillips (A) 702* $125.00

Carey, Matthew **Rhode Island** Phila 1805 8 x 6 Ex-atlas UC engraving *From the Pocket Atlas Phillips (A) 1368* $150.00

Carey, Matthew **The State of Rhode Island** Phila 1814 13.5 x 9.5 Ex-atlas HC engraving *From the General Atlas Phillips (A) 722* $375.00

Carey & Lea **Geographical, ...Historical Map of Rhode Island** Phila 1822-23 17.5 x 22 Ex-atlas HC engraving *Complete Historical, Chronological and Geographical American Atlas Phillips (A) 1373a* $225.00

Lucas, Fielding **Rhode Island** Baltimore 1823 14.5 X 11.5 Ex-atlas HC engraving *From A General Atlas Phillips (A) 742* $225.00

Finley, A. **Rhode Island** Phila 1829 8.5 x 11 Ex-atlas HC engraving *From New General Atlas Phillips (A) 752* $125.00

Bradford, T. G. **Rhode Island** Boston 1838 14.5 x 11.5 Ex-atlas HC engraving *From An Illustrated Atlas* $100.00

Colton, J. W. **Massachusetts & Rhode Island** NY 1854 12 x 16 Folding Map HC Engraving *Cloth folder* $175.00

Colton, J. W. & G. W. **Colton's Massachusetts & Rhode Island** NY 1867 15 x 15 Folding Map Lithograph after engraving *Cloth or leather folder* $150.00

Saint Lawrence

Melish, J. **Map of the River St. Lawrence and Adjacent Country...** Phila 1815 17 x 25 Ex-atlas HC engraving *From Military and Topographical Atlas of the United States* $425.00

Rockwell **Map of Part of the Thousand Islands of the St. Lawrence River** NY 1883 17.5 x 23 Folding Map Lithograph $500.00

St. Louis

Melish, J. **St. Louis and Adjacent Country** Phila 1822 7 x 4 Ex-atlas HC engraving $85.00

Colton, J. W. & G. W. **St. Louis & Chicago** NY 1855-56 15 x 18 Ex-atlas Lithograph after engraving *From Colton's Atlas of the World Phillips (A) 816* $95.00

Mitchell, S. A. **St. Louis** Phila 1879 14 x 11 Ex-atlas Lithograph after engraving *From A New General Atlas Phillips (A) 890* $50.00

San Francisco

Britton & Rey **Map of San Francisco from the latest Surveys** SF 1872 17 x 19.5 Folding Map UC engraving *Cloth Folder. "A Map and Street Directory of San Francisco"* $300.00

Gray **San Francisco** NY 1878 15.5 x 12 Ex-atlas Lithograph after engraving $85.00

Savannah

Colton, J. W. & G. W. **Savannah & Charleston** NY 1855-56 15 x 18 Ex-atlas Lithograph after engraving *From Colton's Atlas of the World Phillips (A) 816* $95.00

South Carolina

also see North Carolina

South Carolina became a state in 1788

Scott **South Carolina** Phila 1795 6 x 7 Ex-atlas Engraving *From the United States Gazeteer. Wheat & Brun 602* $125.00

Arrowsmith & Lewis **South Carolina** Phila 1804 8.5 x 10.5 Ex-atlas Engraving *From New and Elegant General Atlas Phillips (A) 702* $125.00

Carey, Matthew **South Carolina** Phila 1805 6 x 8 Ex-atlas UC engraving *From the Pocket Atlas Phillips (A) 1368* $175.00

Carey, Matthew **The State of South Carolina, From the Best Authorities, by Samuel Lewis** Phila 1814 15 x 17.5 Ex-atlas HC engraving *From the General Atlas Phillips (A) 722* $425.00

Carey & Lea **Geographical, ...Historical Map of South Carolina** Phila 1822-23 17.5 x 22 Ex-atlas HC engraving *Complete Historical, Chronological and Geographical American Atlas Phillips (A) 1373a* $225.00

Lucas, Fielding **South Carolina** Baltimore 1823 11.5 X 14.5 Ex-atlas HC engraving *From A General Atlas Phillips (A) 742* $225.00

Mitchell, S. A. **A New Map of South Carolina** Phila 1850 13 x 16 Ex-atlas HC engraving *From A New Universal Atlas Phillips (A) 831* $85.00

Thomas, Cowperthwait & Co **A New Map of South Carolina With Its Canals, Roads...** Phila 1850-55 11.5 x 14 Ex-atlas HC engraving *From A New Universal Atlas Phillips (A) 800* $85.00

Colton, J. W. **South Carolina** NY 1853 11 x 14 Folding Map HC Engraving *Cloth folder* $425.00

Colton, J. W. & G. W. **South Carolina** NY 1855-56 15 x 18 Ex-atlas Lithograph after engraving *From Colton's Atlas of the World Phillips (A) 816* $95.00

Desilver **A New Map of South Carolina Wit Its Canals, Roads...** Phila 1856-57 12 x 14.5 Ex-atlas HC Engraving *From A New Universal Atlas Phillips (A) 823* $95.00

Gray **Gray's Atlas Map of South Carolina** NY 1873 14.5 x 17 Ex-atlas Lithograph after engraving *Phillips (A) 1390* $75.00

Southern States

Mitchell, S. A. **County Map of Louisiana, Mississippi and Arkansas** Phila 1860 13.5 x 10.5 Ex-atlas Lithograph after engraving *From A New General Atlas Phillips (A) 831* $65.00

Gray **Maryland, Delaware and the District of Columbia** NY 1876 15 x 26 Ex-atlas Lithograph after engraving $75.00

Bradley **County Map of the States of Delaware, Maryland, Virginia, and West Virginia** Phila 1882 14.5 x 22 Ex-atlas Lithograph *From New General Atlas See Phillips (A) 920* $75.00

Morse, J. **Map of the Southern Parts of the United States of America** Phila 1797 8 x 15.5 Ex-atlas Engraving *By Abraham Bradley Phillips (M) 872* $275.00

Johnson & Browning **Johnson's Arkansas, Mississippi, Louisiana** NY 1861 23 x 17 Ex-atlas Lithograph after engraving *Johnson's New Illustrated Family Atlas* $75.00

Lloyd, H. H. **New Military Map of the Border & Southern States** NY 1862 30 x 41.5 Wall Map Lithograph after engraving $650.00

Colton, J. W. & G. W. J. H. **Colton's Map of the Southern States, Including Maryland, Delaware** NY 1864 38 x 54 Folding Map Lithograph after engraving *Cloth folder. Map in two sections* $1,500.00

Lloyd, H. H. **Southern States** NY 1868 14.5 x 26 Ex-atlas Lithograph after engraving *Issued as a supplement to state and county atlases* $150.00

Spanish Possessions

Arrowsmith & Lewis **Spanish Dominions in North America** Boston 1812 8 x 10 Ex-atlas Engraving *From New and Elegant General Atlas Phillips (A) 718* $250.00

Gray **Gray's New Map of St. Louis** NY 1883 17.5 x 14 Ex-atlas Lithograph after engraving $75.00

Tenasee

also see Kentucky

Tennessee became a state in June 1796

Carey, Matthew **A Map of the Tenasee Government Formerly Part of North Carolina** Phila 1794 9 x 20.5 Ex-atlas UC engraving *From Guthrie's Geography* $1,250.00

Carey, Matthew **A Map of the Tenasee State Formerly Part of North Carolina** Phila 1796 9 x 20.5 Ex-atlas UC engraving *From Guthrie's Geography Illustrated* $1,250.00

Carey, Matthew **Tenasee: Lately the S.Wn. Territory** Phila 1805 6 x 8 Ex-atlas UC engraving *From the Pocket Atlas Phillips (A) 1368* $275.00

Arrowsmith & Lewis **Tennessee** Phila 1804 8.5 x 10.5 Ex-atlas Engraving *From New and Elegant General Atlas Phillips (A) 702* $250.00

Arrowsmith & Lewis **Tennessee** Boston 1805 8.5 x 10.5 Ex-atlas Engraving *From New and Elegant General Atlas Phillips (A) 708* $225.00

Carey & Lea **Geographical, ...Historical Map of Tennessee** Phila 1822-23 17.5 x 22 Ex-atlas HC engraving *Complete Historical, Chronological and Geographical American Atlas Phillips (A) 1373a* $275.00

Lucas, Fielding **Tennessee** Baltimore 1823 14.5 X 20.5 Ex-atlas HC engraving *From A General Atlas Phillips (A) 742* $275.00

Finley, A. **Tennessee** Phila 1824 8.5 x 11 Ex-atlas HC engraving *From New General Atlas* $175.00

Burr, David H. **Kentucky & Tennessee** NY 1836 12 x 15 Ex-atlas HC engraving *From The Universal Atlas* $150.00

Tanner, Henry S. **A New Map of Tennessee With Its Roads and Distances** Phila 1836 11 x 15 Ex-atlas HC engraving *From A New Universal Atlas* $175.00

Bradford, T. G. **Tennessee** Boston 1838 11.5 x 15 Ex-atlas HC engraving *From An Illustrated Atlas* $125.00

Mitchell, S. A. **A New Map of Tennessee With Its Roads and Distances** Phila 1846 13 x 16 Ex-atlas HC engraving *From A New Universal Atlas* $125.00

Thomas, Cowperthwait & Co **A New Map of Tennessee With Its Roads and Distances...** Phila 1850-55 11.5 x 15.5 Ex-atlas HC engraving *From A New Universal Atlas Phillips (A)800* $95.00

Colton, J. W. & G. W. **Kentucky & Tennessee** NY 1855-56 15 x 18 Ex-atlas Lithograph after engraving *From Colton's Atlas of the World* $95.00

Johnson & Browning **Johnson's Kentucky & Tennessee** NY 1861 17 x 23 Ex-atlas Lithograph after engraving *3 vignettes* $85.00

Colton, J. W. & G. W. **Colton's Map of the State of Tennessee** NY 1871 20 x 25 Folding Map Lithograph after engraving *Cloth or leather folder. 2 maps* $450.00

Asher & Adams **Kentucky & Tennessee** NY 1872 16.5 x 22.5 Ex-atlas Lithograph *Asher & Adams New Statistical and Topographical Atlas* $75.00

Texas

Texas became a state in Dec. 1845. Annexation 1845

• Bradford, T. G. **Texas** Boston 1835-36 8 x 10.5 Ex-atlas HC engraving *From A Comprehensive Atlas* Illustrated $675.00

Greenleaf **Texas...** Brattleboro 1842 11 x 13 Ex-atlas HC engraving *From New General Atlas Phillips (A) 784* $500.00

Mitchell, S. A. **Map of Texas From the Most Recent Authorities** Phila 1850 13 x 16 Ex-atlas HC engraving *From A New Universal Atlas Phillips (A) 800* $350.00

Thomas, Cowperthwait & Co **Map of Texas from the Most Recent Authorities** Phila 1851 12 x 15 Ex-atlas HC engraving *From A New Universal Atlas Phillips (A)805* $325.00

Colton, J. W. & G. W. **Texas** NY 1855 15 x 18 Ex-atlas Lithograph after engraving *From Colton's Atlas of the World Phillips (A)816* $225.00

Colton, J. W. & G. W. **New Map of the State of Texas** NY 1855-56 16 x 25 Ex-atlas Lithograph after engraving *From Colton's Atlas of the World Phillips (A)816* $275.00

• Colton, J. W. & G. W. **Texas** NY 1856 16 x 25 Folding Map Lithograph after engraving Illustrated $500.00

Colton, J. W. & G. W. **New Map of the State of Texas. Compiled from J. deCordova's Large Map** NY 1857 16 x 25 Ex-atlas Lithograph after engraving *From Colton's Atlas of the World* $275.00

Desilver **Map of the State of Texas From the Latest Authorities by J. H. Young** Phila 1857 12.5 x 15.5 Ex-atlas HC Engraving *Phillips (A)823* $500.00

Colton, J. W. & G. W. **Texas** NY 1858 13 x 10.5 Ex-atlas Lithograph after engraving *From Cabinet Atlas* $150.00

Mitchell, S. A. **County Map of Texas** Phila 1860 10.5 x 13.5 Ex-atlas Lithograph after engraving *Also 1861, 1867. From a New General Atlas Phillips (A)831* $150.00

Johnson & Browning **Johnson's New Map of the State of Texas** NY 1861 17 x 24 Ex-atlas Lithograph after engraving *Johnson's New Illustrated Family Atlas* $175.00

Johnson & Ward **Johnson's New Map of the State of Texas** NY 1866 17 x 24 Ex-atlas Lithograph after engraving *Johnson's New Illustrated Family Atlas* $175.00

Lloyd, H. H. **Texas** NY 1870 12.5 x 16 Ex-atlas Lithograph after engraving *Issued as a supplement to state and county atlases* $250.00

Asher & Adams **Asher & Adams Texas, Eastern Portion (and) Texas, Western Portion** NY 1872-74 16.5 x 22.5 Ex-atlas Lithograph *Asher & Adams New Statistical and Topographical Atlas. 2 sheetss Phillips(A)1272* $225.00

Facing page-Carey, Matthew ***A Map of the Tenasee State Formerly Part of North Carolina*** *Phila 1796 9 x 20.5 Ex-atlas UC engraving From Guthrie's Geography. Tennessee became a state in June 1796. One of the earliest maps of the state.*

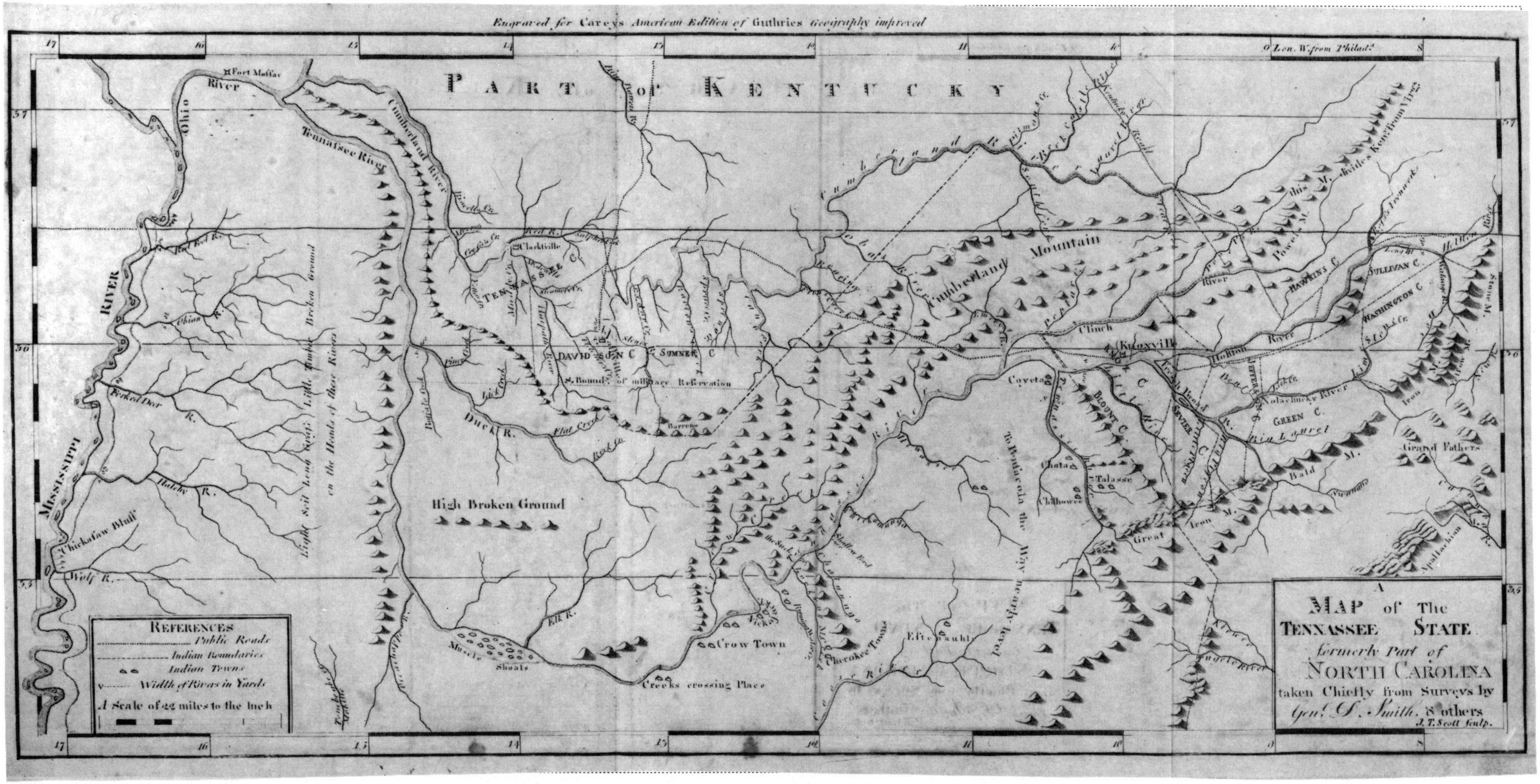
Engraved for Careys American Edition of Guthries Geography improved
A MAP of The TENNASSEE STATE formerly Part of NORTH CAROLINA taken Chiefly from Surveys by Genl. D. Smith, & others
J. T. Scott Sculp.
PART OF KENTUCKY
REFERENCES
Public Roads
Indian Boundaries
Indian Towns
Width of Rivers in Yards
A Scale of 22 miles to the Inch
Lon. W. from Philada.
MISSISSIPPI RIVER
Ohio River
Fort Massac
Tennassee River
Cumberland River
Cumberland Mountain
Clarkville
TENNASSEE C
DAVIDSON C
SUMNER C
Bounds of military Reservation
Duck R.
Elk R.
High Broken Ground
Muscle Shoals
Crow Town
Creeks crossing Place
Cherokee Towns
Chickasaw Bluff
Wolf R.
Forked Deer R.
Hatchy R.
Light Soil level Good Little Timber Broken Ground on the Heads of these Rivers
Knoxville
Clinch River
Holston River
HAWKINS C
SULLIVAN C
WASHINGTON C
GREEN C
JEFFERSON C
SEVIER C
BLOUNT C
Coveta
Chota
Talasse
Chilhowee
To Pensacola the Way nearly level
Nolachucky River
Big Laurel
Grand Fathers
Stone M.
Great Iron M.
Bald M.
Appalachian
Barrens
Big Barren R.
Red R.
Ewalee

Gray **Gray's Atlas Map of Texas** NY 1873 12.5 x 15 Ex-atlas Lithograph after engraving *Phillips (A) 1390* $175.00

Gray **Gray's New Map of Texas and Indian Territory** NY 1875 24 x 16 Ex-atlas Lithograph after engraving *From National Atlas* $225.00

Mitchell, S. A. **County Map of the State of Texas...Showing Adjoining States and Territories** Phila 1877 14 x 21 Ex-atlas Lithograph after engraving *With NM and Indian Territory. From a New General Atlas* $125.00

Gray **Gray's New Map of Texas and Indian Territory** NY 1881 17 x 26.5 Ex-atlas Lithograph after engraving *7 Insets* $250.00

Bradley **Texas** Phila 1885 16.5 x 22.5 Ex-atlas Lithograph *From New General Atlas See Phillips (A) 920* $100.00

Colton, J. W. & G. W. **Texas** NY 1887 17 x 23 Ex-atlas Lithograph after engraving *From Colton's General Atlas* $125.00

Gray **Gray's New Railroad Map of Texas East of the 100th Meridian** NY 1887 25 x 16.5 Ex-atlas Lithograph after engraving $150.00

United States

Bradley, A. **Map of the United States Exhibiting the Post Roads...** Phila 1796 34.5 x 37.5 Folding Map Hand colored engraving $17,500.00

Morse, J. **Map of the Northern Part of the United States of America** Phila 1797 8.5 x 15.5 Ex-atlas Engraving *From The American Gazeteer. Shows proposed NW Terr. states See NW Terr* $350.00

Arrowsmith & Lewis **United States** Phila 1804 8.5 x 10.5 Ex-atlas Engraving *From New and Elegant General Atlas Phillips (A) 702* $200.00

Bradley, A. **Map of the United States Exhibiting the Post Roads...** Phila 1804 38 x 52.5 Folding Map Hand colored engraving *Schwarz & Ehrenberg 222* $12,500.00

Carey, Matthew **United States** Phila 1805 10 x 13 Ex-atlas UC engraving *From the Pocket Atlas Phillips (A) 1368* $325.00

Melish, J. **A Map of the Southern Section of the United States Including the Floridas & Bahama Islands...** Phila 1813 16 x 21 Sep. Iss. HC engraving *Separate issue. Engraved by Tanner* $1,250.00

Carey, Matthew **The Upper Territories of the United States** Phila 1814 17 x 12.5 Ex-atlas HC engraving *From the General Atlas Phillips (A) 722* $750.00

Melish, J. **Northern Section of the United States** Phila 1816 16 x 20 Ex-atlas Engraving *Karpinski 53 & 76* $325.00

Melish, J. **Map of the United States of America** Phila 1816 37 x 58 Folding Map HC engraving $3,500.00

• Melish, J. **United States** Phila, 1816 16 x 20 HC engraving Folding map *From Information and Advice to Emigrants Illustrated* $600.00

Melish, J. **Northern Section of the United States...Southern Section Including Florida** Phila 1816 15 x 21 Ex-atlas HC engraving *Two sheets* $1,250.00

Melish, J. **Map of the U.S.A. Designed to Illustrate...Memoirs of Wm. McClure** Phila 1817 14 x 17 Ex-atlas HC engraving *From Transactions of the American Philosophical Society* $800.00

Melish, J. **United States of America** Phila 1818 16 x 20 Folding Map Engraving $675.00

Melish, J. **United States of America** Phila 1818 16 x 19.5 Folding Map HC engraving $800.00

Melish, J. **United States of America** Phila 1820 17 x 21 Ex-atlas HC engraving $600.00

• Melish, J. **United States of America** Phila 1820-22 16 x 20 Ex-atlas HC engraving *From Lavoisine's Genealogical, Historical...Atlas* $500.00

Melish, J. **United States of America** Phila 1821 17 x 21 Folding Map HC engraving *M. Carey & Son. B. Tanner, engr.* $600.00

Melish, J. **United States** Phila 1816 16 x 20 Folding Map HC engraving *Illustrated* $600.00

Carey & Lea **Geographical, ...Historical Map of United States** Phila 1822-23 17.5 x 22 Ex-atlas HC engraving *Complete Historical, Chronological and Geographical American Atlas Phillips (A) 1373a* $495.00

Lucas, Fielding **United States** Baltimore 1823 14.5 X 20.5 Ex-atlas HC engraving *From A General Atlas Phillips (A) 742* $295.00

Finley, A. **Map of the United States** Phila 1826 17 x 21 Folding Map HC engraving *Leather folder* $650.00

Tanner, Henry S. **A Map of the United States of Mexico** Phila 1826 25 x 30.5 Folding Map HC engraving *2d edition Wheat-TM-529* $3,500.00

Tanner, Henry S. **United States of America** Phila 1829 50 x 62.5 Wall Map HC engraving $1,800.00

Mitchell, S. A. **Map of the United States** Phila 1831 43.5 x 34.5 Folding Map HC engraving *Cloth or leather covers* $750.00

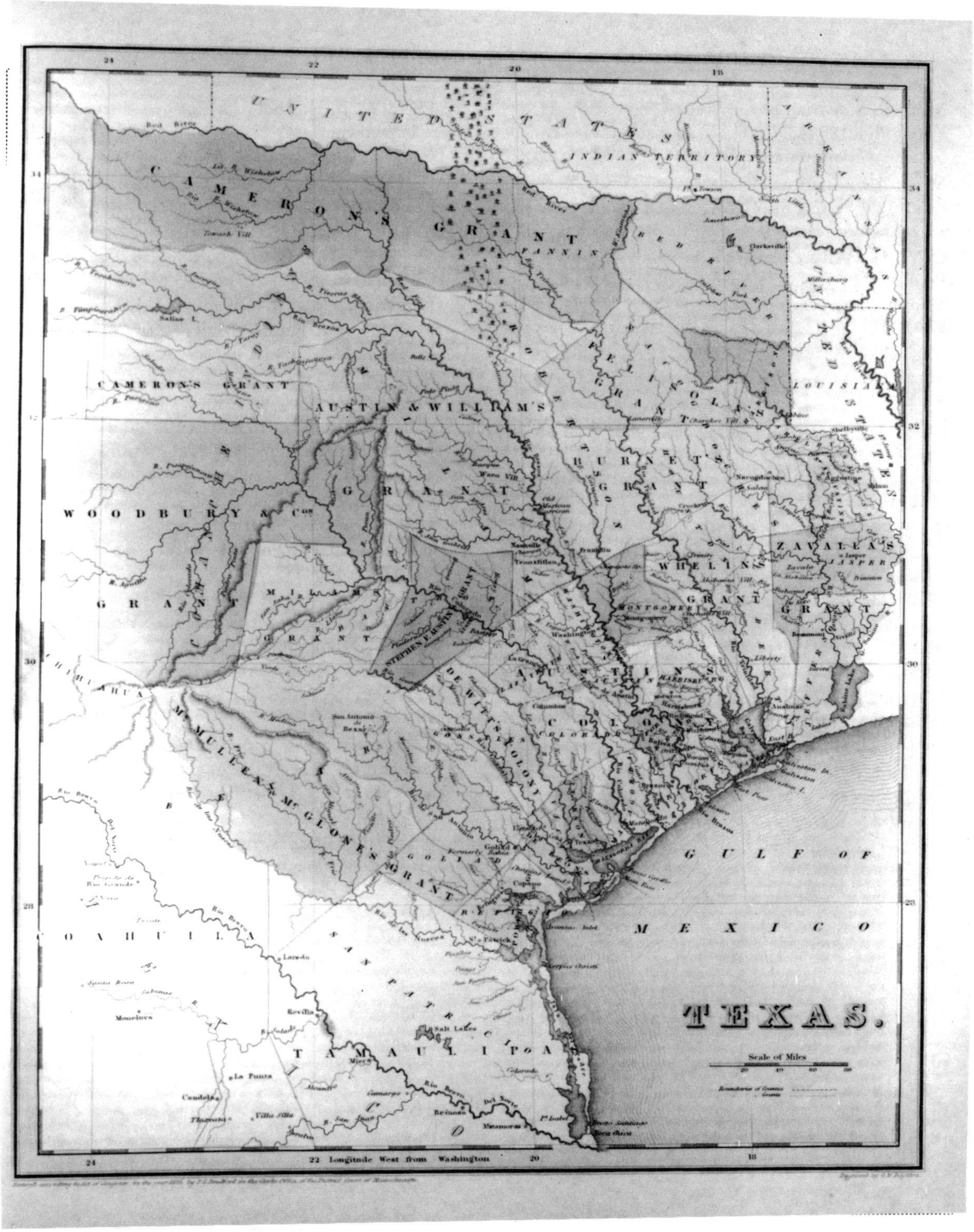

Bradford, T. G. ***Texas*** *Boston 1835-36 8 x 10.5 Ex-atlas HC engraving From A Comprehensive Atlas Phillips (M) 841. One of the earliest maps of Texas, which became a state in 1845.*

Mitchell, S. A.**Map of the United States by J. H. Young**Phila183143.5 x 34.5Wall mapHC engraving *Revised editions published to 1844Ristow 309*$1,000.00

Mitchell, S. A.**Mitchell's Traveller's Guide Through theUnited States**Phila183217.5 x 22Folding MapHC engraving *With booklet & supplementary sheet* $750.00

Colton, J. W.**Burr's Map of the United States Published by J. H. Colton**NY183317 x 21Folding MapHC Engraving*J. H. Colton & Co. 9 Wall Street* $750.00

Mitchell, S. A.**Traveller's Guide Through theUnited States**Phila183321.5 x 22.5Folding MapHC engraving $500.00

Mitchell, S. A.**A New Map of theUnited States**Phila 183352.5 x 78.5Wall mapHC engraving $1,250.00

Mitchell, S. A.**Mitchell's Reference and Distance Map of theUnited States**Phila183452.5 x 66.5Wall mapHC engraving*First edition. 13 Inset maps* $1,000.00

Bradford, T. G.**United States**Boston18358 x 10Ex-atlasHC engraving*From A Comprehensive Atlas* $150.00

Burr, David H.**United States**NY183510.5 x 12.5Ex-atlasHC engraving*From The Universal AtlasPhillips (A) 1379a*$275.00

Mitchell, S. A.**Reference and Distance Map of the United States by J. H. Young**Phila183554.5 x 69 Folding MapHC engraving*With inset Maps* $1,500.00

Bradford, T. G.**United States**Boston183814 x 22.5Ex-atlasHC engraving*From An Illustrated Atlas Wheat (TM) II, 430*$200.00

Bradford, T. G.**United States Exhibiting Ralroads & Canals**Boston18388 x 10Ex-atlasHC engraving*From A Comprehensive Atlas* $125.00

• Tanner, Henry S.**United States**Phila1839-4615 x 12 Ex-atlasHC engraving*From A New Universal Atlas* $200.00

Greenleaf**United States**Brattleboro184211 x 13Ex-atlas HC engraving*From New General AtlasPhillips (A) 784* $200.00

Phelps & Ensign**Phelps & Ensign's Travellers Guide ...United States**NY184217 x 22Folding MapHC engraving*Cloth or leather folder* $650.00

Phelps & Ensign**Phelps & Ensign's Travellers Guide ...United States**NY184326 x 40.5Wall MapHC engraving $875.00

Phelps & Ensign**Phelps & Ensign's Travellers Guide ...United States**NY184517 x 21.5Folding MapHC engraving*Cloth or leather folder* $600.00

Colton, J. W.**Map of theUnited States Showing Routes of U.S. Mail Steam Packets**NY1849Folding MapHC Engraving $1,500.00

Smith, J. C.**New Map for Travellers Through the United States**NY184921.5 x 25.5Folding MapHC Engraving*234pp text* $750.00

Phelps**Phelps National Map of theUnited States**NY 1849-5420.5 x 26Folding MapHC engraving*Cloth or leather folder* $500.00

Colton, J. W. & G. W.**Colton's Map of theUnited States of America**NY185020 x 24Folding Map Lithograph after engraving*Cloth or leather folder. J. H. Colton 86 Cedar St., New York* $300.00

• Thomas, Cowperthwait & Co**A New Map of the United States of America**Phila1850-5216 x 26.5Ex-atlasHC engraving*From A New Universal AtlasPhillips (A)800*Illustrated$275.00

Colton, J. W.**Map of theUnited States of America, The British Provinces, Mexico...**NY185136 x 46Wall MapHC Engraving $600.00

Colton, J. W.**Map of theUnited States, British Provinces...**NY185347 x 54Wall MapHC Engraving $800.00

Colton, J. W.**Map of theUnited States of America, British Provinces, Mexico...**NY185434 x 43Folding MapHC Engraving*Cloth or leather folder* $1,000.00

Colton, J. W. & G. W.**Colton's Map of theUnited States, the Canadas, &c....**NY185424 x 29Folding Map Lithograph after engraving*Cloth or leather folder* $325.00

Gaston & Johnson**A New Map of Our Country**NY 185455 x 62Wall MapHC engraving $750.00

Colton, J. W.**United States of America**NY185518 x 27 Folding MapHC Engraving*Imprint J. H. Colton...172 William St., NY. Separately issued* $350.00

Colton, J. W. & G. W.**United States of America**NY 185516 x 26Ex-atlasLithograph after engraving*From A New Universal Atlas. Eastern Colorado name Colona* $175.00

Colton, J. W. & G. W.**United States of America**NY 1855-5618 x 28Ex-atlasLithograph after engraving*From Colton's Atlas of the WorldPhillips (A)816*$175.00

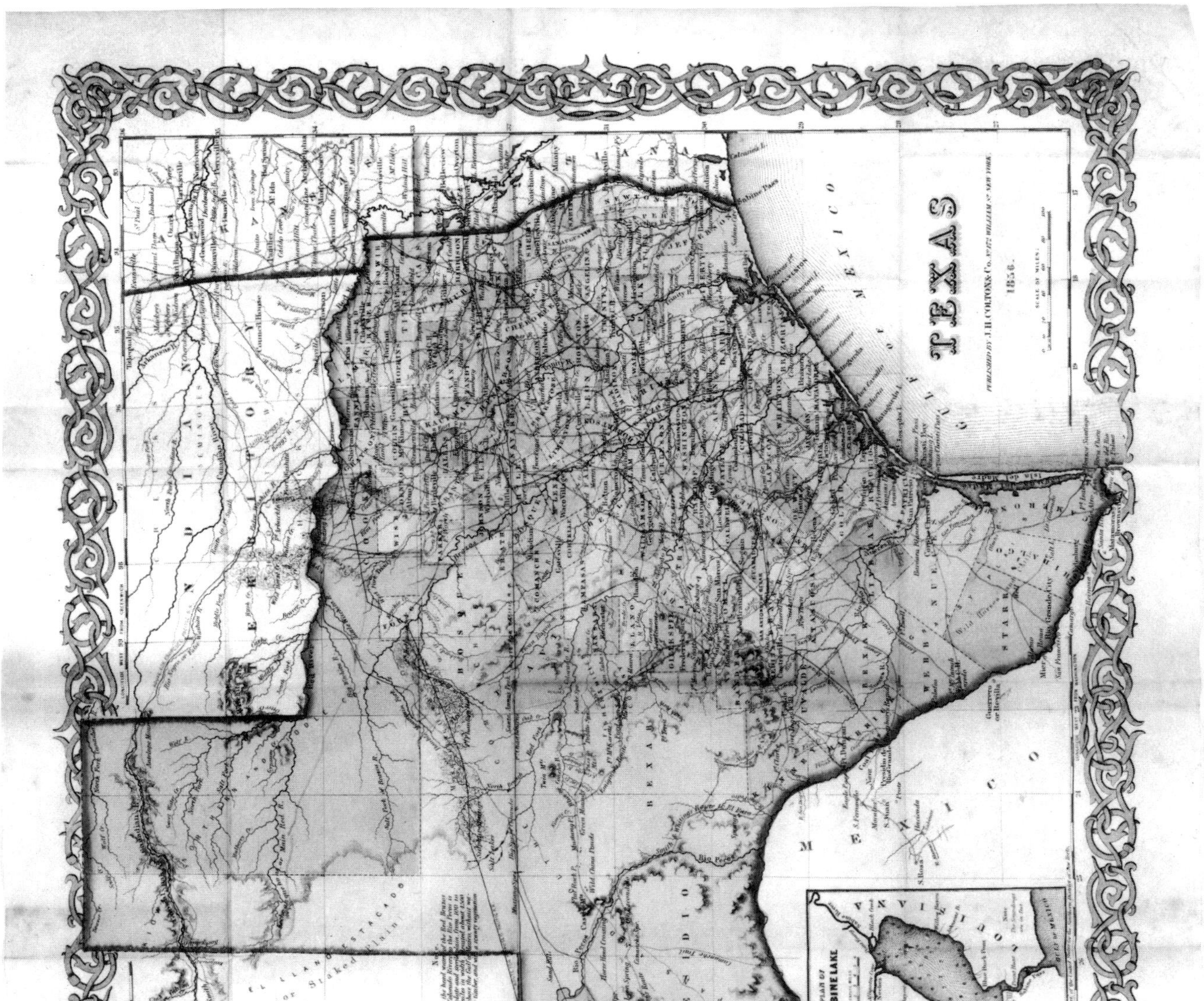

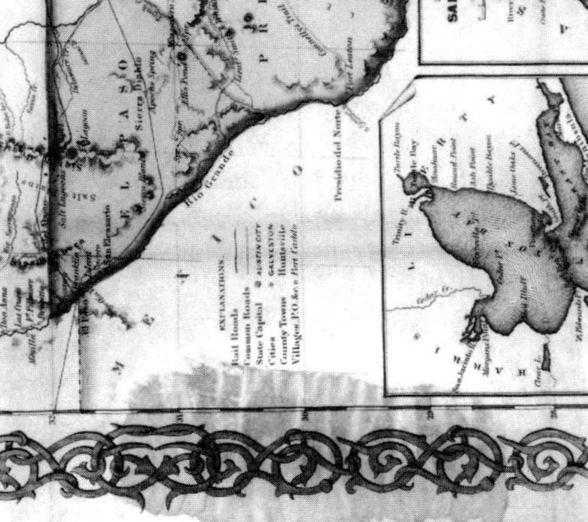

Colton, J. W. & G. W. ***Texas*** *NY 1856 16 x 25 Folding Map Lithograph after engraving. The Colton and Mitchell firms were the most prolific producers of folding maps between 1830 and 1870.*

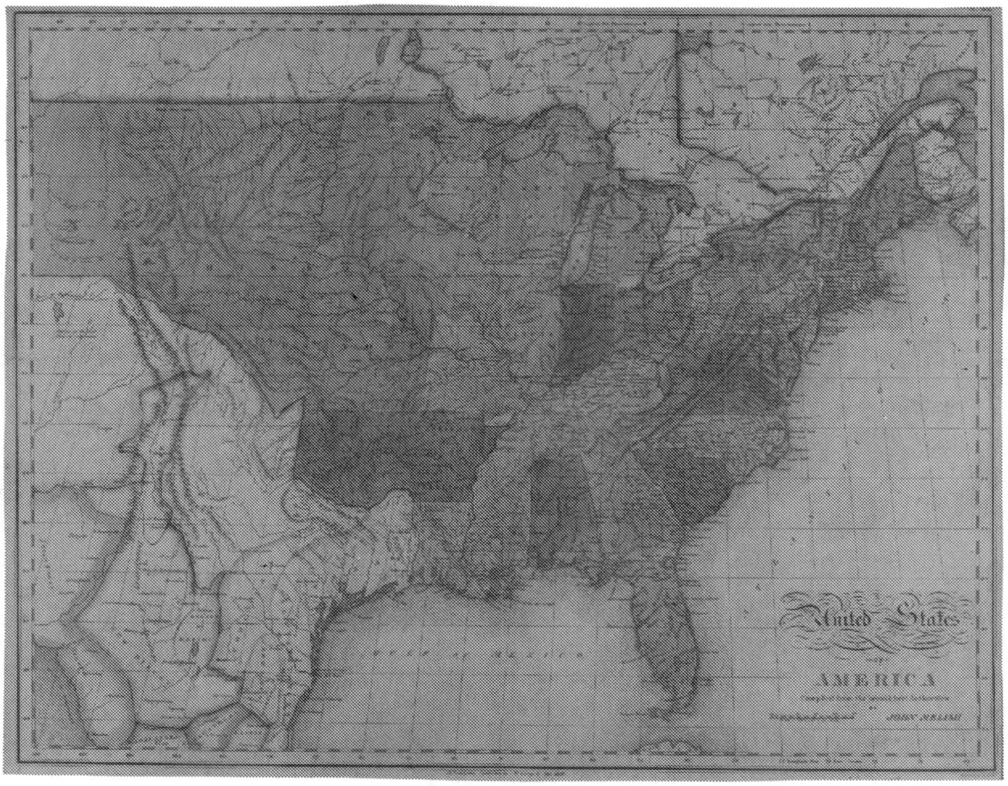

Melish, J. ***United States of America*** *Phila 1820-22 16 x 20 Ex-atlas HC engraving From Lavoisine's Genealogical, Historical and Chronological Atlas*

Morse & Gaston **New Map of Our Country ...United States** NY 1855 55 x 64 Wall map Lithograph after engraving $600.00

Desilver **A New Map of the United States of America** Phila 1857 15.5 x 26 Ex-atlas HC Engraving *By J. Young Phillips (A)823* $250.00

Mitchell, S. A. **Mitchell's New National Map Exhibiting United States** Phila 1859 54 x 55 Wall map HC engraving *Wheat 896* $800.00

Phelps & Watson **Phelps New National Map of the United States** NY 1859 26.5 x 36.5 Wall Map HC engraving $700.00

Mitchell, S. A. **Map of The United States** Phila 1860 13 x 21 Ex-atlas Lithograph after engraving *From A New General Atlas Phillips (A)831* $125.00

Mitchell, S. A. **Map of United States and Territories** Phila 1860 13.5 x 21 Ex-atlas Lithograph after engraving *Phillips (A) 3558, 7. From a New General Atlas Phillips (A)831* $125.00

Colton, J. W. & G. W. **New Railroad and County Map of the United States** NY 1860-62 33 x 40 Folding Map Lithograph after engraving *Cloth or leather folder* $600.00

Colton, J. W. & G. W. **G. W. Colton's New Guide Map of the United States and Canada With Railroads, Counties, etc.** NY 1861 30 x 36 Folding Map Lithograph after engraving *Cloth or leather folder* $600.00

Johnson & Browning **Johnson's New Military Map of the United States** NY 1861 17 x 23 Ex-atlas Lithograph after engraving *Johnson's New Illustrated Family Atlas* $175.00

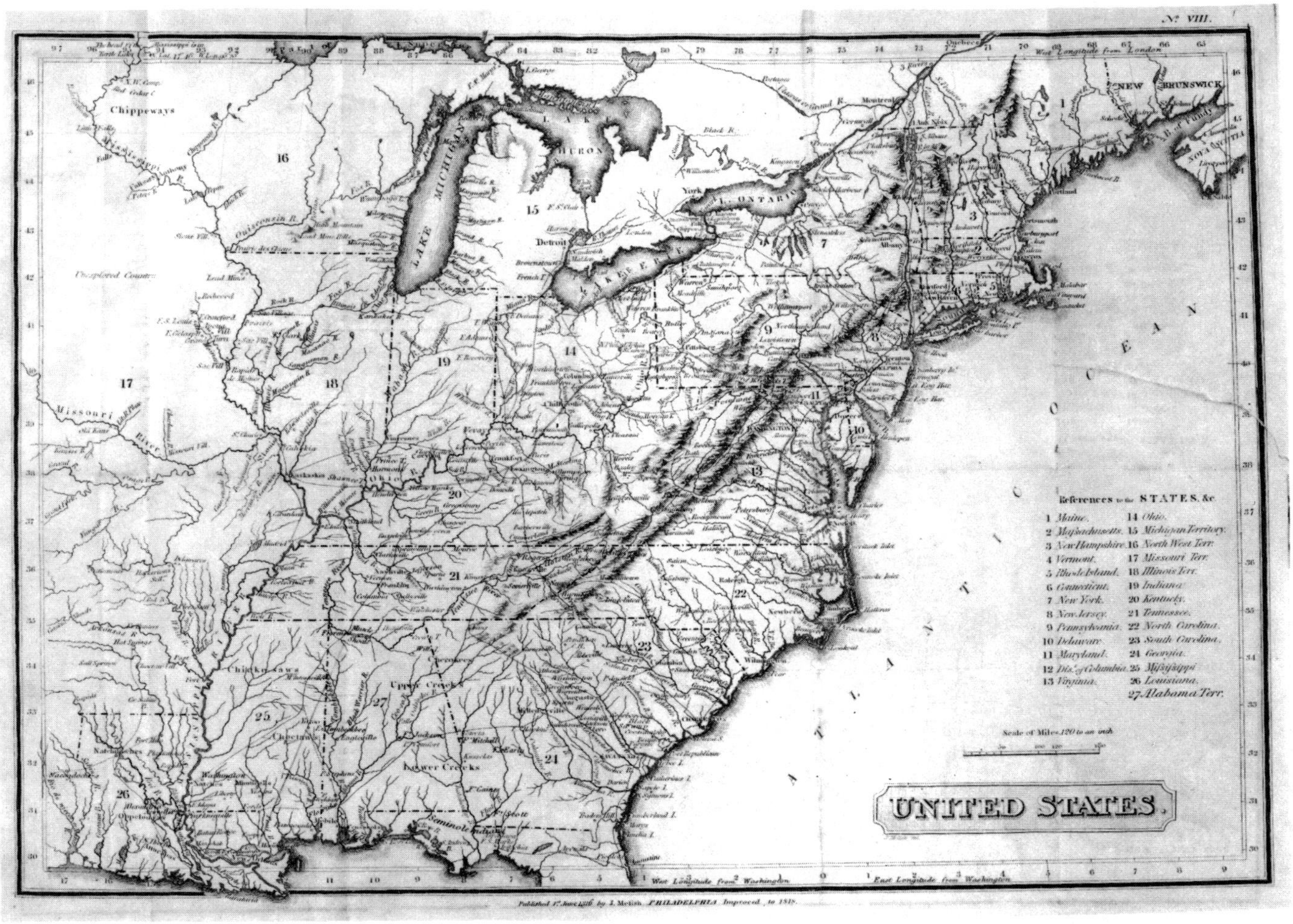

Melish, J. ***United States*** *Phila, 1816 16 x 20 HC engraving Folding map From Information and Advice to Emigrants*

Johnson & Ward**Johnson's New Military Map of the United States**NY 1861 17 x 23 Ex-atlas Lithograph after engraving *U.S. in Military Depts. 9 inset maps of harbors* **$175.00**

Lloyd **Lloyd's New Political Chart...map of the United States Showing Free States, Border Slave States...**NY 1861 34.5 x 25.5 Folding Map Lithograph after engraving **$450.00**

Colton, J. W. & G. W. **New Guide Map of the United States and Canada with Railroads, Counties** NY 1862-66 36 x 31 Folding Map Lithograph after engraving *Cloth or leather folder* **$500.00**

Keeler, W. J. **National Map of the United States** Washington 1867 50 x 60 Folding Map **$800.00**

Colton, J. W. & G. W. **Colton's New Railroad and County Map ...United States...** NY 1869-71 32 x 34 Folding Map Lithograph after engraving *Cloth or leather folder* **$450.00**

Asher & Adams **United States and Territories** NY 1871 16.5 x 22.5 Ex-atlas Lithograph *Asher & Adams New Statistical and Topographical Atlas* **$95.00**

Watson **Watson's New Railroad and Distance Map ... United States and Canada** Chicago 1871 35.5 x 46.5 Folding Map Wax engraving *Cloth folder* **$1,000.00**

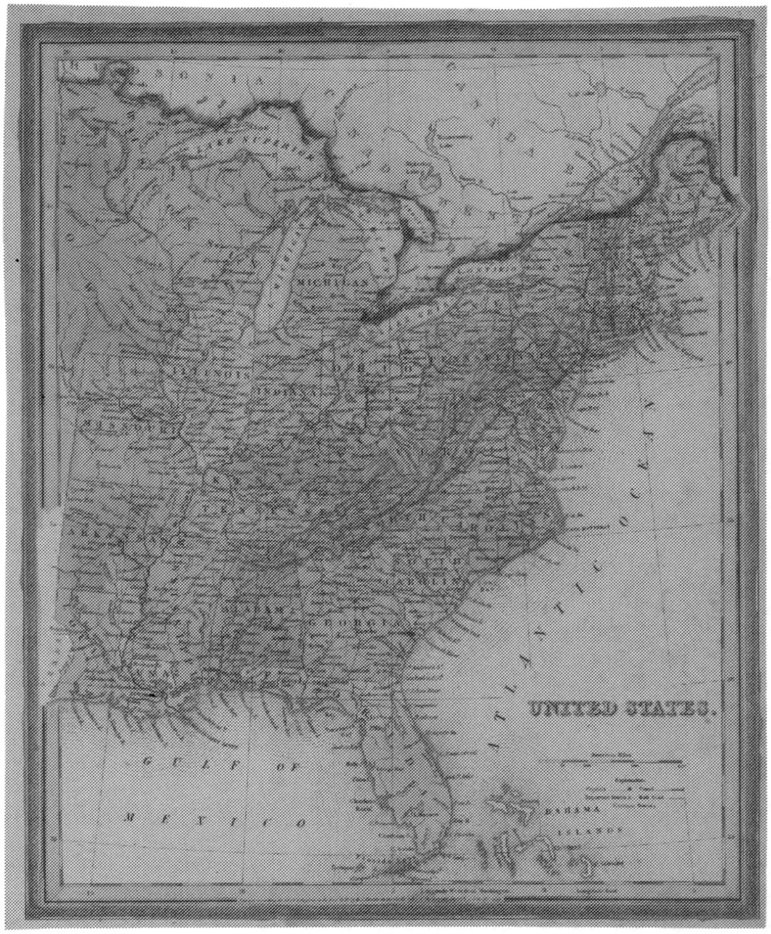

Tanner, Henry S. ***United States*** *Phila 1839-46 15 x 12 Ex-atlas HC engraving*
From A New Universal Atlas

Colton, J. W. & G. W. **G. W. & C. B. Colton's United States of America** NY 1872-76 16 x 28 Folding Map Lithograph after engraving *Cloth folder* $250.00

Gray **Gray's Atlas Map of United States Showing the Principal Geological Formations** NY 1873 16 x 26.5 Ex-atlas Lithograph after engraving *Phillips (A) 1390* $95.00

Rand McNally & Co. **New Railroad & County Map of the United States and Canada** Chicago 1876 52.5 x 96 Folding Map Wax engraving $375.00

Mitchell, S. A. **Railroad Map of the United States Showing...Atlantic to the Pacific** Phila 1880 14 x 22.5 Ex-atlas Lithograph after engraving *From A New General Atlas Phillips (A) 892* $95.00

Bradley **Railroad Map of the United States** Phila 1886 14 x 23 Folding Map Lithograph $175.00

Mitchell, S. A. **Mitchell's National Map of the American Republic** Phila 1843 34 x 24 Wall map HC engraving *First edition. Insets of 32 cities* $800.00

Utah

Utah became a state in Jan. 1896

Mitchell, S. A. **Map of the State of California...Territories of Oregon and Utah...New Mexico** Phila 1845-50 16 x 13 Ex-atlas HC engraving *From A New Universal Atlas* $375.00

Facing Page- Thomas, Cowperthwait & Co ***A New Map of the United States of America*** *Phila 1850-52 16 x 26.5 Ex-atlas HC engraving From A New Universal Atlas Phillips (A) 800*

A NEW
MAP OF THE
UNITED STATES
of America
BY J. H. YOUNG.
GOLD REGION
OF
CALIFORNIA
DISTRICT
OF
COLUMBIA
EXPLANATION
Capitals of States
Principal Cities and Towns
Rail Roads
Common Roads
Battle Fields
Figures attached to Mountains indicate their heights in feet.
PUBLISHED BY
THOMAS, COWPERTHWAIT & Co.
253 Market Street Philadelphia.
GULF OF MEXICO
ATLANTIC OCEAN
PACIFIC OCEAN
BRITISH TERRITORIES
CANADA
OREGON TERRITORY
MISSOURI OR NORTH WEST TERRITORY
MINNESOTA TERRITORY
UTAH TERRITORY
INDIAN TERRITORY
NEW MEXICO
TEXAS
GEORGIA
CALIFORNIA
MEXICO

Thomas, Cowperthwait & Co **A New Map of California...Oregon, Washington, Utah & New Mexico** Phila 1850-52 15.5 x 12.5 Ex-atlas HC engraving $375.00

Colton, J. W. & G. W. **Territories of New Mexico and Utah** NY 1855-56 15 x 18 Ex-atlas Lithograph after engraving *From Colton's Atlas of the World* $175.00

Morse & Gaston **Utah & New Mexico** NY 1857 5 x 6 Ex-atlas Cerograph *From Diamond Atlas* $75.00

Colton, J. W. & G. W. **Colton's Territories of New Mexico and Utah** NY 1861 13 x 15.5 Ex-atlas Lithograph after engraving *Shows Confederate Arizona territory* $200.00

Mitchell, S. A. **County Map of Utah and Nevada** Phila 1865 11.5 x 14 Ex-atlas Lithograph after engraving *Also 1867 and 1869. From a New General Atlas Phillips (A)846* $125.00

Lloyd, H. H. **Map of Utah, Arizona, New Mexico, Kansas, Colorado & Indian Territory** NY 1870 16.5 x 27 Ex-atlas Lithograph after engraving *Issued as a supplement to state and county atlases* $225.00

Asher & Adams **Portions of Utah, Colorado and Wyoming** NY 1872 16.5 x 22.5 Ex-atlas Lithograph *Asher & Adams New Statistical and Topographical Atlas Phillips(A)1272* $85.00

Colton, J. W. & G. W. **Colton's Utah & Colorado** NY 1872-72 12.5 x 16 Ex-atlas Lithograph after engraving *From Colton's General Atlas* $125.00

Colton, J. W. & G. W. **Colorado, Utah, &c.** NY 1873 13 x 16 Ex-atlas Lithograph after engraving *From Colton's General Atlas* $125.00

Asher & Adams **Asher & Adams Utah** NY 1875 16.5 x 22.5 Ex-atlas Lithograph *Asher & Adams New Statistical and Topographical Atlas* $125.00

Mitchell, S. A. **County and Township Map of Utah and Nevada** Phila 1881 15 x23 Ex-atlas Lithograph after engraving *From A New General Atlas Phillips (A)895* $75.00

Rand McNally & Co. **Utah** Chicago 1882 19.5 x 13 Ex-atlas Wax engraving *From Indexed Atlas of the World.* $75.00

Vermont

also see New Hampshire
Vermont became a state in 1791

• Arrowsmith & Lewis **Vermont** Phila 1804 8.5 x 10.5 Ex-atlas Engraving *From New and Elegant General Atlas Phillips (A)702 Illustrated* $125.00

Carey, Matthew **Vermont** Phila 1805 8 x 6 Ex-atlas UC engraving *From the Pocket Atlas Phillips (A) 1368* $150.00

Carey & Lea **Geographical, ... Historical Map of Vermont** Phila 1822-23 17.5 x 22 Ex-atlas HC engraving *Complete Historical, Chronological and Geographical American Atlas Phillips (A) 1373a* $225.00

Lucas, Fielding **Vermont** Baltimore 1823 14.5 X 11.5 Ex-atlas HC engraving *From A General Atlas Phillips (A) 742* $225.00

Tanner, Henry S. **Map of the States of Maine, New Hampshire, Vermont, Massachusetts...** Phila 1823 27 x 22 Ex-atlas HC engraving *From A New American Atlas* $750.00

Finley, A. **Vermont** Phila 1824 8.5 x 11 Ex-atlas HC engraving $125.00

Finley, A. **Map of Maine, New Hampshire and Vermont** Phila 1826 17 x 21.5 Ex-atlas HC engraving *From New American Atlas* $350.00

Robinson, L. **Improved Map of Vermont** 1834 24 x 17.5 Wall Map HC Engraving $750.00

Burr, David H. **Vermont & New Hampshire** NY 1836 15 x 12 Ex-atlas HC engraving *From The Universal Atlas Phillips (A) 1379a* $145.00

Bradford, T. G. **Vermont** Boston 1838 14.5 x 11.5 Ex-atlas HC engraving *From An Illustrated Atlas* $100.00

Greenleaf **Vermont and New Hampshire** Brattleboro 1842 11 x 13 Ex-atlas HC engraving *From New General Atlas Phillips (A) 784* $175.00

Colton, J. W. & G. W. **Vermont** NY 1855-56 15 x 18 Ex-atlas Lithograph after engraving *From Colton's Atlas of the World Phillips (A)816* $95.00

Colton, J. W. & G. W. **Map of Vermont** NY 1859 14 x 11 Folding Map Lithograph after engraving *Cloth folder* $200.00

Walling **Map of the State of Vermont** NY 1859 62 x 59 Wall Map HC Engraving *Published by Johnson & Browning* $600.00

Johnson & Browning **Johnson's New Hampshire and Vermont** NY 1861 17 x 23 Ex-atlas Lithograph after engraving *Johnson's New Illustrated Family Atlas* $95.00

Mitchell, S. A. **New Hampshire and Vermont** Phila 1862 13 x 11 Ex-atlas Lithograph after engraving *From A New General Atlas* $60.00

Virginia

Virginia became a state in 1788

Carey, Matthew **The State of Virgina, From the Best Authorities, by Samuel Lewis** Phila 1795 14 x 20 Ex-atlas UC engraving *From Carey's American Edition of Guthrie's Geography...* $600.00

Scott **Virginia** Phila 1795 6 x 7 Ex-atlas Engraving *From the United States Gazeteer* $200.00

Morse, J. **Virginia** Phila 1796 5.5 x 7.5 Ex-atlas Engraving *From American Universal Geography Wheat & Brun 571* $125.00

Reid **The State of Virginia from the Best Authorities** NY 1796 16 x 19.5 Sep.Iss. Engraving $600.00

• Reid **The State of Virginia from the Best Authorities** NY 1796 16 x 19.5 Ex-atlas $600.00

Arrowsmith & Lewis **Virginia** Phila 1804 10.5 x 8.5 Ex-atlas Engraving *From New and Elegant General Atlas Phillips (A) 702* $175.00

Arrowsmith & Lewis **Virginia** Boston 1805 10.5 x 8.5 Ex-atlas Engraving *From New and Elegant General Atlas Phillips (A) 708* $150.00

Carey, Matthew **Virginia** Phila 1805 6 x 8 Ex-atlas UC engraving *From the Pocket Atlas Phillips (A) 1368* $200.00

Arrowsmith & Lewis **Virginia** Boston 1812 10.5 x 8.5 Ex-atlas Engraving *From New and Elegant General Atlas Phillips (A) 718* $150.00

Carey, Matthew **A Correct Map of Virginia** Phila 1814 14 x 20 Ex-atlas HC engraving *From the General Atlas Phillips (A) 722* $400.00

Arrowsmith & Lewis **Virginia** Boston 1819 10.5 x 8.5 Ex-atlas Engraving *From New and Elegant General Atlas Phillips (A) 734* $150.00

Tanner, Henry S. **Virginia, Maryland and Delaware** Phila 1820 20.5 x 29 Ex-atlas HC engraving *From American Atlas* $875.00

Tanner, Henry S. **Virginia, Maryland and Delaware** Phila 1820-23 20.5 x 29 Ex-atlas HC engraving *From American Atlas* $750.00

Carey & Lea **Geographical, ... Historical Map of Virginia** Phila 1822-23 17.5 x 22 Ex-atlas HC engraving *Complete Historical, Chronological and Geographical American Atlas Phillips (A) 1373a* $295.00

Lucas, Fielding **Virginia** Baltimore 1823 14.5 X 20.5 Ex-atlas HC engraving *From A General Atlas Phillips (A) 742* $275.00

Finley, A. **Virginia** Phila 1825 8.5 x 11 Ex-atlas HC engraving *From New General Atlas* $175.00

Finley, A. **Virginia** Phila 1825 8.5 x 11 Folding Map HC engraving *Leather folder* $500.00

Burr, David H. **Virginia** NY 1834-35 10 x 13.5 Ex-atlas HC engraving *From The Universal Atlas Phillips (A) 1379a* $150.00

Tanner, Henry S. **A New Map of Virginia With Its Canals, Roads and Distances** Phila 1836 11 x 13 Ex-atlas HC engraving *From A New Universal Atlas Phillips (A) 774* $175.00

Mitchell, S. A. **Tourist's Pocket Map of the State of Virginia** Phila 1839 12.5 x 14 Folding Map HC engraving $300.00

Bradford, T. G. **Virginia** Boston 1841 11.5 x 15.5 Ex-atlas HC engraving *From A Universal Illustrated Atlas* ⊙ $150.00

Greenleaf **Virginia** Brattleboro 1842 11 x 13 Ex-atlas HC engraving *From New General Atlas Phillips (A) 784* $150.00

Mitchell, S. A. **A New Map of Virginia With Its Canals, Roads and Distances...** Phila 1846 14.5 x 11.5 Ex-atlas HC engraving *From A New Universal Atlas* $125.00

Thomas, Cowperthwait & Co **A New Map of Virginia With Its Canals, Roads...** Phila 1854 11.5 x 14 Ex-atlas HC engraving *From A New Universal Atlas Phillips (A) 813* $85.00

Colton, J. W. & G. W. **Virginia** NY 1855-56 15 x 18 Ex-atlas Lithograph after engraving *From Colton's Atlas of the World Phillips (A) 816* $95.00

Desilver **A New Map of the State of Virginia Exhibiting Its Internal Improvements** Phila 1856-57 12.5 x 15.5 Ex-atlas HC Engraving *From A New Universal Atlas Phillips (A) 823* $95.00

Morse & Gaston **Virginia** NY 1857 5.5 x 7 Ex-atlas Cerograph *From The World In Miniature* $60.00

Disturnell **Army Map of the Seat of War in Virginia, Showing Battlefields, Fortifications...** Phila 1861 27 x 25 Folding Map HC engraving *Cloth folder* $850.00

Johnson & Browning **Johnson's Pennsylvania, Virginia, Delaware, Maryland** NY 1861 17 x 23 Ex-atlas Lithograph after engraving *Johnson's New Illustrated Family Atlas* $85.00

Arrowsmith & Lewis **Vermont** Phila 1804 8.5 x 10.5 Ex-atlas Engraving *From New and Elegant General Atlas Phillips (A)702. Vermont became a state in 1791*

Colton, J. W. & G. W. **Colton's New Topographical Map of ... Virginia. Maryland and Delaware...East Tennessee...Military Sta..** NY 1862 30.5 x 44.5 Folding Map Lithograph after engraving *Cloth or leather folder* $750.00

Mitchell, S. A. **County Map of Virginia and West Virginia** Phila 1863 11 x 14.5 Ex-atlas Lithograph after engraving *1st Mitchell map showing WV as state. From a New General Atlas* $60.00

West & Johnston **Map of the State of Virginia Containing the Counties...Towns...** Richmond 1864 22.5 x 34.5 Folding Map HC engraving $3,500.00

Colton, J. W. & G. W. **Colton's Virginia and West Virginia** NY 1869 13 x 16 Ex-atlas Lithograph after engraving *From Colton's General Atlas* $75.00

Colton, J. W. & G. W. **Colton's New Topographical Map of ... Virginia, West Virginia, Maryland & Delaware...** NY 1870 28 x 42 Folding Map Lithograph after engraving *Cloth folder* $450.00

Colton, J. W. & G. W. **Colton's Map of Virginia** NY 1872 11 x 15 Folding Map Lithograph after engraving *Cloth folder* $200.00

Gray **Gray's Atlas Map of Virginia & West Virginia** NY 1873 12 x 16 Ex-atlas Lithograph after engraving *Phillips (A)1390* $75.00

Facing page-Reid ***The State of Virginia from the Best Authorities*** *NY 1796 16 x 19.5 Ex-atlas From the American Atlas Phillips (M) 985. Virginia became the 10th state in June, 1788*

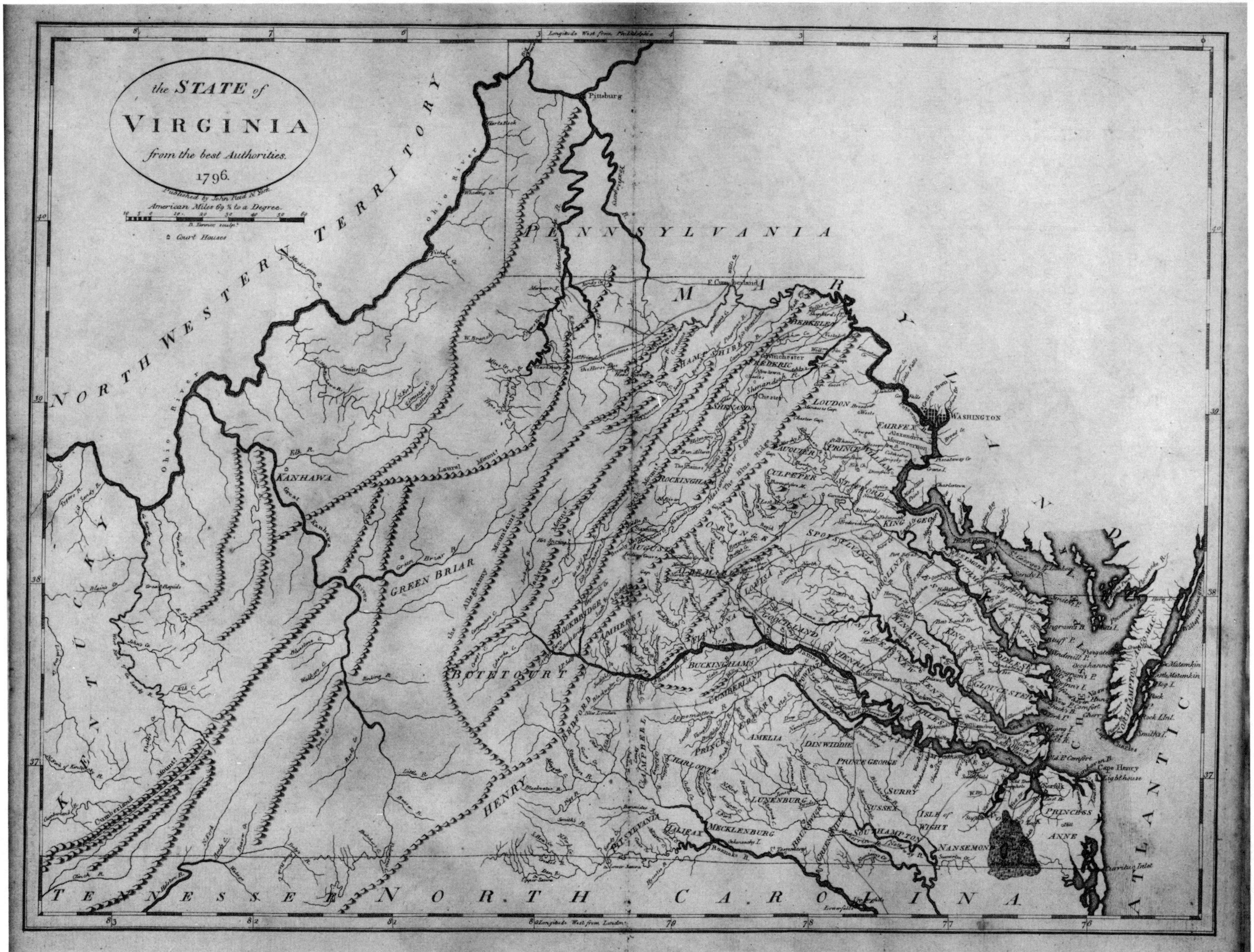
the STATE of
VIRGINIA
from the best Authorities.
1796.
Published by John Reid N. York.
American Miles 69 ½ to a Degree.
B. Tanner sculp.
Court Houses
NORTH WESTERN TERRITORY
PENNSYLVANIA
MARYLAND
NORTH CAROLINA
TENNESSEE
KENTUCKY
ATLANTIC
Longitude West from Philadelphia
Longitude West from London
Ohio River
Pittsburg
WASHINGTON
KANHAWA
GREEN BRIAR
BOTETOURT
HENRY
ROCKINGHAM
AUGUSTA
AMHERST
BUCKINGHAM
CUMBERLAND
AMELIA
DINWIDDIE
PRINCE GEORGE
SURRY
SUSSEX
ISLE of WIGHT
NANSEMOND
SOUTHAMPTON
MECKLENBURG
LUNENBURG
CHARLOTTE
HALIFAX
PRINCESS ANNE
NORTHAMPTON
LOUDON
FAIRFAX
PRINCE WILLIAM
CULPEPER
SPOTSYLVANIA
HAMPSHIRE
BERKELEY
FREDERIC
Winchester
Alexandria
Mount Vernon
Cape Henry
Light house
Smiths I.

Rand McNally & Co. **Indexed Map of Virginia and West Virginia** Chicago 1877 11 x 20 Folding Map Wax engraving *Cloth folder* $175.00

Colton, J. W. & G. W. **Map of the Virginia, Kentucky and Ohio Railroad....** NY 1881 28.5 x 41.5 Wall Map Lithograph after engraving $275.00

Rand McNally & Co. **Virginia** Chicago 1889 18.5 x 25.5 Ex-atlas Wax engraving *From Indexed Atlas of the World* $75.00

Rand McNally & Co. **Indexed County and Railroad Pocket Map... Virginia** Chicago 1893 19 x 26 Folding Map Wax engraving $95.00

Washington

Washington became a state in Nov. 1889

Thomas, Cowperthwait & Co **A New Map of California...Oregon, Washington, Utah & New Mexico** Phila 1850-52 15.5 x 12.5 Ex-atlas HC engraving *The Chief Part of New Mexico"* $375.00

Colton, J. W. & G. W. **Washington and Oregon** NY 1855-56 15 x 18 Ex-atlas Lithograph after engraving *From Colton's Atlas of the World* $125.00

Colton, J. W. & G. W. **The Territories of Washington and Oregon** NY 1856 12.5 x 16 Ex-atlas Lithograph after engraving *From Colton's Atlas of the World Phillips (A)816* $125.00

Morse & Gaston **Washington & Oregon Territories** NY 1857 5 x 6 Ex-atlas Cerograph *From Diamond Atlas* $75.00

Colton, J. W. & G. W. **Oregon, Washington, Idaho, California, Utah and New Mexico** NY 1858 13 x 11 Ex-atlas Lithograph after engraving *From Colton's General Atlas* $175.00

Mitchell, S. A. **Map of Oregon, Washington and Part of British Columbia** Phila 1860-62 10.5 x 13.5 Ex-atlas Lithograph after engraving *From A New General Atlas* $125.00

Johnson & Browning **Johnson's Washington & Oregon** NY 1861 11 x 14 Ex-atlas Lithograph after engraving *Johnson's New Illustrated Family Atlas* $75.00

• Johnson & Browning **Johnson's Washington Oregon and Idaho** NY 1864 11 x 14 Ex-atlas Lithograph after engraving *Johnson's New Illustrated Family Atlas Illustrated* $75.00

Mitchell, S. A. **Plan of Washington** Phila 1861 11 x 13 Ex-atlas Lithograph after engraving *From A New General Atlas* $85.00

Mitchell, S. A. **Map of Oregon, Washington, Idaho and Part of Montana** Phila 1866-77 11 x 13.5 Ex-atlas Lithograph after engraving *From A New General Atlas* $75.00

Colton, J. W. & G. W. **Oregon, Washington, Idaho, Montana & British Columbia** NY 1868 16.5 x 27 Ex-atlas Lithograph after engraving *From Colton's General Atlas* $175.00

Gray **Washington** NY 1873 14 x 17 Ex-atlas Lithograph after engraving $95.00

Gray **Washington** NY 1875 12 x 15 Ex-atlas Lithograph after engraving $95.00

Mitchell, S. A. **County and Township Map of Oregon and Washington** Phila 1883 20 x 14.5 Ex-atlas Lithograph after engraving *From A New General Atlas* $60.00

Bradley **Washington and Oregon** Phila 1885 23 x 17 Ex-atlas Lithograph *From New General Atlas Phillips (A)870* $85.00

Bradley **County and Township Map of Oregon and Washington** Phila 1887 21.5 x 15 Ex-atlas Lithograph *From New General Atlas* $95.00

Washington, District of Columbia

Carey & Lea **Geographical... and Historical Map of District of Columbia** Phila 1822-23 17.5 x 22 Ex-atlas HC engraving *Complete Historical... Geographical American Atlas Phillips (A) 1373a* $325.00

Melish, J. **District of Columbia** Phila 1834 7 x 5 Ex-atlas HC engraving $85.00

Bradford, T. G. **District of Columbia** Boston 1835 10 x 8 Ex-atlas HC engraving *From a Comprehensive Atlas* $75.00

Tanner, Henry S. **City of Washington** Phila 1836-44 11.5 x 14.5 Ex-atlas HC engraving *Carey & Hart Publishers Phillips (A)774* $200.00

Bradford, T. G. **Washington-Cincinnati-New Orleans-Louisville** Boston 1838 11.5 x 14 Ex-atlas HC engraving *4 city plans* $85.00

Tanner, Henry S. **City of Washington** Phila 1846 12.5 x 15.5 Ex-atlas HC engraving *Phila: S. A. Mitchell* $150.00

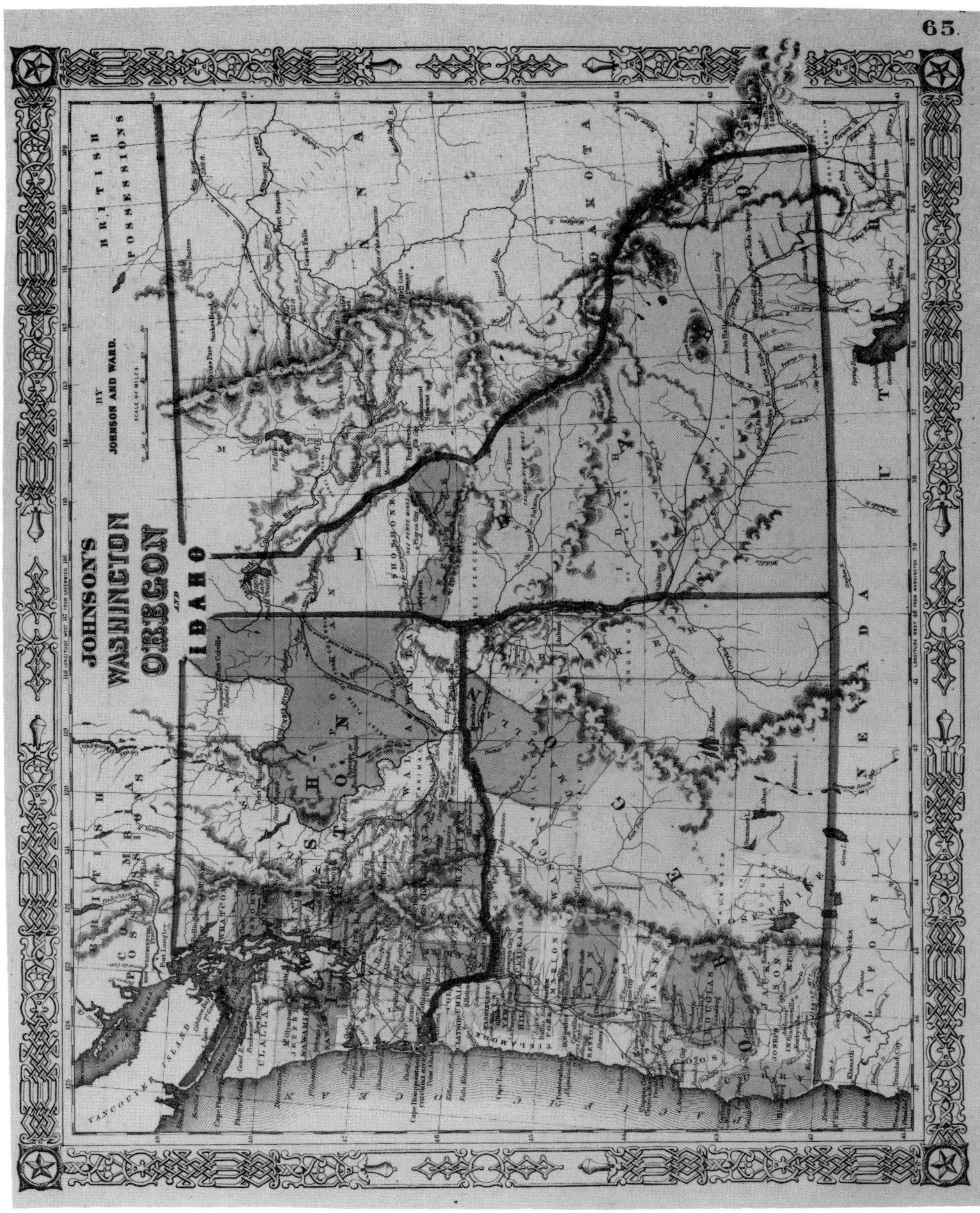

Johnson & Ward ***Johnson's Washington Oregon and Idaho****NY186411 x 14Ex-atlasLithograph after engravingJohnson's New Illustrated Family Atlas. Washington became a state in Nov. 1889,Oregon became a state in Feb. 1859. Idaho became a state in July 1890*

Mitchell, S. A. **City of Washington** Phila 1850 13 x 16 Ex-atlas HC engraving *From A New Universal Atlas Phillips (A) 800* $125.00

Mitchell, S. A. **City of Washington** Phila 1850 13 x 16 Ex-atlas HC engraving *From A New Universal Atlas Phillips (A) 800* $125.00

Thomas, Cowperthwait & Co **City of Washington** Phila 1851 12 x 15 Ex-atlas HC engraving *From A New Universal Atlas Phillips (A) 805* $125.00

Desilver **City of Washington** Phila 1856 13 x 15.5 Ex-atlas HC Engraving *From A New Universal Atlas Phillips (A) 823* $95.00

Colton, J. W. & G. W. **Georgetown and the City of Washington** NY 1855-56 15 x 18 Ex-atlas Lithograph after engraving *From Colton's Atlas of the World Phillips (A) 816* $150.00

Johnson & Browning **Johnson's Georgetown and the City of Washington** NY 1861 13 x 16 Ex-atlas Lithograph after engraving *Johnson's New Illustrated Family Atlas* $75.00

Mitchell, S. A. **Plan of the City of Washington...Capitol of the United States** Phila 1870 11 x 13 Ex-atlas Lithograph after engraving *From A New General Atlas Phillips (A) 859* $85.00

Entwhistle **Entwhistle's Handy Map of Washington and Vicinity...** Wash 1876 16 x 21 Folding Map Lithograph $175.00

West Indies

Lucas, Fielding **Antigua** Baltimore 1823 11.5 X 14.5 Ex-atlas HC engraving *From A General Atlas Phillips (A) 742* $225.00

Lucas, Fielding **Bahamas** Baltimore 1823 11.5 X 14.5 Ex-atlas HC engraving *From A General Atlas Phillips (A) 742* $350.00

Lucas, Fielding **Barbadoes** Baltimore 1823 14.5 X 11.5 Ex-atlas HC engraving *From A General Atlas Phillips (A) 742* $350.00

Lucas, Fielding **Bermudas** Baltimore 1823 11.5 X 14.5 Ex-atlas HC engraving *From A General Atlas Phillips (A) 742* $250.00

Lucas, Fielding **Cuba** Baltimore 1823 14.5 X 20.5 Ex-atlas HC engraving *From A General Atlas Phillips (A) 742* $275.00

Carey & Lea **Geographical, ... Historical Map of Cuba and Bahama Islands** Phila 1822-23 17.5 x 22 Ex-atlas HC engraving *Complete Historical, Chronological and Geographical American Atlas Phillips (A) 1373a* $275.00

Colton, J. W. & G. W. **Cuba, Jamaica & Porto Rico** NY 1855-56 15 x 18 Ex-atlas Lithograph after engraving *From Colton's Atlas of the World Phillips (A) 816* $95.00

Johnson & Browning **Johnson's Cuba, Jamaica, Puerto Rico** NY 1861 17 x 26 Ex-atlas Lithograph after engraving *Johnson's New Illustrated Family Atlas* $75.00

Lucas, Fielding **Curacao** Baltimore 1823 14.5 X 11.5 Ex-atlas HC engraving *From A General Atlas Phillips (A) 742* $175.00

Lucas, Fielding **Dominica** Baltimore 1823 11.5 X 14.5 Ex-atlas HC engraving *From A General Atlas Phillips (A) 742* $150.00

Lucas, Fielding **Grenada** Baltimore 1823 14.5 X 11.5 Ex-atlas HC engraving *From A General Atlas Phillips (A) 742* $175.00

Lucas, Fielding **Guadeloupe** Baltimore 1823 11.5 X 14.5 Ex-atlas HC engraving *From A General Atlas Phillips (A) 742* $150.00

Lucas, Fielding **Hayti or St. Domingo** Baltimore 1823 14.5 X 20.5 Ex-atlas HC engraving *From A General Atlas Phillips (A) 742* $250.00

Carey & Lea **Geographical, ... Historical Map of Hispaniola** Phila 1822-23 17.5 x 22 Ex-atlas HC engraving *Complete Historical, Chronological and Geographical American Atlas Phillips (A) 1373a* $275.00

Lucas, Fielding **Jamaica** Baltimore 1823 11.5 X 14.5 Ex-atlas HC engraving *From A General Atlas Phillips (A) 742* $225.00

Carey & Lea **Geographical, ... Historical Map of Jamaica** Phila 1822-23 17.5 x 22 Ex-atlas HC engraving *Complete Historical, Chronological and Geographical American Atlas Phillips (A) 1373a* $275.00

Carey & Lea **Geographical, ... Historical Map of Leeward Islands** Phila 1822-23 17.5 x 22 Ex-atlas HC engraving *Complete Historical, Chronological and Geographical American Atlas Phillips (A) 1373a* $275.00

Lucas, Fielding **Martinico** Baltimore 1823 11.5 X 14.5 Ex-atlas HC engraving *From A General Atlas Phillips (A) 742* $150.00

Lucas, Fielding **Nevis** Baltimore 1823 11.5 X 14.5 Ex-atlas HC engraving *From A General Atlas Phillips (A) 742* $175.00

Carey & Lea **Geographical, ... Historical Map of Porto Rico and Virgin Islands** Phila 1822-23 17.5 x 22 Ex-atlas HC engraving *Complete Historical, Chronological and Geographical American Atlas Phillips (A) 1373a* $275.00

Lucas, Fielding **Porto Rico** Baltimore 1823 11.5 X 14.5 Ex-atlas HC engraving *From A General Atlas Phillips (A) 742* $225.00

Lucas, Fielding **St. Christophers** Baltimore 1823 11.5 X 14.5 Ex-atlas HC engraving *From A General Atlas Phillips (A) 742* $225.00

Lucas, Fielding **St. Lucia** Baltimore 1823 11.5 X 14.5 Ex-atlas HC engraving *From A General Atlas Phillips (A) 742* $150.00

Lucas, Fielding **St. Vincent** Baltimore 1823 14.5 X 11.5 Ex-atlas HC engraving *From A General Atlas Phillips (A) 742* $225.00

Lucas, Fielding **Tobago** Baltimore 1823 14.5 X 11.5 Ex-atlas HC engraving *From A General Atlas Phillips (A) 742* $175.00

Lucas, Fielding **Virgin Islands** Baltimore 1823 11.5 X 14.5 Ex-atlas HC engraving *From A General Atlas Phillips (A) 742* $175.00

Lucas, Fielding **West Indies** Baltimore 1823 11.5 X 14.5 Ex-atlas HC engraving *From A General Atlas Phillips (A) 742* $225.00

Lucas, Fielding **Trinidad** Baltimore 1824 14.5 X 11.5 Ex-atlas HC engraving *From A General Atlas Phillips (A) 742* $225.00

Morse, J. **West Indies According to the Best Authorities** Phila 1793 8 x 12 Ex-atlas Engraving *From American Universal Geography Wheat & Brun 686* $175.00

Tanner, Henry S. **West Indies** 1834 11.5 x 14.5 Ex-atlas HC engraving *Carey & Hart Publishers* $125.00

Burr, David H. **West Indies** NY 1836 12 x 15 Ex-atlas HC engraving *From The Universal Atlas Phillips (A) 1379a* $125.00

Bradford, T. G. **West Indies** Boston 1842 14 x 17 Ex-atlas HC engraving *From A Universal Illustrated Atlas* $150.00

Carey & Lea **Geographical, ... Historical Map of West Indies** Phila 1822-23 17.5 x 22 Ex-atlas HC engraving *Complete Historical, Chronological and Geographical American Atlas Phillips (A) 1373a* $275.00

Colton, J. W. **Topographical Map of the West Indies and Adjacent Coasts by John Pinkerton** NY 1852 19 x 27 Folding Map HC Engraving *Cloth or leather folder.* $750.00

Colton, J. W. & G. W. **West Indies** NY 1855-56 15 x 18 Ex-atlas Lithograph after engraving *From Colton's Atlas of the World Phillips (A)816* $95.00

Carey & Lea **Geographical, ... Historical Map of Windward Islands** Phila 1822-23 17.5 x 22 Ex-atlas HC engraving *Complete Historical, Chronological and Geographical American Atlas Phillips (A) 1373a* $275.00

Gray **West Indies and Central America** NY 1870 14 x 17 Ex-atlas Lithograph after engraving $95.00

West Virginia- also see Virginia

West Virginia became a state in 1863

Mitchell, S. A. **County Map of Virginia and North Carolina** Phila 1860 10 x 12 Ex-atlas Lithograph after engraving *From A New General Atlas* $60.00

Mitchell, S. A. **County Map of Virginia and West Virginia** Phila 1863 11 x 14.5 Ex-atlas Lithograph after engraving *1st Mitchell map showing WV as state. From A New General Atlas* $60.00

Colton, J. W. & G. W. **Colton's Map of the Oil District of West Virginia and Ohio** NY 1865 31 x 36 Folding Map Lithograph after engraving *Cloth or leather folder* $600.00

Colton, J. W. & G. W. **Colton's Virginia and West Virginia** NY 1869 13 x 16 Ex-atlas Lithograph after engraving *From Colton's General Atlas* $75.00

Colton, J. W. & G. W. **Colton's New Topographical Map of ... Virginia, West Virginia, Maryland & Delaware...** NY 1870 28 x 42 Folding Map Lithograph after engraving *Cloth folder* $450.00

Colton, J. W. & G. W. **Colton's Map of the State of West Virginia & Portions of Adjoining States** NY 1873 23 x 25.5 Folding Map Lithograph after engraving *Cloth or leather folder* $450.00

Gray **Gray's Atlas Map of Virginia & West Virginia** NY 1873 12 x 16 Ex-atlas Lithograph after engraving $75.00

Rand McNally & Co. **Indexed Map of Virginia and West Virginia** Chicago 1877 11 x 20 Folding Map Wax engraving *Cloth folder* $175.00

Western States

Mitchell, S. A. **Map of the State of California...Territories of Oregon and Utah...New Mexico** Phila 1845-50 16 x 13 Ex-atlas HC engraving *From A New Universal Atlas* $375.00

Mitchell, S. A. **Oregon, Upper California and New Mexico** Phila 1849-50 16 x 13 Ex-atlas HC engraving *From A New Universal Atlas* $375.00

Thomas, Cowperthwait & Co **A New Map of California...Oregon, Washington, Utah & New Mexico** Phila 1850-52 15.5 x 12.5 Ex-atlas HC engraving $375.00

Colton, J. W. **Map of the Western States** NY 1854 17.5 x 22 Folding Map HC Engraving *Cloth or leather folder* $350.00

Colton, J. W. **Colton's Railroad & Township Map ... Western States** NY 1856 43 x 43 Folding Map HC Engraving *Cloth or leather folder* $600.00

Colton, J. W. **Railroad & Township Map Western States** NY 1856 33 x 40 Folding Map HC Engraving *Cloth or leather folder* $600.00

Desilver **A New Map of the State of California, Territories of Oregon, Washington, Utah & New Mexico** Phila 1856-59 15.5 x 12.5 Ex-atlas HC Engraving *Baltimore: Cushing & Bailey Phillips (A) 823* $400.00

Colton, J. W. & G. W. **Oregon, Washington, Idaho, California, Utah and New Mexico** NY 1858 13 x 11 Ex-atlas Lithograph after engraving *From Colton's General Atlas* $175.00

Johnson & Browning **Johnson's California, Territories of New Mexico and Utah** NY 1861 18 x 24 Ex-atlas Lithograph after engraving *Johnson's New Illustrated Family Atlas* $125.00

Johnson & Browning **Johnson's Nebraska, Dakota, Colorado & Kansas** NY 1861 12 x 15 Ex-atlas Lithograph after engraving *Johnson's New Illustrated Family Atlas* $95.00

Mitchell, S. A. **Map of Kansas, Nebraska and Colorado...Idaho** Phila 1861 11 x 13 Ex-atlas Lithograph after engraving *From a New General Atlas* $85.00

Johnson & Ward **Johnson's Nebraska, Dakota, Colorado, Idaho & Kansas** NY 1862 12 x 15 Ex-atlas Lithograph after engraving *Johnson's New Illustrated Family Atlas Phillips (A) 837* $85.00

Johnson & Ward **Johnson's Nebraska, Dakota, Idaho, Montana and Wyoming** NY 1865 17 x 23 Ex-atlas Lithograph after engraving *Johnson's New Illustrated Family Atlas* $125.00

Mitchell, S. A. **Map of Oregon, Washington, Idaho and Part of Montana** Phila 1866-77 11 x 13.5 Ex-atlas Lithograph after engraving *From A New General Atlas* $75.00

Colton, J. W. & G. W. **Colton's Map of the States & Territories West of the Mississippi...to the Pacific Ocean...** NY 1867 28 x44 Folding Map Lithograph after engraving *Cloth or leather folder.* $700.00

Johnson & Ward **Johnson's Nebraska, Dakota, Idaho and Montana** NY 1867 17 x 23 Ex-atlas Lithograph after engraving *Johnson's New Illustrated Family Atlas* $95.00

Colton, J. W. & G. W. **Map of California, Nevada, Utah, Colorado, Arizona & New Mexico** NY 1868 15 x 24.5 Ex-atlas Lithograph after engraving *From Colton's General Atlas* $200.00

Colton, J. W. & G. W. **Oregon, Washington, Idaho, Montana & British Columbia** NY 1868 16.5 x 27 Ex-atlas Lithograph after engraving *From Colton's General Atlas* $175.00

Watson **Watson's New Map of the Western States, Territories, Mexico and Central America** Chicago 1869 36.5 x 27.5 Folding Map Wax engraving *Cloth folder* $1,250.00

Colton, J. W. & G. W. **Colton's Map of the States & Territories West of the Mississippi...to the Pacific Ocean...** NY 1871 28 x44 Folding Map Lithograph after engraving *Cloth or leather folder.* $700.00

Lloyd, H. H. **Nebraska, and the Territories of Dakota, Idaho, Montana, Wyoming** NY 1872 15.5 x 24.5 Ex-atlas Lithograph after engraving *Issued as a supplement to state and county atlases* $225.00

Mitchell, S. A. **County Map of Kansas, Nebraska, Colorado, Dakota, Wyoming** Phila 1872 20 x 14 Ex-atlas Lithograph after engraving *From A New General Atlas* $125.00

Colton, J. W. & G. W. **Colton's Oregon, Washington, Idaho, Montana & British Columbia** NY 1873 16.5 x 27 Ex-atlas Lithograph after engraving *From Colton's General Atlas Phillips (A) 866* $125.00

Mitchell, S. A. **County Map of Colorado, Wyoming, Dakota, Montana** Phila 1874-78 19.5 x 14 Ex-atlas Lithograph after engraving *From A New General Atlas* $95.00

Mitchell, S. A. **County Map of Dakota, Wyoming, Kansas, Nebraska and Colorado** Phila 1879 19.5 x 15 Ex-atlas Lithograph after engraving *From A New General Atlas* $95.00

Bradley **Montana, Idaho and Wyoming** Phila 1884 15 x 22 Ex-atlas Lithograph *From New General Atlas* $85.00

Bradley **County and Township Map of Montana, Idaho and Wyoming** Phila 1887 15.5 x 23.5 Ex-atlas Lithograph *From New General Atlas* $95.00

Colton, J. W. & G. W. **Montana, Idaho & Wyoming** NY 1887 17.5 x 25 Ex-atlas Lithograph after engraving *From Colton's General Atlas* $125.00

Colton, J. W. & G. W. **Wyoming, Colorado and Utah** NY 1887 17 x 25 Ex-atlas Lithograph after engraving *From Colton's General Atlas* $125.00

Wisconsin

Wisconsin became a state in May, 1848

Bradford, T. G. **Iowa and Wisconsin** Boston 1838 14.5 x 11.5 Ex-atlas HC engraving *From An Illustrated Atlas* $175.00

Greenleaf **Wisconsin and Iowa** Brattleboro 1842 11 x 13 Ex-atlas HC engraving *From New General Atlas* $275.00

Morse & Breese **Wisconsin, Southern Part** NY 1844-46 12.5 x 15.5 Ex-atlas Cerographic prtd color *From North American Atlas Phillips (A) 1228,31 Karrow 6, 1663* $175.00

Tanner, Henry S. **Wisconsin** Phila 1846 16 x 13.5 Ex-atlas HC engraving *From A New Universal Atlas* $175.00

• Thomas, Cowperthwait & Co **Map of the State of Wisconsin** Phila 1850-55 16 x 13 Ex-atlas HC engraving *From A New Universal Atlas Phillips (A)800* Illustrated $125.00

Lapham **The State of Wisconsin** Milwaukee 1852 31.5 x 48 Folding Map HC engraving *Phillips (M) 1077* $600.00

Colton, J. W. **Wisconsin** NY 1854 15 x 12 Folding Map HC Engraving *Separately issued* $350.00

Colton, J. W. & G. W. **Wisconsin** NY 1855-56 15 x 18 Ex-atlas Lithograph after engraving *From Colton's Atlas of the World Phillips (A)816* $125.00

Desilver **A New Map of the State of Wisconsin** Phila 1856 16 x 13.5 Ex-atlas HC Engraving *From A New Universal Atlas Phillips (A)823* $125.00

Mitchell, S. A. **County Map of Michigan and Wisconsin** Phila 1860 11 x 13.5 Ex-atlas Lithograph after engraving *From A New General Atlas* $65.00

Asher & Adams **Wisconsin** NY 1872 16.5 x 22.5 Ex-atlas Lithograph *Asher & Adams New Statistical and Topographical Atlas Phillips(A)1272* $75.00

World

Lucas, Fielding **Mercator's Chart** Baltimore 1823 14.5 X 20 Ex-atlas HC engraving *From A General Atlas Phillips (A) 742* $225.00

Tanner, Henry S. **World on Mercator's Projection** Phila 1823 23 x 29 Ex-atlas HC engraving *From American Atlas 2d Edition* $600.00

Mitchell, S. A. **A Map of the World on Mercator's Projection** Phila 1843 47 x 74 Wall map HC engraving *Independent Texas* $1,000.00

Colton, J. W. **Colton's New Illustrated Map of the World** NY 1849 31 x 42 Folding Map HC Engraving *Cloth or leather folder. First edition.* $950.00

Colton, J. W. **Colton's New Illustrated Map of the World** NY 1851 31 x 42 Folding Map HC Engraving *Cloth or leather folder. Title moved to top* $875.00

Johnson & Browning **Johnson's Western & Eastern Hemisphere** NY 1861 17 x 26 Ex-atlas Lithograph after engraving *Johnson's New Illustrated Family Atlas* $95.00

Johnson & Browning **Johnson's World** NY 1861 17 x 26 Ex-atlas Lithograph after engraving *Johnson's New Illustrated Family Atlas* $100.00

Wyoming

Wyoming became a state in July 1890

Colton, J. W. & G. W. **Dakota and Wyoming** NY 1868-72 13.5 x 16.5 Ex-atlas Lithograph after engraving *From Colton's General Atlas* $150.00

Mitchell, S. A. **County Map of Dakota, Wyoming, Kansas, Nebraska and Colorado** Phila 1870 19.5 x 15 Ex-atlas Lithograph after engraving *From A New General Atlas* $95.00

Asher & Adams **Wyoming** NY 1873 16.5 x 22.5 Ex-atlas Lithograph *Asher & Adams New Statistical and Topographical Atlas* $150.00

Mitchell, S. A. **County Map of Colorado, Wyoming, Dakota, Montana** Phila 1874-78 19.5 x 14 Ex-atlas Lithograph after engraving *From A New General Atlas Phillips (A) 888* $95.00

Colton, J. W. & G. W. **Montana, Idaho & Wyoming** NY 1876-77 17.5 x 25 Ex-atlas Lithograph after engraving *From Colton's General Atlas* $150.00

Mitchell, S. A. **Territory of Wyoming** Phila 1879 11 x 14 Ex-atlas HC engraving *From A New General Atlas Phillips (A)890* $95.00

Mitchell, S. A. **Territory of Wyoming** Phila 1880 11 x 14 Ex-atlas Lithograph after engraving *From A New General Atlas Phillips (A) 892* $85.00

Bradley **Montana, Idaho and Wyoming** Phila 1884 15 x 22 Ex-atlas Lithograph *From New General Atlas Phillips (A) 920* $85.00

Colton, J. W. & G. W. **Wyoming, Colorado and Utah** NY 1887 17 x 25 Ex-atlas Lithograph after engraving *From Colton's General Atlas* $125.00

Mitchell, S. A. **County and Township Map of Montana, Idaho and Wyoming** Phila 1887 15 x 22 Ex-atlas Lithograph after engraving *From A New General Atlas* $95.00

Thomas, Cowperthwait & Co **Map of the State of Wisconsin** Phila 1850-55 16 x 13 Ex-atlas HC engraving From A New Universal Atlas Phillips (A)800

LIST OF MAPS BY PUBLISHER

• *Illustrated*

Arrowsmith & Lewis

Delaware Phila 1804 10.5 x 8.5 Ex-atlas Engraving *From New and Elegant General Atlas* Phillips (A)702 $150.00

Delaware Boston 1805 10.5 x 8.5 Ex-atlas Engraving *From New and Elegant General Atlas* Phillips (A) 708 $150.00

Delaware Boston 1819 10.5 x 8.5 Ex-atlas Engraving *Phila: John Conrad & Co.* Phillips (A)734 $150.00

Georgia Phila 1804 8.5 x 10.5 Ex-atlas Engraving *From New and Elegant General Atlas* Phillips (A)702 $150.00

Kentucky Phila 1804 8.5 x 10.5 Ex-atlas Engraving *From New and Elegant General Atlas* Phillips (A)702 $175.00

Maine Phila 1804 8.5 x 10.5 Ex-atlas Engraving *From New and Elegant General Atlas* Phillips (A)702 $125.00

Maryland Phila 1804 8.5 x 10.5 Ex-atlas Engraving *From New and Elegant General Atlas* Phillips (A)702 $150.00

Maryland Boston 1805 8.5 x 10.5 Ex-atlas Engraving *From New and Elegant General Atlas* Phillips (A) 708 $150.00

Maryland Boston 1819 8.5 x 10.5 Ex-atlas Engraving *From New and Elegant General Atlas* Phillips (A)734 $150.00

Massachusetts Phila 1804 8.5 x 10.5 Ex-atlas Engraving *From New and Elegant General Atlas* Phillips (A)702 $125.00

Mississippi Territory Phila 1804 8.5 x 10.5 Ex-atlas Engraving *From New and Elegant General Atlas* Phillips (A)702 $275.00

Mississippi Territory Boston 1805 8.5 x 10.5 Ex-atlas Engraving *From New and Elegant General Atlas* Phillips (A) 708 $250.00

New Hampshire Phila 1804 10.5 x 8.5 Ex-atlas Engraving *From New and Elegant General Atlas* Phillips (A)702 $100.00

• **New Jersey** Phila 1804 10.5 x 8.5 Ex-atlas Engraving *From New and Elegant General Atlas* Phillips (A)702 Illustrated $125.00

New Jersey Boston 1819 10.5 x 8.5 Ex-atlas Engraving *From New and Elegant General Atlas* Phillips (A)734 $125.00

• **New York** Phila 1804 8.5 x 10.5 Ex-atlas Engraving *From New and Elegant General Atlas* Phillips (A)702 Illustrated $125.00

North Carolina Phila 1804 8.5 x 10.5 Ex-atlas Engraving *From New and Elegant General Atlas* Phillips (A)702 $150.00

Ohio Phila 1804 10.5 x 8.5 Ex-atlas Engraving *First separate map of the new state. From New and Elegant General Atlas* Phillips (A)702 Illustrated $325.00

Pennsylvania Phila 1804 8.5 x 10.5 Ex-atlas Engraving *From New and Elegant General Atlas* Phillips (A)702 $125.00

Rhode Island Phila 1804 10.5 x 8.5 Ex-atlas Engraving *From New and Elegant General Atlas* Phillips (A)702 $125.00

South Carolina Phila 1804 8.5 x 10.5 Ex-atlas Engraving *From New and Elegant General Atlas* Phillips (A)702 $125.00

Spanish Dominions in North America Boston 1812 8 x 10 Ex-atlas Engraving *From New and Elegant General Atlas* Phillips (A) 718 $250.00

Tennessee Phila 1804 8.5 x 10.5 Ex-atlas Engraving *From New and Elegant General Atlas* Phillips (A)702 $250.00

Tennessee Boston 1805 8.5 x 10.5 Ex-atlas Engraving *From New and Elegant General Atlas* Phillips (A) 708 $225.00

United States Phila 1804 8.5 x 10.5 Ex-atlas Engraving *From New and Elegant General Atlas* Phillips (A)702 $200.00

• **Vermont** Phila 1804 8.5 x 10.5 Ex-atlas Engraving *From New and Elegant General Atlas* Phillips (A)702 Illustrated $125.00

Virginia Phila 1804 10.5 x 8.5 Ex-atlas Engraving *From New and Elegant General Atlas* Phillips (A)702 $175.00

Virginia Boston 1805 10.5 x 8.5 Ex-atlas Engraving *From New and Elegant General Atlas* Phillips (A) 708 $150.00

Virginia Boston 1812 10.5 x 8.5 Ex-atlas Engraving *From New and Elegant General Atlas* Phillips (A) 718 $150.00

VirginiaBoston 1819 10.5 x 8.5 Ex-atlas Engraving *From New and Elegant General Atlas* Phillips (A)734 $150.00
Aschbach **Pocket Map Showing the Probable Theatre of War** Phila 1861 15 x 13 Folding Map HC engraving $800.00

Asher & Adams

Arkansas and Portion of Indian territory NY 1872 16.5 x 22.5 Ex-atlas Lithograph *Asher & Adams New Statistical and Topographical Atlas* Phillips(A)1272 $85.00
Asher & Adams California & Nevada. North (and) South NY 1872 16.5 x 22.5 Ex-atlas Lithograph *Asher & Adams New Statistical and Topographical Atlas. 2 sheets.* Phillips(A)1272 $175.00
Asher & Adams Dakota NY 1875 22.5 x 16.5 Ex-atlas Lithograph *Asher & Adams New Statistical and Topographical Atlas* $85.00
Florida NY 1872 16.5 x 22.5 Ex-atlas Lithograph *Asher & Adams New Statistical and Topographical Atlas* Phillips(A)1272 $75.00
Georgia & Alabama NY 1872 16.5 x 22.5 Ex-atlas Lithograph *Asher & Adams New Statistical and Topographical Atlas* Phillips(A)1272 $75.00
Asher & Adams Idaho, Montana Western Portion NY 1875 16.5 x 22.5 Ex-atlas Lithograph *Asher & Adams New Statistical and Topographical Atlas* $125.00
Illinois NY 1872 22.5 x 16.5 Ex-atlas Lithograph *Asher & Adams New Statistical and Topographical Atlas* Phillips(A)1272 $75.00
Asher & Adams Indian Territory and Texas North West Portion NY 1875 16.5 x 22.5 Ex-atlas Lithograph *Asher & Adams New Statistical and Topographical Atlas* $95.00
Kentucky & Tennessee NY 1872 16.5 x 22.5 Ex-atlas Lithograph *Asher & Adams New Statistical and Topographical Atlas* Phillips(A)1272 $75.00
Kentucky & Tennessee NY 1872 16.5 x 22.5 Ex-atlas Lithograph *Asher & Adams New Statistical and Topographical Atlas* $75.00
Louisiana & Mississippi NY 1872 16.5 x 22.5 Ex-atlas Lithograph *Asher & Adams New Statistical and Topographical Atlas* Phillips(A)1272 $75.00
Louisiana & Mississippi NY 1872 16.5 x 22.5 Ex-atlas Lithograph *Asher & Adams New Statistical and Topographical Atlas* $75.00
Minnesota NY 1874 16.5 x 22.5 Ex-atlas Lithograph *Asher & Adams New Statistical and Topographical Atlas* $75.00
Asher & Adams Montana Eastern Portion NY 1875 16.5 x 22.5 Ex-atlas Lithograph *Asher & Adams New Statistical and Topographical Atlas* $125.00
Nebraska NY 1873 16.5 x 22.5 Ex-atlas Lithograph *Asher & Adams New Statistical and Topographical Atlas* $75.00
Asher & Adams New Mexico NY 1873 16.5 x 22.5 Ex-atlas Lithograph *Asher & Adams New Statistical and Topographical Atlas* $150.00
North Carolina & South Carolina NY 1872 16.5 x 22.5 Ex-atlas Lithograph *Asher & Adams New Statistical and Topographical Atlas* Phillips(A)1272 $75.00
Ohio and Indiana NY 1872 16.5 x 22.5 Ex-atlas Lithograph *Asher & Adams New Statistical and Topographical Atlas* Phillips(A)1272 $75.00
Asher & Adams Oregon NY 1875 16.5 x 22.5 Ex-atlas Lithograph *Asher & Adams New Statistical and Topographical Atlas* $85.00
Asher & Adams Texas, Eastern Portion (and) Texas, Western Portion NY 1872-74 16.5 x 22.5 Ex-atlas Lithograph *Asher & Adams New Statistical and Topographical Atlas. 2 sheetss* Phillips(A)1272 $225.00
United States and Territories NY 1871 16.5 x 22.5 Ex-atlas Lithograph *Asher & Adams New Statistical and Topographical Atlas* $95.00
Asher & Adams Utah NY 1875 16.5 x 22.5 Ex-atlas Lithograph *Asher & Adams New Statistical and Topographical Atlas* $125.00
Portions ofUtah, Colorado and Wyoming NY 1872 16.5 x 22.5 Ex-atlas Lithograph *Asher & Adams New Statistical and Topographical Atlas* Phillips(A)1272 $85.00
Wisconsin NY 1872 16.5 x 22.5 Ex-atlas Lithograph *Asher & Adams New Statistical and Topographical Atlas* Phillips(A)1272 $75.00
Wyoming NY 1873 16.5 x 22.5 Ex-atlas Lithograph *Asher & Adams New Statistical and Topographical Atlas* $150.00

Asher & Co.

The Historical War Map Baltimore 1862 24 x 33 Folding Map HC engraving *Imprint of E. F. Hazelton, Baltimore* $600.00
The Historical War Map Baltimore 1863 24 x 33 Folding Map HC engraving *Imprint of Barnitz, Cincinnati. With 72p text* $600.00

Aspin

North and South America Phila 1823 13.5 x 17 Sep. Issue HC engraving *From Abbe Gaultiers Geographical Game. Shows Franklinia in eastern TN* $275.00

Barnes, R. L.

County, Township and Railroad Map of ...
Pennsylvania Phila 1857 32.5 x 49 Wall Map HC engraving $500.00
12 Miles Around Philadelphia Phila 1858 21 x 21 Folding Map HC engraving *Cloth folder* $400.00
Barnes Driving Map of Phildelphia and Surroundings Phila 1874 24.5 x 28.5 Folding Map HC engraving *Cloth folder* $250.00
Map of Venango County, Pennsylvania Phila 1865 24 x 32.5 Folding Map HC engraving *Cloth folder* $750.00

Bradford & Goodrich

Alabama Boston 1838-42 11.5 x 14 Ex-atlas HC engraving *From Universal Illustrated Atlas* Phillips (A) 783 $150.00
Arkansas Boston 1842 11.5 x 14 Ex-atlas HC engraving *From Universal Illustrated Atlas* Phillips (A) 783 $125.00
Baltimore Boston 1841 11.5 x 14.5 Ex-atlas HC engraving *From Universal Illustrated Atlas* Phillips (A) 783 $100.00
Delaware Boston 1838-46 14.5 x 11.5 Ex-atlas HC engraving *From Universal Illustrated Atlas* Phillips (A) 783 $100.00
Florida Boston 1846 14.5 x 11.5 Ex-atlas HC engraving *From Universal Illustrated Atlas* Phillips (A) 783 $150.00
Georgia Boston 1841 14.5 x 11.5 Ex-atlas HC engraving *From Universal Illustrated Atlas* Phillips (A) 783 $125.00
Indiana Boston 1842 14.5 x 11.5 Ex-atlas HC engraving *From Universal Illustrated Atlas* Phillips (A) 783 $100.00
Mississippi Boston 1842 14.5 x 11.5 Ex-atlas HC engraving *From Universal Illustrated Atlas* Phillips (A) 783 $100.00
New York Boston 1838-46 11 x 14 Ex-atlas Lithograph after engraving *From Universal Illustrated Atlas* Phillips (A) 783 $85.00

Bradford, T. G.

Alabama Boston 1838 14.5 x 11.5 Ex-atlas HC engraving *From An Illustrated Atlas* $150.00
Arkansas Boston 1838 11 x 14 Ex-atlas HC engraving *From An Illustrated Atlas* $100.00
Baltimore Boston 1838 11.5 x 14.5 Ex-atlas HC engraving *From An Illustrated Atlas* $125.00
Baltimore Boston 1842 11.5 x 14.5 Ex-atlas HC engraving *Another issue.* $100.00
Boston Boston 1842 11.5 x 14.5 Ex-atlas HC engraving *From An Illustrated Atlas* $175.00
Connecticut Boston 1838 11.5 x 14.5 Ex-atlas HC engraving *From An Illustrated Atlas* $100.00
Delaware Boston 1838 14.5 x 11.5 Ex-atlas HC engraving *From An Illustrated Atlas* $125.00
District of Columbia Boston 1835 10 x 8 Ex-atlas HC engraving *From a Comprehensive Atlas* $75.00
Florida Boston 1838 14 x 13 Ex-atlas HC engraving *From An Illustrated Atlas* $150.00
Georgia Boston 1838 10 x 8 Ex-atlas HC engraving *From A Comprehensive Atlas* $85.00
Illinois Boston 1838 14.5 x 11.5 Ex-atlas HC engraving *From An Illustrated Atlas* $100.00
Indiana Boston 1838 14.5 x 11.5 Ex-atlas HC engraving *From An Illustrated Atlas* $125.00
Indiana & Ohio Boston 1835 8 x 10 Ex-atlas HC engraving *From a Comprehensive Atlas* $85.00
Iowa and Wisconsin Boston 1838 14.5 x 11.5 Ex-atlas HC engraving *From An Illustrated Atlas* $175.00
Kentucky Boston 1838-42 10.5 x 14 Ex-atlas HC engraving *From An Illustrated Atlas* $100.00
Louisiana and Part of Arkansas Boston 1838 10 x 8 Ex-atlas HC engraving *From a Comprehensive Atlas* $75.00
Maine Boston 1835 10 x 8 Ex-atlas HC engraving *From a Comprehensive Atlas* $75.00
Maryland Boston 1838-41 11.5 x 14.5 Ex-atlas HC engraving *From An Illustrated Atlas* $100.00
Massachusetts Boston 1842 11.5 x 14.5 Ex-atlas HC engraving *From An Illustrated Atlas* $125.00
Mexico, Guatemala and the West Indies Boston 1835 8 x 11 Ex-atlas HC engraving *From a Comprehensive Atlas* $125.00
Michigan and the Great Lakes Boston 1835 7.5 x 10 Ex-atlas HC engraving *From a Comprehensive Atlas* $175.00
Mississippi Boston 1838 14 x 11 Ex-atlas HC engraving *From An Illustrated Atlas* $150.00
Mississippi Boston 1839 10 x 8 Ex-atlas HC engraving *From a Comprehensive Atlas* $95.00
Mississippi & Alabama Boston 1835 8 x 10 Ex-atlas HC engraving *From a Comprehensive Atlas* $125.00
Missouri Boston 1838 11 x 14 Ex-atlas HC engraving *From An Illustrated Atlas* $150.00
• **Missouri, Illinois and Iowa** Boston 1835 10.5 x 8 Ex-atlas HC Engraving *From a Comprhensive Atlas* Illustrated $150.00
New Hampshire Boston 1838 14.5 x 11.5 Ex-atlas HC engraving *From An Illustrated Atlas* $100.00
New Hampshire & Vermont Boston 1835 10 x 7.5 Ex-atlas HC engraving *From a Comprehensive Atlas* $95.00
New Hampshire & Vermont Boston 1835 10 x 7.5 Ex-atlas HC engraving *From a Comprehensive Atlas* $95.00

New Jersey Boston 1838 14 x 11 Ex-atlas HC engraving *From An Illustrated Atlas* $125.00
New York Boston 1838 14 x 11 Ex-atlas HC engraving *From An Illustrated Atlas* $125.00
Ohio Boston 1838 13.5 x 11 Ex-atlas HC engraving *From An Illustrated Atlas* $125.00
PennsylvaniaBoston 1838 11.5 x 14.5 Ex-atlas HC engraving *From An Illustrated Atlas* $100.00
Pennsylvania & New Jersey Boston 1835 8 x 10 Ex-atlas HC engraving *From a Comprehensive Atlas* $75.00
Rhode Island Boston 1838 14.5 x 11.5 Ex-atlas HC engraving *From An Illustrated Atlas* $100.00
TennesseeBoston 1838 11.5 x 15 Ex-atlas HC engraving *From An Illustrated Atlas* $125.00
Texas Boston 1835-36 8 x 10.5 Ex-atlas HC engraving *From A Comprehensive Atlas* Illustrated $675.00
United States Boston 1835 8 x 10 Ex-atlas HC engraving *From A Comprehensive Atlas* $150.00
United States Boston 1838 14 x 22.5 Ex-atlas HC engraving *From An Illustrated Atlas* Wheat (TM) II, 430 $200.00
United States Exhibiting Ralroads & Canals Boston 1838 8 x 10 Ex-atlas HC engraving *From A Comprehensive Atlas* $125.00
VermontBoston 1838 14.5 x 11.5 Ex-atlas HC engraving *From An Illustrated Atlas* $100.00
VirginiaBoston 1841 11.5 x 15.5 Ex-atlas HC engraving *From A Universal Illustrated Atlas* $150.00
Washington-Cincinnati-New Orleans-Louisville Boston 1838 11.5 x 14 Ex-atlas HC engraving *4 city plans* $85.00
West Indies Boston 1842 14 x 17 Ex-atlas HC engraving *From A Universal Illustrated Atlas* $150.00

Bradley

Publishers of (Mitchell's) New General Atlas

Arizona and New Mexico Phila 1886 14.5 x 22 Ex-atlas Lithograph *From New General Atlas*See Phillips (A)920 $75.00
County and Township Map of Arizona and New Mexico Phila 1887 14 x 22 Ex-atlas Lithograph *From New General Atlas*See Phillips (A)920 $85.00
Colorado Phila 1887 17 x 21 Ex-atlas Lithograph *From New General Atlas*See Phillips (A)920 $100.00
Colorado Phila 1889 17 x 21 Ex-atlas Lithograph *From New General Atlas*See Phillips (A)920 $100.00
County and Township Map of Dakota Phila 1887 15 x 12.5 Ex-atlas Lithograph *From New General Atlas*See Phillips (A)920 $85.00
County Map of the States of Delaware, Maryland, Virginia, and West Virginia Phila 1882 14.5 x 22 Ex-atlas Lithograph *From New General Atlas*See Phillips (A)920 $75.00
County Map of Florida Phila 1887 12 x 15 Ex-atlas Lithograph *From New General Atlas*See Phillips (A)920 $95.00
County Map of Georgia and Alabama Phila 1887 12.5 x 20 Ex-atlas Lithograph *From New General Atlas*See Phillips (A)920 $65.00
Indian Territory Phila 1889 12.5 x 17 Ex-atlas Lithograph *From New General Atlas*See Phillips (A)920 $95.00
Kansas Phila 1885 16 x 22 Ex-atlas Lithograph *From New General Atlas*See Phillips (A)920 $75.00
Kentucky and Tennessee Phila 1888 14 x 21 Ex-atlas Lithograph *From New General Atlas*See Phillips (A)920 $65.00
Montana, Idaho and Wyoming Phila 1884 15 x 22 Ex-atlas Lithograph *From New General Atlas* $85.00
County and Township Map of Montana, Idaho and Wyoming Phila 1887 15.5 x 23.5 Ex-atlas Lithograph *From New General Atlas*See Phillips (A)920 $95.00
North and South Dakota Phila 1889 21 x 17 Ex-atlas Lithograph *From New General Atlas*See Phillips (A)920 See Dakota $85.00
County and Township Map of Oregon and Washington Phila 1887 21.5 x 15 Ex-atlas Lithograph *From New General Atlas*See Phillips (A)920 $95.00
Texas Phila 1885 16.5 x 22.5 Ex-atlas Lithograph *From New General Atlas*See Phillips (A)920 $100.00
Railroad Map of the United States Phila 1886 14 x 23 Folding Map Lithograph $175.00
Washington and Oregon Phila 1885 23 x 17 Ex-atlas Lithograph *From New General Atlas*Phillips (A)870 $85.00

Bradley, Abraham

Map of the United States Exhibiting the Post Roads... Phila 1796 34.5 x 37.5 Folding Map Hand colored engraving $17,500.00
Map of the United States Exhibiting the Post Roads... Phila 1804 38 x 52.5 Folding Map Hand colored engraving *Schwarz & Ehrenberg 222* $12,500.00

Britton & Rey

Map of San Francisco from the latest Surveys SF 1872 17 x 19.5 Folding Map UC engraving *Cloth Folder. "A Map and Street Directory of San Francisco"* $300.00

Burr, David H.

Map of New Jersey and Pennsylvania Washington 1839 37.5 x 50.5 Folding Map HC engraving *2 sheets* $800.00
Map of the State of Alabama NY 1836 15 x 12 Ex-atlas HC engraving *From The Universal Atlas* Phillips (A) 1379a $175.00
Arkansas NY 1835 11 x 13 Ex-atlas HC engraving *From The Universal Atlas* Phillips (A) 1379a $175.00
Delaware & Maryland NY 1836 12 x 15 Ex-atlas HC engraving *From The Universal Atlas* Phillips (A) 1379a $175.00
Map of the Territory of Florida NY 1834-36 13 x 11 Ex-atlas HC engraving *From The Universal Atlas* Phillips (A) 1379a $250.00
Map of Florida Washington 1839 50 x 35 Folding Map HC engraving $1,500.00
Georgia NY 1836 13 x 11 Ex-atlas HC engraving *From The Universal Atlas* $175.00
Illinois NY 1836 15 x 12 Ex-atlas HC engraving *From The Universal Atlas* Phillips (A) 1379a Phillips (M) 327 $200.00
Indiana NY 1836 15 x 12 Ex-atlas HC engraving *From The Universal Atlas* Phillips (A) 1379a $200.00
Kentucky & Tennessee NY 1836 12 x 15 Ex-atlas HC engraving *From The Universal Atlas* Phillips (A) 1379a $150.00
Kentucky & Tennessee NY 1836 12 x 15 Ex-atlas HC engraving *From The Universal Atlas* $150.00
Map of Kentucky and Tennessee Washington 1839 36 x 50 Folding Map HC engraving $1,500.00
Louisiana NY 1836 12 x 15 Ex-atlas HC engraving *From The Universal Atlas* Phillips (A) 1379a $175.00
Maine NY 1836 15 x 12 Ex-atlas HC engraving *From The Universal Atlas* Phillips (A) 1379a $145.00
Massachusetts, Rhose Island & Connecticut NY 1836 12 x 15 Ex-atlas HC engraving *From The Universal Atlas* Phillips (A) 1379a $175.00
United States of Mexico NY 1836 15 x 12 Ex-atlas HC engraving *From The Universal Atlas* Phillips (A) 1379a $425.00
Michigan NY 1831-36 15 x 12 Ex-atlas HC engraving *From The Universal Atlas* Phillips (A) 1379a Phillips (M) 424 $325.00
Mississippi NY 1835-36 14 x 11 Ex-atlas HC engraving *From The Universal Atlas* $185.00
Missouri NY 1834-36 11 x 12.5 Ex-atlas HC engraving *From The Universal Atlas* Phillips (A) 1379a $275.00
New Jersey NY 1836 12 x 15 Ex-atlas HC engraving *From The Universal Atlas* Phillips (A) 1379a $150.00
Map of New Jersey & Pennsylvania Washington 1839 36 x 50 Folding Map HC engraving $1,500.00
Map of the State of New York NY 1836 12 x 15 Ex-atlas HC engraving *From The Universal Atlas* Phillips (A) 1379a $175.00
Map of the State of New York Ithaca 1839 19 x 24 Folding Map HC engraving *Leather covers* $350.00
Map of the Country ...Round New York City NY 1836 15 x 12 Ex-atlas HC engraving *From The Universal Atlas. Circular Map* Phillips (A) 1379a $250.00
Map of the City and County of New York With the Adjacent Country NY 1829 20 x 49.5 Ex-atlas HC engraving *From Atlas of the State of New York* Phillips (A) 1379a $900.00
North America NY 1836 15 x 12 Ex-atlas HC engraving *From The Universal Atlas* Phillips (A) 1379a $175.00
North and South Carolina NY 1836 12 x 15 Ex-atlas HC engraving *From The Universal Atlas* Phillips (A) 1379a $145.00
Ohio NY 1836 12 x 15 Ex-atlas HC engraving *From The Universal Atlas* Phillips (A) 1379a $145.00
Oregon Territory NY 1833-36 10.5 x 12.5 Ex-atlas HC engraving *From The Universal Atlas* Phillips (A) 1379a $300.00
Pennsylvania NY 1836 12 x 15 Ex-atlas HC engraving *From The Universal Atlas* Phillips (A) 1379a $175.00
United States NY 1835 10.5 x 12.5 Ex-atlas HC engraving *From The Universal Atlas* Phillips (A) 1379a $275.00
Vermont & New Hampshire NY 1836 15 x 12 Ex-atlas HC engraving *From The Universal Atlas* $145.00
Virginia NY 1834-35 10 x 13.5 Ex-atlas HC engraving *From The Universal Atlas* Phillips (A) 1379a $150.00
West Indies NY 1836 12 x 15 Ex-atlas HC engraving *From The Universal Atlas* Phillips (A) 1379a $125.00

Carey & Lea

Geographical, ...Historical Map of Alabama Phila 1822-23 17.5 x 22 Ex-atlas HC engraving *Complete Historical, Chronological and Geographical American Atlas* Phillips (A) 1373a Phillips (M) 92 $225.00
Geographical, ...Historical Map of Americas Phila 1822-23 17.5 x 22 Ex-atlas HC engraving *Complete Historical, Chronological and Geographical American Atlas* Phillips (A) 1373a $250.00
• **Geographical, ...Historical Map of Arkansas Territory** Phila 1822-23 17.5 x 22 Ex-atlas HC engraving *Complete Historical, Chronological and Geographical American Atlas* Phillips (A) 1373a Illustrated $475.00

Geographical, ...Historical Map ofBritish Possessions Phila 1822-23 17.5 x 22 Ex-atlas HC engraving *Complete Historical, Chronological and Geographical American Atlas* Phillips (A) 1373a $250.00
Geographical, ...Historical Map ofConnecticut Phila 1822-23 17.5 x 22 Ex-atlas HC engraving *Complete Historical, Chronological and Geographical American Atlas* Phillips (A) 1373a $275.00
Geographical, ... Historical Map ofCuba and Bahama Islands Phila 1822-23 17.5 x 22 Ex-atlas HC engraving *Complete Historical, Chronological and Geographical American Atlas* Phillips (A) 1373a $275.00
Geographical, ... Historical Map ofDelaware Phila 1822-23 17.5 x 22 Ex-atlas HC engraving *Complete Historical, Chronological and Geographical American Atlas* Phillips (A) 1373a $225.00
Geographical, ... Historical Map ofDistrict of Columbia Phila 1822-23 17.5 x 22 Ex-atlas HC engraving *Complete Historical... Geographical American Atlas* Phillips (A) 1373a $325.00
Geographical, ... Historical Map ofFlorida Phila 1822-23 17.5 x 22 Ex-atlas HC engraving *Complete Historical, Chronological and Geographical American Atlas* Phillips (A) 1373a $325.00
Geographical, ... Historical Map ofGeorgia Phila 1822-23 17.5 x 22 Ex-atlas HC engraving *Complete Historical, Chronological and Geographical American Atlas* Phillips (A) 1373a $250.00
Geographical, ... Historical Map ofHispaniola Phila 1822-23 17.5 x 22 Ex-atlas HC engraving *Complete Historical, Chronological and Geographical American Atlas* Phillips (A) 1373a $275.00
Geographical, ... Historical Map ofIllinois Phila 1822-23 17.5 x 22 Ex-atlas HC engraving *Complete Historical, Chronological and Geographical American Atlas* Phillips (A) 1373a Illustrated $295.00
Geographical, ... Historical Map ofIndiana Phila 1822-23 17.5 x 22 Ex-atlas HC engraving *Complete Historical, Chronological and Geographical American Atlas* Phillips (A) 1373a $295.00
Geographical, ... Historical Map ofJamaica Phila 1822-23 17.5 x 22 Ex-atlas HC engraving *Complete Historical, Chronological and Geographical American Atlas* Phillips (A) 1373a $275.00
Geographical, ... Historical Map ofKentucky Phila 1822-23 17.5 x 22 Ex-atlas HC engraving *Complete Historical, Chronological and Geographical American Atlas* Phillips (A) 1373a $295.00
Geographical, ... Historical Map ofLeeward Islands Phila 1822-23 17.5 x 22 Ex-atlas HC engraving *Complete Historical, Chronological and Geographical American Atlas* Phillips (A) 1373a $275.00
Geographical, ... Historical Map ofLouisiana Phila 1822-23 17.5 x 22 Ex-atlas HC engraving *Complete Historical, Chronological and Geographical American Atlas* Phillips (A) 1373a $275.00
Geographical, ... Historical Map ofMaine Phila 1822-23 17.5 x 22 Ex-atlas HC engraving *Complete Historical, Chronological and Geographical American Atlas* Phillips (A) 1373a $225.00
Geographical, ... Historical Map ofMaryland Phila 1822-23 17.5 x 22 Ex-atlas HC engraving *Complete Historical, Chronological and Geographical American Atlas* Phillips (A) 1373a $295.00
Geographical, ... Historical Map ofMassachusets Phila 1822-23 17.5 x 22 Ex-atlas HC engraving *Complete Historical, Chronological and Geographical American Atlas* Phillips (A) 1373a $275.00
Geographical, ... Historical Map ofMexico (California) Phila 1822-23 17.5 x 22 Ex-atlas HC engraving *Complete Historical, Chronological and Geographical American Atlas* Phillips (A) 1373a $675.00
Geographical, ... Historical Map ofMichigan Territory Phila 1822-23 17.5 x 22 Ex-atlas HC engraving *Complete Historical, Chronological and Geographical American Atlas* Phillips (A) 1373a Illustrated $675.00
Geographical, ... Historical Map ofMississippi Phila 1822-23 17.5 x 22 Ex-atlas HC engraving *Complete Historical, Chronological and Geographical American Atlas* Phillips (A) 1373a $225.00
Geographical, ... Historical Map ofMissouri Phila 1822-23 17.5 x 22 Ex-atlas HC engraving *Complete Historical, Chronological and Geographical American Atlas* Phillips (A) 1373a $295.00
Geographical, ... Historical Map ofNew Hampshire Phila 1822-23 17.5 x 22 Ex-atlas HC engraving *Complete Historical, Chronological and Geographical American Atlas* Phillips (A) 1373a $225.00
Geographical, ... Historical Map ofNew Jersey Phila 1822-23 17.5 x 22 Ex-atlas HC engraving *Complete Historical, Chronological and Geographical American Atlas* Phillips (A) 1373a $225.00
Geographical, ... Historical Map ofNew York Phila 1822-23 17.5 x 22 Ex-atlas HC engraving *Complete Historical, Chronological and Geographical American Atlas* Phillips (A) 1373a $295.00

Geographical, ... Historical Map ofNorth America Phila 1822-23 17.5 x 22 Ex-atlas HC engraving *Complete Historical, Chronological and Geographical American Atlas* Phillips (A) 1373a **$295.00**

Geographical, ... Historical Map ofNorth Carolina Phila 1822-23 17.5 x 22 Ex-atlas HC engraving *Complete Historical, Chronological and Geographical American Atlas* Phillips (A) 1373a **$225.00**

Geographical, ... Historical Map ofOhio Phila 1822-23 17.5 x 22 Ex-atlas HC engraving *Complete Historical, Chronological and Geographical American Atlas* Phillips (A) 1373a **$295.00**

Geographical, ... Historical Map ofPennsylvania Phila 1822-23 17.5 x 22 Ex-atlas HC engraving *Complete Historical, Chronological and Geographical American Atlas* Phillips (A) 1373a **$295.00**

Geographical, ... Historical Map ofPorto Rico and Virgin Islands Phila 1822-23 17.5 x 22 Ex-atlas HC engraving *Complete Historical, Chronological and Geographical American Atlas* Phillips (A) 1373a **$275.00**

Geographical, ... Historical Map ofRhode Island Phila 1822-23 17.5 x 22 Ex-atlas HC engraving *Complete Historical, Chronological and Geographical American Atlas* Phillips (A) 1373a **$225.00**

Geographical, ... Historical Map ofSouth Carolina Phila 1822-23 17.5 x 22 Ex-atlas HC engraving *Complete Historical, Chronological and Geographical American Atlas* Phillips (A) 1373a **$225.00**

Geographical, ... Historical Map ofTennessee Phila 1822-23 17.5 x 22 Ex-atlas HC engraving *Complete Historical, Chronological and Geographical American Atlas* Phillips (A) 1373a **$275.00**

Geographical, ... Historical Map ofUnited States Phila 1822-23 17.5 x 22 Ex-atlas HC engraving *Complete Historical, Chronological and Geographical American Atlas* Phillips (A) 1373a **$495.00**

Geographical, ... Historical Map ofVermont Phila 1822-23 17.5 x 22 Ex-atlas HC engraving *Complete Historical, Chronological and Geographical American Atlas* Phillips (A) 1373a **$225.00**

Geographical, ... Historical Map ofVirginia Phila 1822-23 17.5 x 22 Ex-atlas HC engraving *Complete Historical, Chronological and Geographical American Atlas* Phillips (A) 1373a **$295.00**

Geographical, ... Historical Map ofWest Indies Phila 1822-23 17.5 x 22 Ex-atlas HC engraving *Complete Historical, Chronological and Geographical American Atlas* Phillips (A) 1373a **$275.00**

Geographical, ... Historical Map ofWindward Islands Phila 1822-23 17.5 x 22 Ex-atlas HC engraving *Complete Historical, Chronological and Geographical American Atlas* Phillips (A) 1373a **$275.00**

Carey, Matthew

Connecticut Phila 1805 6 x 7.5 Ex-atlas UC engraving *From the Pocket Atlas* Phillips (A) 1368 **$150.00**

- **Delaware** Phila 1795 16 x 9 Ex-atlas UC engraving *From Carey's American Edition of Guthrie's Geography...* Illustrated **$500.00**

Delaware Phila 1801 8 x 6 Ex-atlas UC engraving *From the Pocket Atlas* **$150.00**

Delaware, from the Best Authorities Phila 1814 16 x 9 Ex-atlas HC engraving *From the General Atlas* Phillips (A) 722 **$400.00**

Georgia Phila 1795 9 x 15.5 Ex-atlas HC engraving *From Carey's American Edition of Guthrie's Geography...* **$650.00**

Georgia Phila 1805 8 x 6 Ex-atlas HC engraving *From the Pocket Atlas* Phillips (A) 1368 **$200.00**

Kentuckey Phila 1805 8 x 6 Ex-atlas HC engraving *From the Pocket Atlas* Phillips (A) 1368 Illustrated **$200.00**

Kentucky Phila 1814 10 x 18.5 Ex-atlas HC engraving *From the General Atlas* Phillips (A) 722 **$400.00**

Louisiana Phila 1805 8 x 6 Ex-atlas UC engraving *From the Pocket Atlas* Phillips (A) 1368 **$275.00**

- **Louisiana** Phila 1814 15.5 x 17.5 Ex-atlas HC engraving *From the General Atlas* Phillips (A) 722 Illustrated **$500.00**

Maine Phila 1805 8 x 6 Ex-atlas UC engraving *From the Pocket Atlas* Phillips (A) 1368 **$150.00**

- **The District of Maine** Phila 1814 15.5 x 11 Ex-atlas HC engraving *From the General Atlas* Phillips (A) 722 Illustrated **$375.00**

Maryland Phila 1801 6 x 8 Ex-atlas UC engraving *From the Pocket Atlas* **$200.00**

The State ofMaryland, From the Best Authorities Phila 1795 17 x 21 Ex-atlas UC engraving *From Carey's American Edition of Guthrie's Geography...* **$700.00**

Massachusetts Phila 1805 6 x 8 Ex-atlas UC engraving *From the Pocket Atlas* Phillips (A) 1368 Illustrated **$150.00**

Mississippi Territory Phila 1814 6 x 8 Ex-atlas UC engraving *From the Pocket Atlas* Phillips (A) 1370 **$200.00**

Mississippi Territory & Georgia Phila 1805 6 x 8 Ex-atlas UC engraving *From the Pocket Atlas* Phillips (A) 1368 **$250.00**

Missouri Territory Phila 181412 x 14 Ex-atlas UC engraving *From the General Atlas* Phillips (A) 722 $675.00
Missouri Territory Phila 181812 x 14 Ex-atlas UC engraving *From the General Atlas* Phillips (A)732 $650.00
N.W. Territory Phila 18056 x 8 Ex-atlas UC engraving *From the Pocket Atlas* Phillips (A) 1368 $250.00
New Hampshire Phila 18058 x 6 Ex-atlas UC engraving *From the Pocket Atlas* Phillips (A) 1368 $150.00
• **The State of New Hampshire**Phila 179417.5 x 11 Ex-atlas UC engraving *From the General Atlas* Illustrated $400.00
The State of New Jersey Phila 179518.5 x 12 Ex-atlas UC engraving *From the General Atlas* $400.00
New Jersey Phila 17968 x 6 Ex-atlas UC engraving *From the Pocket Atlas* Phillips (A) 1364 $175.00
New Jersey Phila 18058 x 6 Ex-atlas UC engraving *From the Pocket Atlas* Phillips (A) 1368 $150.00
New York Phila 18056 x 8 Ex-atlas UC engraving *From the Pocket Atlas* Phillips (A) 1368 $150.00
North Carolina Phila 18056 x 8 Ex-atlas UC engraving *From the Pocket Atlas* Phillips (A) 1368 $175.00
• **North Carolina**Phila 181411 x 18 Ex-atlas HC engraving *From the General Atlas* Illustrated $475.00
North Carolina, From the Latest Surveys, By Samuel Lewis Phila 181811 x 18.5 Ex-atlas HC engraving *From the General Atlas* Phillips (A)732 $475.00
OhioPhila 18146 x 8 Ex-atlas UC engraving *From the Pocket Atlas* Phillips (A) 1370 $150.00
The State of Ohio With Part of Upper Canada Phila 181414.5 x 14 Ex-atlas HC engraving *From the General Atlas* Phillips (A) 722 $500.00
PennsylvainaPhila 181811.5 x 18.5 Ex-atlas HC engraving *From the General Atlas* Phillips (A)732 $475.00
PennsylvaniaPhila 18056 x 8 Ex-atlas UC engraving *From the Pocket Atlas* Phillips (A) 1368 $150.00
Rhode Island Phila 18058 x 6 Ex-atlas UC engraving *From the Pocket Atlas* Phillips (A) 1368 $150.00
The State of Rhode Island Phila 181413.5 x 9.5 Ex-atlas HC engraving *From the General Atlas* Phillips (A) 722 $375.00
Plat of the Seven Ranges of Townships Phila 181424 x 13 Ex-atlas UC engraving *From the General Atlas* Phillips (A) 722 $450.00
South Carolina Phila 18056 x 8 Ex-atlas UC engraving *From the Pocket Atlas* Phillips (A) 1368 $175.00
The State of South Carolina, From the Best Authorities, by Samuel Lewis Phila 181415 x 17.5 Ex-atlas HC engraving *From the General Atlas* Phillips (A) 722 $425.00
A Map of the Tenasee Government Formerly Part of North Carolina Phila 17949 x 20.5 Ex-atlas UC engraving *From Guthrie's Geography* $1,250.00
• **A Map of the Tenasee State Formerly Part of North Carolina**Phila 17969 x 20.5 Ex-atlas UC engraving *From Guthrie's Geography* Illustrated $1,250.00
Tenasee: Lately the S.Wn. Territory Phila 18056 x 8 Ex-atlas UC engraving *From the Pocket Atlas* Phillips (A) 1368 $275.00
United States Phila 180510 x 13 Ex-atlas UC engraving *From the Pocket Atlas* Phillips (A) 1368 $325.00
The Upper Territories of the United States Phila 1814 8 x 6 Ex-atlas UC engraving *From the Pocket Atlas* Phillips (A) 1370 $175.00
The Upper Territories of the United States Phila 1814 17 x 12.5 Ex-atlas HC engraving *From the General Atlas* Phillips (A) 722 $750.00
VermontPhila 18058 x 6 Ex-atlas UC engraving *From the Pocket Atlas* Phillips (A) 1368 $150.00
The State of Virgina, From the Best Authorities, by Samuel Lewis Phila 179514 x 20 Ex-atlas UC engraving *From Carey's American Edition of Guthrie's Geography...* $600.00
VirginiaPhila 18056 x 8 Ex-atlas UC engraving *From the Pocket Atlas* Phillips (A) 1368 $200.00
A Correct Map of Virginia Phila 181414 x 20 Ex-atlas HC engraving *From the General Atlas* Phillips (A) 722 $400.00

Carleton, Osgood

Map of Massachusetts Proper Boston 183232 x 47 Folding Map HC engraving $2,250.00

Chapman

Chapman's Sectional Map of Illinois Milwaukee 1857 38.5 x 23 Folding Map HC engraving *Cloth folder* $750.00
Chapman's Township Map of Illinois Milwaukee 1857 17 x 13.5 Folding Map HC engraving *Cloth folder* $450.00

Colby

Map of the State of Maine Houlton 188933.5 x 25 Folding Map Lithograph *Cloth folder* $325.00

Colton, (J. W. & G. W.)

Alabama NY 1855-56 15 x 18 Ex-atlas Lithograph after engraving *From Colton's Atlas of the World* Phillips (A)816 $95.00

Map of the State of Alabama NY 1885 36 x 27 Folding Map Lithograph after engraving *Cloth folder. Separately issued.* $325.00

Map of the Territory of Alaska NY 1886 13 x 16 Ex-atlas Lithograph after engraving *From Colton's General Atlas* $85.00

Arkansas NY 1855-56 15 x 18 Ex-atlas Lithograph after engraving *From Colton's Atlas of the World* Phillips (A)816 $95.00

Baltimore NY 1855-56 15 x 18 Ex-atlas Lithograph after engraving *From Colton's Atlas of the World* Phillips (A)816 $150.00

• **Boston and Adjacent Cities** NY 1855-56 15 x 18 Ex-atlas Lithograph after engraving *From Colton's Atlas of the World* Phillips (A)816 Illustrated $125.00

California NY 1854 15.5 x 12 Folding Map HC engraving *Cloth folder* $1,250.00

California NY 1855-56 15 x 18 Ex-atlas Lithograph after engraving *From Colton's Atlas of the World* Phillips (A)816 $175.00

California NY 1857 15 x 12 Ex-atlas Lithograph after engraving *From Colton's General Atlas* $125.00

California NY 1860 13 x 10 Ex-atlas Lithograph after engraving *Shows 39 counties* $95.00

Colton's California & Nevada NY 1873 25 x 17 Folding Map Lithograph after engraving *Cloth or leather folder* $500.00

Colton's California and Nevada NY 1873 29 x 17 Ex-atlas Lithograph after engraving *From Colton's General Atlas* Phillips (A) 866 $125.00

Colton's California and Nevada NY 1887 25 x 17 Ex-atlas Lithograph after engraving *From Colton's General Atlas* $100.00

Map of California, Nevada, Utah, Colorado, Arizona & New Mexico NY 1868 15 x 24.5 Ex-atlas Lithograph after engraving *From Colton's General Atlas* $200.00

City of Chicago, Illinois NY 1856 12.5 x 8.5 Folding Map HC engraving *Cloth folder* $850.00

Colorado, Utah, &c. NY 1873 13 x 16 Ex-atlas Lithograph after engraving *From Colton's General Atlas* Phillips (A) 866 $125.00

Connecticut NY 1855-56 15 x 18 Ex-atlas Lithograph after engraving *From Colton's Atlas of the World* Phillips (A)816 $95.00

Cuba, Jamaica & Porto Rico NY 1855-56 15 x 18 Ex-atlas Lithograph after engraving *From Colton's Atlas of the World* Phillips (A)816 $95.00

Dakota NY 1873-1887 16 x 13 Ex-atlas Lithograph after engraving *From Colton's General Atlas* Phillips (A) 866 $85.00

Dakota and Wyoming NY 1868-72 13.5 x 16.5 Ex-atlas Lithograph after engraving *From Colton's General Atlas* $150.00

Delaware and Maryland NY 1855-56 15 x 18 Ex-atlas Lithograph after engraving *From Colton's Atlas of the World* Phillips (A)816 $95.00

Florida NY 1855-56 15 x 18 Ex-atlas Lithograph after engraving *From Colton's Atlas of the World* Phillips (A)816 $95.00

Florida NY 1877 17 x 28 Ex-atlas Lithograph after engraving *From Colton's General Atlas* $125.00

Georgetown and the City of Washington NY 1855-56 15 x 18 Ex-atlas Lithograph after engraving *From Colton's Atlas of the World* Phillips (A)816 $150.00

Georgia NY 1855-56 15 x 18 Ex-atlas Lithograph after engraving *From Colton's Atlas of the World* Phillips (A)816 $95.00

Colton's Georgia NY 1864 14 x 11 Folding Map Lithograph after engraving *Cloth or leather folder* $300.00

Colton's Map of the State of Georgia NY 1866 38 x 24.5 Folding Map Lithograph after engraving *Cloth or leather folder* $850.00

Map of Georgia Central RR and Connections NY 1859 10 x 14.5 Folding Map Lithograph after engraving *Lang & Lang imprint* $200.00

Hawaiian Group or Sandwich Islands NY 1855 16 x 13 Ex-atlas Lithograph after engraving *From Colton's Atlas of the World* Phillips (A)816 $85.00

New Sectional Map of the State of Illinois NY 1852 30 x 25 Folding Map HC Engraving *Cloth or leather folder* $500.00

Map of Illinois NY 1854 14 x 11 Folding Map HC Engraving *Cloth folder* $325.00

Illinois NY 1855-56 15 x 18 Ex-atlas Lithograph after engraving *From Colton's Atlas of the World* Phillips (A)816 $95.00

Colton's Indian Territory NY 1867-68 13 x 16 Ex-atlas Lithograph after engraving *From Colton's General Atlas* $175.00

Indian Territory NY 1872-73 13 x 16 Ex-atlas Lithograph after engraving *From Colton's General Atlas* Phillips (A) 866 $125.00

Colton's Indian Territory NY 1887 13 x 16 Ex-atlas Lithograph after engraving *From Colton's General Atlas* $125.00

Indiana NY 1855-56 15 x 18 Ex-atlas Lithograph after engraving *From Colton's Atlas of the World* Phillips (A)816 $95.00

Colton's Map of the State of Indiana Compiled from...United States Surveys... NY 1877 40 x 26 Folding Map Lithograph after engraving *Cloth or leather folder* $500.00

New Railroad Map of Indiana, Ohio and Part of Illinois NY 1875 16 x 28 Folding Map Lithograph after engraving $75.00

Map of Iowa NY 1854 12.5 x 14.5 Folding Map HC Engraving *Cloth or leather folder* $325.00

Iowa NY 1855-56 15 x 18 Ex-atlas Lithograph after engraving *From Colton's Atlas of the World* Phillips (A)816 $95.00

Colton's Township Map of ... Iowa NY 1863-66 16 x 22 Folding Map Lithograph after engraving *Cloth folder* $275.00

Kansas NY 1866-72 16.5 x 24 Ex-atlas Lithograph after engraving *From Colton's General Atlas* See Phillips (A)856 $85.00

Colton's New Sectional Map of ... Kansas NY 1869 29 x 56 Folding Map Lithograph after engraving *Cloth folder* $650.00

Kansas and Nebraska NY 1860 24 x 15 Ex-atlas Lithograph after engraving *From Colton's General Atlas* $75.00

Kentucky & Tennessee NY 1855-56 15 x 18 Ex-atlas Lithograph after engraving *From Colton's Atlas of the World* $95.00

Lake Superior and the Northern Part of Michigan NY 1854 13 x 16 Ex-atlas Lithograph after engraving $85.00

Lake Superior and the Northern Part of Michigan NY 1854 13 x 16 Folding Map Lithograph after engraving *Cloth folder* $350.00

Colton's Map of Lake Superior and Upper Peninsula of Michigan... NY 1868 16.5 x 24.5 Folding Map Lithograph after engraving *Cloth folder. "Showing...Portage Lake...Canal...Iron Lands...Separate issue"* $350.00

Louisiana NY 1855-56 15 x 18 Ex-atlas Lithograph after engraving *From Colton's Atlas of the World* Phillips (A)816 $95.00

Colton's Map of the State of Louisiana and Eastern Part of Texas NY 1871 30 x 39.5 Folding Map Lithograph after engraving *Cloth folder* $650.00

Louisville & New Orleans NY 1855-56 15 x 18 Ex-atlas Lithograph after engraving *From Colton's Atlas of the World* Phillips (A)816 $95.00

Maine NY 1855-56 15 x 18 Ex-atlas Lithograph after engraving *From Colton's Atlas of the World* Phillips (A)816 $95.00

Colton's Maine NY 1877 17 x 13 Folding Map Lithograph after engraving *Cloth or leather folder* $150.00

Massachusetts & Rhode Island NY 1854 12 x 16 Folding Map HC Engraving *Cloth folder* $175.00

Colton's Massachusetts & Rhode Island NY 1867 15 x 15 Folding Map Lithograph after engraving *Cloth or leather folder* $150.00

Massachusetts and Rhode Island NY 1855-56 15 x 18 Ex-atlas Lithograph after engraving *From Colton's Atlas of the World* Phillips (A)816 $95.00

Mexico NY 1855-56 15 x 18 Ex-atlas Lithograph after engraving *From Colton's Atlas of the World* Phillips (A)816 $95.00

Colton's Mexico NY 1861 11 x 14 Folding Map Lithograph after engraving *Cloth folder* $450.00

Michigan NY 1855-56 15 x 18 Ex-atlas Lithograph after engraving *From Colton's Atlas of the World* Phillips (A)816 $125.00

Minnesota NY 1855-56 15 x 18 Ex-atlas Lithograph after engraving *From Colton's Atlas of the World* Phillips (A)816 $125.00

Minnesota NY 1857 13 x 16 Ex-atlas Lithograph after engraving *Last year as territory* Phillips (A)827 $175.00

Minnesota NY 1858 13 x 16 Ex-atlas Lithograph after engraving *First Year of Statehood* Phillips (A)827 $175.00

Colton's New Sectional Map of the State of Minnesota NY 1873 20 x 25 Folding Map Lithograph after engraving *Cloth folder. 2 maps* $400.00

Minnesota and Dakota NY 1860 13 x 16 Ex-atlas Lithograph after engraving *From Colton's General Atlas* $85.00

Mississippi NY 1855-56 15 x 18 Ex-atlas Lithograph after engraving *From Colton's Atlas of the World* Phillips (A)816 $95.00

Missouri NY 1855-56 15 x 18 Ex-atlas Lithograph after engraving *From Colton's Atlas of the World* Phillips (A)816 Illustrated $95.00

Colton's New Map of Missouri NY 1869 21 x 27 Folding Map Lithograph after engraving *Cloth folder* $250.00

Montana, Idaho & WyomingNY1876-7717.5 x 25 Ex-atlas Lithograph after engraving *From Colton's General Atlas*Phillips (A)879 $150.00
Montana, Idaho & WyomingNY188717.5 x 25 Ex-atlas Lithograph after engraving *From Colton's General Atlas* $125.00
Nebraska & Kanzas NY1855-5615 x 18 Ex-atlas Lithograph after engraving *From Colton's Atlas of the World. 1st state of this map "Kanzas"* $175.00
Colton's New Sectional Map of Nebraska and Part of DakotaNY187028 x 37 Folding Map Lithograph $300.00
Sectional Map ofNebraska and Part of DakotaNY 187233 x 40 Folding Map Lithograph after engraving *Cloth or leather folder* $400.00
New HampshireNY1855-5615 x 18 Ex-atlas Lithograph after engraving *From Colton's Atlas of the World*Phillips (A)816 $95.00
New JerseyNY1855-5615 x 18 Ex-atlas Lithograph after engraving *From Colton's Atlas of the World*Phillips (A)816 $95.00
New Mexico and ArizonaNY187317 x 25 Ex-atlas Lithograph after engraving *From Colton's General Atlas* Phillips (A) 866 $150.00
Colton's Map ofNew Mexico and ArizonaNY187720 x 24 Folding Map Lithograph after engraving *Cloth or leather folder* $450.00
Territories ofNew Mexico and UtahNY1855-5615 x 18 Ex-atlas Lithograph after engraving *From Colton's Atlas of the World*Phillips (A)816 $175.00
Colton's Territories ofNew Mexico and UtahNY 186113 x 15.5 Ex-atlas Lithograph after engraving *Shows Confederate Arizona territory* $200.00
New YorkNY183317 x 21 Folding Map HC Engraving *Cloth folder. First Colton publication* $600.00
Map of the State ofNew York....Embracing Plans of the Cities...by David A. BurrNY183446 x 56 Wall Map HC Engraving $800.00
Colton's Railroad and Township Map of ... New YorkNY1853-6028 x 24 Folding Map Lithograph after engraving *Cloth folder* $275.00
Colton's Map ofNew YorkNY185020 x 20 Folding Map HC Engraving $275.00
New YorkNY185411 x 14 Folding Map Lithograph after engraving *Cloth folder* $250.00
New YorkNY1855-5615 x 18 Ex-atlas Lithograph after engraving *From Colton's Atlas of the World*Phillips (A)816 $95.00
New York, Brooklyn, Williamsburgh, Jersey City & the Adjacent..NY185325 x 51 Wall Map HC Engraving $650.00
Map ... Thirty Three Miles AroundNew York City NY185524.5 x 23 Folding Map HC Engraving *Cloth folder* $500.00
Map ofNew York CityNY1855-5618 x 28 Ex-atlas Lithograph after engraving *From Colton's Atlas of the World*Phillips (A)816 $175.00
Map of the City of Brooklyn...City of Williamsburgh...Part of the City of New YorkNY 185532.5 x 46 Wall Map HC engraving $425.00
Map ... Thirty Three Miles AroundCity of New York NY187924.5 x 23.5 Circular Map Lithograph after engraving $600.00
Colton's New York City, Brooklyn, Jersey City, Hoboken..NY187322.5 x 15 Folding Map Lithograph after engraving *Cloth folder* $375.00
North AmericaNY1855-5615 x 18 Ex-atlas Lithograph after engraving *From Colton's Atlas of the World*Phillips (A)816 $95.00
North CarolinaNY1855-5615 x 18 Ex-atlas Lithograph after engraving *From Colton's Atlas of the World*Phillips (A)816 $95.00
Colton's North CarolinaNY1869-7114 x 16 Folding Map Lithograph after engraving *Cloth folder* $350.00
Northern America, British, Russian, and Danish NY 185615 x 18 Ex-atlas Lithograph after engraving *From Colton's Atlas of the World* $95.00
Guide Through Ohio, Michigan, Indiana, Illinois, Missouri, Wisconsin & IowaNY185520.5 x 25.5 Folding Map HC Engraving *Bound with Colton's Western Tourist and Emigrant's Guide* $450.00
Guide Through Ohio, Michigan, Indiana, Illinois NY 185720 x 27 Folding Map HC Engraving *Cloth folder stamped "Map of the Western States"* $400.00
Ohio NY1855-5615 x 18 Ex-atlas Lithograph after engraving *From Colton's Atlas of the World*Phillips (A)816 $95.00
Colton's Railroad and Township Map ofOhio NY 186720 x 24 Folding Map Lithograph after engraving $250.00
Oregon, Washington and Idaho NY1876-7717 x 25 Ex-atlas Lithograph after engraving *From Colton's General Atlas*Phillips (A) 879 $125.00
Oregon, Washington, Idaho, California, Utah and New Mexico NY185813 x 11 Ex-atlas Lithograph after engraving *From Colton's General Atlas*Phillips (A)827 $175.00

Oregon, Washington, Idaho, California, Utah and New Mexico NY 1858 13 x 11 Ex-atlas Lithograph after engraving *From Colton's General Atlas* $175.00

Oregon, Washington, Idaho, Montana & British Columbia NY 1868 16.5 x 27 Ex-atlas Lithograph after engraving *From Colton's General Atlas* $175.00

Colton's Oregon, Washington, Idaho, Montana & British Columbia NY 1873 16.5 x 27 Ex-atlas Lithograph after engraving *From Colton's General Atlas* Phillips (A) 866 $125.00

Pennsylvania NY 1855-56 15 x 18 Ex-atlas Lithograph after engraving *From Colton's Atlas of the World* Phillips (A)816 $95.00

Colton's New Township Map of ... Pennsylvania NY 1866 17 x 27 Folding Map Lithograph after engraving *Cloth folder* $175.00

Colton's Map of Pennsylvania NY 1871 14 x 18 Folding Map Lithograph after engraving $225.00

Philadelphia NY 1855-56 15 x 18 Ex-atlas Lithograph after engraving *From Colton's Atlas of the World* Phillips (A)816 $125.00

Pittsburgh & Cincinnati NY 1855-56 15 x 18 Ex-atlas Lithograph after engraving *From Colton's Atlas of the World* $95.00

Portsmouth on the Ohio River NY 1836 21 x 30 Folding Map HC Engraving *Cloth or leather folder. Bound with Burr's map of Ohio* $1,250.00

Map of the Richmond and Louisville RR Connecting...Virginia...Kentucky... NY 1882 30 x 40 Folding Map Lithograph after engraving *Cloth folder* $350.00

Savanah & Charleston NY 1855-56 15 x 18 Ex-atlas Lithograph after engraving *From Colton's Atlas of the World* $95.00

South Carolina NY 1855-56 15 x 18 Ex-atlas Lithograph after engraving *From Colton's Atlas of the World* Phillips (A)816 $95.00

J. H. Colton's Map of the Southern States, Including Maryland, Delaware NY 1864 38 x 54 Folding Map Lithograph after engraving *Cloth folder. Map in two sections* $1,500.00

St. Louis & Chicago NY 1855-56 15 x 18 Ex-atlas Lithograph after engraving *From Colton's Atlas of the World* $95.00

South Carolina NY 1853 11 x 14 Folding Map HC Engraving *Cloth folder* $425.00

Colton's Map of the State of Tennessee NY 1871 20 x 25 Folding Map Lithograph after engraving *Cloth or leather folder. 2 maps* $450.00

Texas NY 1855 15 x 18 Ex-atlas Lithograph after engraving *From Colton's Atlas of the World* Phillips (A)816 $225.00

New Map of the State of Texas NY 1855-56 16 x 25 Ex-atlas Lithograph after engraving *From Colton's Atlas of the World* Phillips (A)816 $275.00

• **Texas** NY 1856 16 x 25 Folding Map Lithograph after engraving Illustrated $500.00

Texas NY 1858 13 x 10.5 Ex-atlas Lithograph after engraving *From Cabinet Atlas* $150.00

Texas NY 1887 17 x 23 Ex-atlas Lithograph after engraving *From Colton's General Atlas* $125.00

New Map of the State of Texas. Compiled from J. deCordova's Large Map NY 1857 16 x 25 Ex-atlas Lithograph after engraving *From Colton's Atlas of the World* $275.00

New Railroad and County Map of the United States NY 1860-62 33 x 40 Folding Map Lithograph after engraving *Cloth or leather folder* $600.00

New Guide Map of the United States and Canada with Railroads, Counties NY 1862-66 36 x 31 Folding Map Lithograph after engraving *Cloth or leather folder* $500.00

G. W. Colton's New Guide Map of the United States and Canada With Railroads, Counties, etc. NY 1861 30 x 36 Folding Map Lithograph after engraving *Cloth or leather folder* $600.00

Colton's Map of the United States of America NY 1850 20 x 24 Folding Map Lithograph after engraving *Cloth or leather folder. J. H. Colton 86 Cedar St., New York* $300.00

United States of America NY 1855 18 x 27 Folding Map HC Engraving *Imprint J. H. Colton...172 William St., NY. Separately issued* $350.00

Map of the United States of America, British Provinces, Mexico... NY 1854 34 x 43 Folding Map HC Engraving *Cloth or leather folder* $1,000.00

Map of the United States of America, The British Provinces, Mexico... NY 1851 36 x 46 Wall Map HC Engraving $600.00

Burr's Map of the United States Published by J. H. Colton NY 1833 17 x 21 Folding Map HC Engraving *J. H. Colton & Co. 9 Wall Street* $750.00

Map of the United States Showing Routes of U.S. Mail Steam Packets NY 1849 Folding Map HC Engraving $1,500.00

Map of the United States, British Provinces... NY 1853 47 x 54 Wall Map HC Engraving $800.00

United States of AmericaNY185516 x 26 Ex-atlas Lithograph after engraving *From A New Universal Atlas. Eastern Colorado name Colona* $175.00

United States of AmericaNY1855-5618 x 28 Ex-atlas Lithograph after engraving *From Colton's Atlas of the World*Phillips (A)816 $175.00

G. W. & C. B. Colton's United States of AmericaNY 1872-7616 x 28 Folding Map Lithograph after engraving *Cloth folder* $250.00

Colton's Map of the United States, the Canadas, &c.... NY185424 x 29 Folding Map Lithograph after engraving *Cloth or leather folder* $325.00

Colton's New Railroad and County Map ...United States... NY1869-7132 x 34 Folding Map Lithograph after engraving *Cloth or leather folder* $450.00

Colton's Utah & Colorado NY1872-7212.5 x 16 Ex-atlas Lithograph after engraving *From Colton's General Atlas* $125.00

Colton's Map of the Oil District of Venango, Crawford, and Warren Counties, PennsylvaniaNY 186531 x 37 Folding Map Lithograph after engraving *Cloth or leather folder* $600.00

VermontNY1855-5615 x 18 Ex-atlas Lithograph after engraving *From Colton's Atlas of the World*Phillips (A)816 $95.00

Map of VermontNY185914 x 11 Folding Map Lithograph after engraving *Cloth folder* $200.00

VirginiaNY1855-5615 x 18 Ex-atlas Lithograph after engraving *From Colton's Atlas of the World*Phillips (A)816 $95.00

Colton's Map of VirginiaNY187211 x 15 Folding Map Lithograph after engraving *Cloth folder* $200.00

Colton's Virginia and West VirginiaNY186913 x 16 Ex-atlas Lithograph after engraving *From Colton's General Atlas* $75.00

Map of the Virginia, Kentucky and Ohio Railroad.... NY188128.5 x 41.5 Wall Map Lithograph after engraving $275.00

Colton's... Map of the Seat of War in Virginia, Maryland, &c. NY186226.5 x 19 Folding Map Lithograph after engraving *Cloth or leather folder* $1,000.00

Colton's New Topographical Map of ... Virginia, West Virginia, Maryland & Delaware... NY187028 x 42 Folding Map Lithograph after engraving *Cloth folder* $450.00

Colton's New ...Map of the States of Virginia. Maryland and Delaware... NY186230.5 x 44.5 Folding Map Lithograph after engraving *Cloth or leather folder* $750.00

Washington and OregonNY1855-5615 x 18 Ex-atlas Lithograph after engraving *From Colton's Atlas of the World* $125.00

The Territories of Washington and OregonNY1856 12.5 x 16 Ex-atlas Lithograph after engraving *From Colton's Atlas of the World* $125.00

West IndiesNY1855-5615 x 18 Ex-atlas Lithograph after engraving *From Colton's Atlas of the World*Phillips (A)816 $95.00

Topographical Map of the West Indies and Adjacent Coasts by John PinkertonNY185219 x 27 Folding Map HC Engraving *Cloth or leather folder.* $750.00

Colton's Map of the States & Territories West of the Mississippi...to the Pacific Ocean... NY186728 x44 Folding Map Lithograph after engraving *Cloth or leather folder.* $700.00

Colton's Map of the States & Territories West of the Mississippi...to the Pacific Ocean... NY187128 x44 Folding Map Lithograph after engraving *Cloth or leather folder.* $700.00

Colton's Map of the State of West Virginia & Portions of Adjoining StatesNY187323 x 25.5 Folding Map Lithograph after engraving *Cloth or leather folder* $450.00

Colton's Map of the Oil District of West Virginia and OhioNY186531 x 36 Folding Map Lithograph after engraving *Cloth or leather folder* $600.00

Map of the Western StatesNY185417.5 x 22 Folding Map HC Engraving *Cloth or leather folder* $350.00

Colton's Railroad & Township Map ...Western StatesNY185643 x 43 Folding Map HC Engraving *Cloth or leather folder* $600.00

Railroad & Township Map Western StatesNY185633 x 40 Folding Map HC Engraving *Cloth or leather folder* $600.00

WisconsinNY185415 x 12 Folding Map HC Engraving *Separately issued* $350.00

WisconsinNY1855-5615 x 18 Ex-atlas Lithograph after engraving *From Colton's Atlas of the World*Phillips (A)816 $125.00

Colton's New Illustrated Map of the WorldNY1849 31 x 42 Folding Map HC Engraving *Cloth or leather folder. First edition.* $950.00

Colton's New Illustrated Map of the World NY 1851 31 x 42 Folding Map HC Engraving *Cloth or leather folder. Title moved to top* $875.00

Wyoming, Colorado and Utah NY 1887 17 x 25 Ex-atlas Lithograph after engraving *From Colton's General Atlas* $125.00

Cram, George F.

Railroad and Twonship Map of Indian Ty. Chicago 1875 19.5 x 14 Ex-atlas Lithograph *From New Commercial Atlas of the U.S. and Territories* $200.00

Desilver

Publishers of (Mitchell's) New Universal Atlas

A New Map of Alabama With Its Roads and Distances... Phila 1856-57 14.5 x 11.5 Ex-atlas HC Engraving *From A New Universal Atlas* Phillips (A)823 $125.00

A New Map of Arkansas With Its Counties, Towns... Phila 1856-57 16 x 13.5 Ex-atlas HC Engraving *From A New Universal Atlas* Phillips (A)823 $125.00

A New Map of the State of California, Territories of Oregon, Washington, Utah & New Mexico Phila 1856-59 15.5 x 12.5 Ex-atlas HC Engraving *Baltimore: Cushing & Bailey* Phillips (A)823 $400.00

Map of Connecticut Phila 1856-57 12.5 x 14.5 Ex-atlas HC Engraving *From A New Universal Atlas* Phillips (A)823 $85.00

A New Map of the State of Georgia Exhibiting Its Internal Improvements Phila 1856-57 16 x 13 Ex-atlas HC Engraving *From A New Universal Atlas* Phillips (A)823 $95.00

A New Map of the State of Illinois Phila 1856-57 15.5 x 13 Ex-atlas HC Engraving *From A New Universal Atlas* Phillips (A)823 $100.00

A New Map of Indiana Exhibiting Its Internal Improvements... Phila 1857 16 x 13.5 Ex-atlas HC Engraving *From A New Universal Atlas* Phillips (A)823 $100.00

A New Map of Indiana With Its Roads and Distances... Phila 1856 16 x 13.5 Ex-atlas HC Engraving *From A New Universal Atlas* Phillips (A)823 $100.00

A New Map of the State of Iowa Phila 1856-57 13.5 x 16 Ex-atlas HC Engraving *From A New Universal Atlas* Phillips (A)823 $100.00

A New Map of Kentucky With Its Roads and Distances Phila 1856-59 11.5 x 14 Ex-atlas HC Engraving *Baltimore: Cushing & Bailey* Phillips-A-6135,28 $95.00

A New Map of Louisiana With Its Canals, Roads & Distances... Phila 1856-57 11.5 x 14 Ex-atlas HC Engraving *From A New Universal Atlas* Phillips (A)823 $125.00

A New Map of Maine Phila 1856-59 15.5 x 12.5 Ex-atlas HC Engraving *From A New Universal Atlas* Phillips (A)823 $85.00

A New Map of Maryland and Delaware... Phila 1856 11.5 x 15 Ex-atlas HC Engraving *From A New Universal Atlas* Phillips (A)823 $95.00

A New Map of Michigan With Its Canals, Roads... Phila 1856-57 14.5 x 11.5 Ex-atlas HC Engraving *From A New Universal Atlas* Phillips (A)823 $125.00

A New Map of Mississippi With Its Roads and Distances... Phila 1856 14.5 x 11.5 Ex-atlas HC Engraving *From A New Universal Atlas* Phillips (A)823 $85.00

A New Map of the State of Missouri Phila 1856-57 13 x 16 Ex-atlas HC Engraving *From A New Universal Atlas* Phillips (A)823 $125.00

Map of New Jersey Compiled From the Latest Authorities Phila 1856 15.5 x 12.5 Ex-atlas HC Engraving *20 Counties* Phillips (A)823 $95.00

Map of the State of New York Compiled From the Latest Authorities Phila 1857 16 x 26 Ex-atlas HC Engraving *Five insets, two columns of data* Phillips (A)823 $150.00

A New Map of Nth. Carolina With Its Canals, Roads... Phila 1856 12 x 14.5 Ex-atlas HC Engraving *From A New Universal Atlas* Phillips (A)823 $95.00

A New Map of the State of Ohio Phila 1856-57 16 x 13 Ex-atlas HC Engraving *From A New Universal Atlas* Phillips (A)823 $100.00

A New Map of the State of Pennsylvania Including New Jersey Phila 1860 16 x 26.5 Ex-atlas HC Engraving Phillips (A)823 $100.00

A New Map of South Carolina Wit Its Canals, Roads... Phila 1856-57 12 x 14.5 Ex-atlas HC Engraving *From A New Universal Atlas* Phillips (A)823 $95.00

Map of the State of Texas From the Latest Authorities by J. H. Young Phila 1857 12.5 x 15.5 Ex-atlas HC Engraving Phillips (A)823 $500.00

A New Map of the United States of America Phila 1857 15.5 x 26 Ex-atlas HC Engraving *By J. Young* Phillips (A)823 $250.00

A New Map of the State of Virginia Exhibiting Its Internal Improvements Phila 1856-57 12.5 x 15.5 Ex-atlas HC Engraving *From A New Universal Atlas* Phillips (A)823 $95.00

City ofWashington Phila 1856 13 x 15.5 Ex-atlas HC Engraving *From A New Universal Atlas* Phillips (A)823 $95.00
A New Map of the State ofWisconsin Phila 1856 16 x 13.5 Ex-atlas HC Engraving *From A New Universal Atlas* Phillips (A)823 $125.00

Disturnell

Routes Between New York and Washington Phila 1837 23.4 x 4.5 Folding Map HC engraving *Cloth folder* $800.00
Army Map of the Seat of War in Virginia, Showing Battlefields, Fortifications... Phila 1861 27 x 25 Folding Map HC engraving *Cloth folder* $850.00

Duncan & Co.

Plan of the City and Environs ofNew Orleans... Phila 1865 15.5 x 18.5 Folding Map HC engraving $700.00

Entwhistle

Entwhistle's Handy Map ofWashington and Vicinity... Wash 1876 16 x 21 Folding Map Lithograph $175.00

Farmer

An Improved ... Map of the Surveyed Part of... Michigan NY 1835 21 x 31 Folding Map HC engraving *Cloth or leather folder. Second Issue* Phillips (M) 425 $1,500.00
An Improved ... Map of the Surveyed Part of... Michigan NY 1836 21 x 31 Folding Map HC engraving *Cloth or leather folder. Second Issue* $1,500.00
Map of the Territories ofMichigan and Ouisconsin Detroit 1830 40 x 34 Folding Map HC engraving Phillips (M)424 $1,250.00
Improved Map of the Territories of Michigan and Ouisconsin Albany 1835 20 x 34 Folding Map HC engraving Phillips (M)424 $1,000.00
Map of the Surveyed Part ...Territory of Michigan on a Scale of 8 miles... Detroit 1826 20 x 21 Folding Map HC engraving Phillips (M)424 $1,250.00

Finley, A.

Alabama Phila 1829 8.5 x 11 Folding Map HC engraving *Cloth or leather folder* Phillips (A)752 $600.00
Connecticut Phila 1831-34 8.5 x 11 Ex-atlas HC engraving $125.00
Delaware Phila 1829 11.5 x 8.5 Ex-atlas HC engraving *From New General Atlas* Phillips (A)752 $175.00
Map ofFlorida According to the Latest Authorities (with) West Indies Phila 1827 na Folding Map HC engraving *Leather folder* $1,000.00
Illinois Phila 1824-26 11.5 x 8.5 Ex-atlas HC engraving *From New General Atlas* Phillips (A)1378 $175.00
Illinois Phila 1834 18.5 x 13 Ex-atlas HC engraving *Inset map of "Lead Mine Region" (Michigan & Wisc.)* Phillips (M)327 $275.00
Kentucky Phila 1825 11.5 x 8.5 Ex-atlas HC engraving *From New General Atlas* $175.00
Map ofLouisiana, Mississippi, and Alabama... Phila 1827 17 x 20 Folding Map HC engraving $850.00
Maine Phila 1828 11.5 x 8.5 Folding Map HC engraving $225.00
Map of Maine, New Hampshire and Vermont Phila 1826 17 x 21.5 Ex-atlas HC engraving *From New American Atlas* Phillips (A)1378 $350.00
Maryland Phila 1825 8.5 x 11 Ex-atlas HC engraving *From New General Atlas* Phillips (A)1378 $200.00
Massachusetts Phila 1826 9 x 11 Folding Map HC engraving *Leather folder* $375.00
• **Missouri** Phila 1832 12 x 9.5 Ex-atlas HC engraving *From New General Atlas* Illustrated $175.00
New Hampshire Phila 1832 11 x 9 Ex-atlas HC engraving *From New General Atlas* Phillips (A)1378 $200.00
New Jersey Phila 1826 11.5 x 8.5 Ex-atlas HC engraving *From New General Atlas* Phillips (A)1378 $125.00
New York Phila 1824 8.5 x 11 Ex-atlas HC engraving *From New General Atlas* $125.00
Map of Ohio and the Settled Parts of Michigan Phila 1834 19 x 13 Folding Map HC engraving *Leather folder* $750.00
Pennsylvania Phila 1824 8.5 x 11 Ex-atlas HC engraving *From New General Atlas* $125.00
Rhode Island Phila 1829 8.5 x 11 Ex-atlas HC engraving *From New General Atlas* Phillips (A)752 $125.00
Tennessee Phila 1824 8.5 x 11 Ex-atlas HC engraving *From New General Atlas* $175.00
Map of the United States Phila 1826 17 x 21 Folding Map HC engraving *Leather folder* $650.00
Vermont Phila 1824 8.5 x 11 Ex-atlas HC engraving $125.00
Virginia Phila 1825 8.5 x 11 Ex-atlas HC engraving *From New General Atlas* $175.00
Virginia Phila 1825 8.5 x 11 Folding Map HC engraving *Leather folder* $500.00

Frey, A. C.

Topographical Railroad & County Map of ... California and Nevada NY 1868 38.5 x 30.5 Folding Map Lithograph after engraving $850.00

Gaston & Johnson

A New Map of Our Country NY 1854 55 x 62 Wall Map HC engraving $750.00

Goodrich

Florida Boston 1841 15 x 13 Ex-atlas HC engraving $275.00

Map of the Hudson Between Sandy Hook & Sandy Hill... NY 1820 47 x 9 Folding Map Engraving *Half leather folder* $1,500.00

Gray

Gray's New Map of Alabama NY 1880 28 x 17.5 Ex-atlas Lithograph after engraving $75.00

Gray's New Map of Baltimore NY 1878 15 x 12.5 Ex-atlas Lithograph after engraving $75.00

Boston and Adjacent Cities NY 1881 16.5 x 22 Ex-atlas Lithograph after engraving $75.00

Gray's California and Nevada NY 1874 27 x 17 Ex-atlas Lithograph after engraving $100.00

Gray's Atlas Map of California, Nevada, Utah, Colorado, Arizona & New Mexico NY 1873 15.5 x 25.5 Ex-atlas Lithograph after engraving *From Atlas of the United States. Based on Colton* $125.00

Map of Cayuga and Seneca Counties, New York...by O. W. Gray NY 1859 58 x 58 Wall Map HC engraving $375.00

Chicago NY 1876 15.5 x 12.5 Ex-atlas Lithograph after engraving $85.00

Colorado NY 1878 12 x 15 Ex-atlas Lithograph after engraving $85.00

Gray's Atlas Map of Connecticut With Portions of New York & Rhode Island NY 1874 14 x 17.5 Ex-atlas Lithograph after engraving $75.00

Dakota NY 1873 15.5 x 12.5 Ex-atlas Lithograph after engraving $100.00

Georgia NY 1887-81 26 x 16 Ex-atlas Lithograph after engraving $85.00

Indiana NY 1877 25 x 15.5 Ex-atlas Lithograph after engraving *Frank Gray: O. W. Gray & Son* $75.00

Gray's Atlas Map of Louisiana NY 1875 14 x 17 Ex-atlas Lithograph after engraving $75.00

Louisiana NY 1878-81 16 x 26 Ex-atlas Lithograph after engraving $75.00

City of Louisville NY 1876 12 x 14.5 Ex-atlas Lithograph after engraving $75.00

Maryland, Delaware and the District of Columbia NY 1876 15 x 26 Ex-atlas Lithograph after engraving $75.00

Gray's New Map of Mississippi NY 1878 28 x 17.5 Ex-atlas Lithograph after engraving $75.00

Gray's Atlas Map of Missouri NY 1875 12.5 x 15 Ex-atlas Lithograph after engraving $75.00

New Jersey NY 1873 15 x 12 Ex-atlas Lithograph after engraving Phillips (A)1390 $75.00

New York NY 1878 17.5 x 27.5 Ex-atlas Lithograph after engraving $75.00

Map of the Railroads of New York and Part of New England NY 1874 16.5 x 25.5 Ex-atlas Lithograph after engraving *With Colton copyright* $95.00

Gray's Atlas Map of New York City NY 1873 17 x 14 Ex-atlas Lithograph after engraving Phillips (A)1390 $95.00

Gray's Atlas Map of North Carolina NY 1873 14.5 x 17 Ex-atlas Lithograph after engraving Phillips (A)1390 $75.00

Map of Orleans & Niagara Counties, New York...by O. W. Gray Phila 1860 60 x 60 Wall Map HC engraving *Phila: A. R. Z. Dawson* $375.00

San Francisco NY 1878 15.5 x 12 Ex-atlas Lithograph after engraving $85.00

Gray's Atlas Map of South Carolina NY 1873 14.5 x 17 Ex-atlas Lithograph after engraving Phillips (A)1390 $75.00

Gray's New Map of St. Louis NY 1883 17.5 x 14 Ex-atlas Lithograph after engraving $75.00

Gray's Atlas Map of Texas NY 1873 12.5 x 15 Ex-atlas Lithograph after engraving Phillips (A)1390 $175.00

Gray's New Map of Texas and Indian Territory NY 1875 24 x 16 Ex-atlas Lithograph after engraving *From National Atlas* $225.00

Gray's New Map of Texas and Indian Territory NY 1881 17 x 26.5 Ex-atlas Lithograph after engraving *7 Insets* $250.00

Gray's New Map of Texas and Indian Territory NY 1881 17 x 26.5 Ex-atlas Lithograph after engraving *7 Insets* $250.00

Gray's New Railroad Map of Texas East of the 100th Meridian NY 1887 25 x 16.5 Ex-atlas Lithograph after engraving $150.00

Gray's Atlas Map ofUnited States Showing the Principal Geological Formations NY 1873 16 x 26.5 Ex-atlas Lithograph after engraving Phillips (A)1390 $95.00

Gray's Atlas Map ofVirginia & West Virginia NY 1873 12 x 16 Ex-atlas Lithograph after engraving Phillips (A)1390 $75.00

Gray's Atlas Map ofVirginia & West Virginia NY 1873 12 x 16 Ex-atlas Lithograph after engraving $75.00

Washington NY 1873 14 x 17 Ex-atlas Lithograph after engraving $95.00

Washington NY 1875 12 x 15 Ex-atlas Lithograph after engraving $95.00

West Indies and Central America NY 1870 14 x 17 Ex-atlas Lithograph after engraving $75.00

Greenleaf, J.

Arkansas Brattleboro 1842 11 x 13 Ex-atlas HC engraving *From New General Atlas* Phillips (A) 784 $175.00

Illinois Brattleboro 1848 11 x 13 Ex-atlas HC engraving *From A New Universal Atlas* $175.00

- **Indiana** Brattleboro 1842 11 x 13 Ex-atlas HC engraving *From New General Atlas* Phillips (A) 784 Illustrated $175.00

Louisiana Brattleboro 1842 11 x 13 Ex-atlas HC engraving *From New General Atlas* Phillips (A) 784 $125.00

Maine Brattleboro 1842 11 x 13 Ex-atlas HC engraving *From New General Atlas* Phillips (A) 784 $150.00

Map of the State ofMaine with the Province of New Brunswick Brattleboro 1844 50 x 42 Wall Map HC engraving $2,000.00

Michigan Brattleboro 1842 14 x 12 Ex-atlas HC engraving *From New General Atlas* Phillips (A) 784 $375.00

Mississippi Brattleboro 1842 13 x 11 Ex-atlas HC engraving *From New General Atlas* Phillips (A) 784 $150.00

Missouri Brattleboro 1842 13 x 11 Ex-atlas HC engraving *From New General Atlas* Phillips (A) 784 $175.00

New Jersey Brattleboro 1842 12.5 x 10.5 Ex-atlas HC engraving *From New General Atlas* Phillips (A) 784 $125.00

New York Brattleboro 1842 12.5 x 10.5 Ex-atlas HC engraving *From New General Atlas* Phillips (A) 784 $125.00

North America Brattleboro 1848 13 x 11 Ex-atlas HC engraving *From A New Universal Atlas* $175.00

Ohio Brattleboro 1842 13 x 11 Ex-atlas HC engraving *From New General Atlas* Phillips (A) 784 $175.00

Oregon Territory Brattleboro 1842 11 x 13 Ex-atlas HC engraving *From New General Atlas* Phillips (A) 784 $325.00

Texas... Brattleboro 1842 11 x 13 Ex-atlas HC engraving *From New General Atlas* Phillips (A) 784 $500.00

United States Brattleboro 1842 11 x 13 Ex-atlas HC engraving *From New General Atlas* Phillips (A) 784 $200.00

Vermont and New Hampshire Brattleboro 1842 11 x 13 Ex-atlas HC engraving *From New General Atlas* Phillips (A) 784 $175.00

Virginia Brattleboro 1842 11 x 13 Ex-atlas HC engraving *From New General Atlas* Phillips (A) 784 $150.00

Wisconsin and Iowa Brattleboro 1842 11 x 13 Ex-atlas HC engraving *From New General Atlas* Phillips (A) 784 $275.00

Ide

Ide's Map ofMontana Helena 1891 21 x 38 Folding Map Lithograph $800.00

Johnson & Browning

Johnson's Arkansas, Mississippi, Louisiana NY 1861 23 x 17 Ex-atlas Lithograph after engraving *Johnson's New Illustrated Family Atlas* $75.00

Johnson's California, Territories of New Mexico and Utah NY 1861 18 x 24 Ex-atlas Lithograph after engraving *Johnson's New Illustrated Family Atlas* $125.00

Johnson's Cuba, Jamaica, Puerto Rico NY 1861 17 x 26 Ex-atlas Lithograph after engraving *Johnson's New Illustrated Family Atlas* $75.00

Johnson's Delaware & Maryland NY 1861 12 x 17 Ex-atlas Lithograph after engraving *Johnson's* $65.00

Johnson's Florida NY 1861 12 x 16 Ex-atlas Lithograph after engraving *Johnson's New Illustrated Family Atlas* $85.00

Johnson's Georgetown and the City of Washington NY 1861 13 x 16 Ex-atlas Lithograph after engraving *Johnson's New Illustrated Family Atlas* $75.00

Johnson's Georgia & Alabama NY 1861 17 x 23 Ex-atlas Lithograph after engraving *Johnson's New Illustrated Family Atlas* $75.00

Johnson's Illinois NY 1861 17 x 13 Ex-atlas Lithograph after engraving *Johnson's New Illustrated Family Atlas* $75.00

Johnson's Iowa & Nebraska NY 1861 16 x 13 Ex-atlas Lithograph after engraving *Johnson's New Illustrated Family Atlas* $65.00

Johnson's Kentucky & Tennessee NY 1861 17 x 23 Ex-atlas Lithograph after engraving *3 vignettes* $85.00
Johnson's Maine NY 1861 17 x 13 Ex-atlas Lithograph after engraving *Johnson's New Illustrated Family Atlas* $60.00
Johnson's Massachusetts, Connecticut, Rhode Island NY 1861 Ex-atlas Lithograph after engraving *Johnson's New Illustrated Family Atlas* $85.00
Johnson's Mexico NY 1861 12 x 15 Ex-atlas Lithograph after engraving *Johnson's New Illustrated Family Atlas* $75.00
Johnson's Michigan & Indiana NY 1861 17 x 23 Ex-atlas Lithograph after engraving *Johnson's New Illustrated Family Atlas* $85.00
Johnson's Minnesota & Dakota NY 1861 13 x 16 Ex-atlas Lithograph after engraving *Johnson's New Illustrated Family Atlas* $75.00
Johnson's Missouri & Kansas NY 1861 17 x 23 Ex-atlas Lithograph after engraving *3 vignettes* Illustrated $95.00
Johnson's Nebraska and Kansas NY 1861 13 x 16 Ex-atlas Lithograph after engraving *Johnson's New Illustrated Family Atlas* $175.00
Johnson's Nebraska, Dakota, Colorado & Kansas NY 1861 12 x 15 Ex-atlas Lithograph after engraving *Johnson's New Illustrated Family Atlas* $95.00
Johnson's New England NY 1861 17 x 23 Ex-atlas Lithograph after engraving *Johnson's New Illustrated Family Atlas* $95.00
Johnson's New Hampshire and Vermont NY 1861 17 x 23 Ex-atlas Lithograph after engraving *Johnson's New Illustrated Family Atlas* $95.00
Johnson's New Jersey NY 1861 16 x 13 Ex-atlas Lithograph after engraving *Johnson's New Illustrated Family Atlas* $50.00
Johnson's New York NY 1861 17 x 23 Ex-atlas Lithograph after engraving *Johnson's New Illustrated Family Atlas* $85.00
Johnson's North America NY 1861 17 x 22 Ex-atlas Lithograph after engraving *Johnson's New Illustrated Family Atlas* $95.00
Johnson's North and South Carolina NY 1861 17 x 22 Ex-atlas Lithograph after engraving *Johnson's New Illustrated Family Atlas* $75.00
Johnson's Ohio & Indiana NY 1861 17 x 23 Ex-atlas Lithograph after engraving *Johnson's New Illustrated Family Atlas* $85.00
Johnson's Pennsylvania, Virginia, Delaware, Maryland NY 1861 17 x 23 Ex-atlas Lithograph after engraving *Johnson's New Illustrated Family Atlas* $85.00
Johnson's New Map of the State of Texas NY 1861 17 x 24 Ex-atlas Lithograph after engraving *Johnson's New Illustrated Family Atlas* $175.00
• **Johnson's New Military Map of the United States** NY 1861 17 x 23 Ex-atlas Lithograph after engraving *Johnson's New Illustrated Family Atlas. U.S. in States* Illustrated $175.00

Johnson's New Military Map of the United States NY 1861 17 x 23 Ex-atlas Lithograph after engraving *Johnson's New Illustrated Family Atlas U.S. in Military Depts.* $175.00
Johnson's Washington & Oregon NY 1861 11 x 14 Ex-atlas Lithograph after engraving *Johnson's New Illustrated Family Atlas* $75.00
Johnson's Western & Eastern Hemispheres NY 1861 17 x 26 Ex-atlas Lithograph after engraving *Johnson's New Illustrated Family Atlas* $95.00
Johnson's World NY 1861 17 x 26 Ex-atlas Lithograph after engraving *Johnson's New Illustrated Family Atlas* $100.00

Johnson & Ward

Johnson's California, Territories of Utah, Nevada, Colorado, New Mexico... NY 1864 18 x 24 Ex-atlas Lithograph after engraving *Shows Arizona* $150.00
Johnson's Florida NY 1863-64 12 x 16 Ex-atlas Lithograph after engraving *Johnson's New Illustrated Family Atlas* Phillips (A) 840 $85.00
Johnson's Minnesota & Dakota NY 1864 12 x 15 Ex-atlas Lithograph after engraving *Johnson's New Illustrated Family Atlas* Phillips (A) 843 $75.00
Johnson's Nebraska, Dakota, Idaho and Montana NY 1867 17 x 23 Ex-atlas Lithograph after engraving *Johnson's New Illustrated Family Atlas* $95.00
Johnson's Nebraska, Dakota, Idaho, Montana and Wyoming NY 1865 17 x 23 Ex-atlas Lithograph after engraving *Johnson's New Illustrated Family Atlas* $125.00
Johnson's Nebraska, Dakota, Idaho, Montana and Wyoming NY 1865 17 x 23 Ex-atlas Lithograph after engraving *Johnson's New Illustrated Family Atlas* $125.00
Johnson's Nebraska, Dakota, Colorado, Idaho & Kansas NY 1862 12 x 15 Ex-atlas Lithograph after engraving *Johnson's New Illustrated Family Atlas* Phillips (A) 837 $85.00

• **Johnson's Nebraska, Dakota, Colorado, Montana & Kansas** NY 1862 12 x 15 Ex-atlas Lithograph after engraving *Johnson's New Illustrated Family Atlas* Illustrated **$95.00**

Johnson's New Map of the State of Texas NY 1866 17 x 24 Ex-atlas Lithograph after engraving *Johnson's New Illustrated Family Atlas* **$175.00**

Johnson's New Military Map of the United States NY 1862 17 x 23 Ex-atlas Lithograph after engraving *U.S. in States. Variant Scrollwork border* **$175.00**

Johnson's New Military Map of the United States NY 1862 17 x 23 Ex-atlas Lithograph after engraving *U.S. in Military Depts. 9 inset maps of harbors* **$175.00**

Keeler, W. J.

National Map of the United States Washington 1867 50 x 60 Folding Map **$800.00**

Lapham

The State of Wisconsin Milwaukee 1852 31.5 x 48 Folding Map HC engraving Phillips (M) 1077 **$600.00**

Lawson, J. T.

Lawson's Map... of the Gold Regions of Upper California NY 1849 15 x 21 Folding Map HC engraving **$2,000.00**

Lloyd, H. H.

Lloyd's New Political Chart...map of the United States Showing Free States, Border Slave States... NY 1861 34.5 x 25.5 Folding Map Lithograph after engraving **$450.00**

California and Nevada NY 1872 15.5 x 12 Ex-atlas Lithograph after engraving *Issued as a supplement to state and county atlases* **$150.00**

Nebraska, and the Territories of Dakota, Idaho, Montana, Wyoming NY 1872 15.5 x 24.5 Ex-atlas Lithograph after engraving *Issued as a supplement to state and county atlases* **$225.00**

New Military Map of the Border & Southern States NY 1862 30 x 41.5 Wall Map Lithograph after engraving **$650.00**

Southern States NY 1868 14.5 x 26 Ex-atlas Lithograph after engraving *Issued as a supplement to state and county atlases* **$150.00**

Texas NY 1870 12.5 x 16 Ex-atlas Lithograph after engraving *Issued as a supplement to state and county atlases* **$250.00**

Map of Utah, Arizona, New Mexico, Kansas, Colorado & Indian Territory NY 1870 16.5 x 27 Ex-atlas Lithograph after engraving *Issued as a supplement to state and county atlases* **$225.00**

Lucas, Fielding

Alabama Baltimore 1823 14.5 X 11.5 Ex-atlas HC engraving *From A General Atlas* Phillips (A) 742 **$250.00**

Antigua Baltimore 1823 11.5 X 14.5 Ex-atlas HC engraving *From A General Atlas* Phillips (A) 742 **$225.00**

Arkansas Territory Baltimore 1823 11.5 X 14.5 Ex-atlas HC engraving *From A General Atlas* Phillips (A) 742 **$350.00**

Bahamas Baltimore 1823 11.5 X 14.5 Ex-atlas HC engraving *From A General Atlas* Phillips (A) 742 **$350.00**

Plan of Baltimore Baltimore 1823 14.5 X 20.5 Folding Map HC engraving Illustrated **$475.00**

Barbadoes Baltimore 1823 14.5 X 11.5 Ex-atlas HC engraving *From A General Atlas* Phillips (A) 742 **$350.00**

Bermudas Baltimore 1823 11.5 X 14.5 Ex-atlas HC engraving *From A General Atlas* Phillips (A) 742 **$250.00**

Connecticut Baltimore 1823 11.5 X 14.5 Ex-atlas HC engraving *From A General Atlas* Phillips (A) 742 **$225.00**

Cuba Baltimore 1823 14.5 X 20.5 Ex-atlas HC engraving *From A General Atlas* Phillips (A) 742 **$275.00**

Curacao Baltimore 1823 14.5 X 11.5 Ex-atlas HC engraving *From A General Atlas* Phillips (A) 742 **$175.00**

Delaware Baltimore 1823 14.5 X 11.5 Ex-atlas HC engraving *From A General Atlas* Phillips (A) 742 **$225.00**

Dominica Baltimore 1823 11.5 X 14.5 Ex-atlas HC engraving *From A General Atlas* Phillips (A) 742 **$150.00**

Florida Baltimore 1823 11.5 X 14.5 Ex-atlas HC engraving *From A General Atlas* Phillips (A) 742 **$275.00**

Georgia Baltimore 1823 14.5 X 11.5 Ex-atlas HC engraving *From A General Atlas* Phillips (A) 742 **$225.00**

Grenada Baltimore 1823 14.5 X 11.5 Ex-atlas HC engraving *From A General Atlas* Phillips (A) 742 **$175.00**

Guadeloupe Baltimore 1823 11.5 X 14.5 Ex-atlas HC engraving *From A General Atlas* Phillips (A) 742 **$150.00**

Hayti or St. Domingo Baltimore 1823 14.5 X 20.5 Ex-atlas HC engraving *From A General Atlas* Phillips (A) 742 **$250.00**

Illinois Baltimore 1823 14.5 X 11.5 Ex-atlas HC engraving *From A General Atlas* Phillips (A) 742 **$295.00**

Indiana Baltimore 1823 14.5 X 11.5 Ex-atlas HC engraving *From A General Atlas* Phillips (A) 742 **$295.00**

Jamaica Baltimore 1823 11.5 X 14.5 Ex-atlas HC engraving *From A General Atlas* Phillips (A) 742 **$225.00**

Kentucky Baltimore 1823 14.5 X 20.5 Ex-atlas HC engraving *From A General Atlas* Phillips (A) 742 $295.00
Louisiana Baltimore 1823 14.5 X 20.5 Ex-atlas HC engraving *From A General Atlas* Phillips (A) 742 $400.00
Maine Baltimore 1823 14.5 X 11.5 Ex-atlas HC engraving *From A General Atlas* Phillips (A) 742 $225.00
Martinico Baltimore 1823 11.5 X 14.5 Ex-atlas HC engraving *From A General Atlas* Phillips (A) 742 $150.00
Maryland-City of Baltimore Baltimore 1823 14.5 X 20.5 Ex-atlas HC engraving *From A General Atlas* Phillips (A) 742 $375.00
Massachusetts Baltimore 1823 14.5 X 20.5 Ex-atlas HC engraving *From A General Atlas* Phillips (A) 742 $295.00
Mercator's Chart Baltimore 1823 14.5 X 20 Ex-atlas HC engraving *From A General Atlas* Phillips (A) 742 $225.00
Mexico Baltimore 1823 11.5 X 14.5 Ex-atlas HC engraving *From A General Atlas* Phillips (A) 742 $325.00
Michigan Territory Baltimore 1823 11.5 X 14.5 Ex-atlas HC engraving *From A General Atlas* Phillips (A) 742 $425.00
• **Mississippi** Baltimore 1823 14.5 X 11.5 Ex-atlas HC engraving *From A General Atlas* Phillips (A) 742 Illustrated $250.00
Missouri Baltimore 1823 14.5 X 11.5 Ex-atlas HC engraving *From A General Atlas* Phillips (A) 742 $300.00
Nevis Baltimore 1823 11.5 X 14.5 Ex-atlas HC engraving *From A General Atlas* Phillips (A) 742 $175.00
New Hampshire Baltimore 1823 14.5 X 11.5 Ex-atlas HC engraving *From A General Atlas* Phillips (A) 742 $225.00
New Jersey Baltimore 1823 14.5 X 11.5 Ex-atlas HC engraving *From A General Atlas* Phillips (A) 742 $225.00
New York Baltimore 1823 14.5 X 20.5 Ex-atlas HC engraving *From A General Atlas* Phillips (A) 742 $295.00
• **North America** Baltimore 1823 14.5 X 11.5 Ex-atlas HC engraving *From A General Atlas* Phillips (A) 742 $225.00
North Carolina Baltimore 1823 14.5 X 20.5 Ex-atlas HC engraving *From A General Atlas* Phillips (A) 742 $250.00
Ohio Baltimore 1823 14.5 X 11.5 Ex-atlas HC engraving *From A General Atlas* Phillips (A) 742 $250.00
Pennsylvania Baltimore 1823 14.5 X 20.5 Ex-atlas HC engraving *From A General Atlas* Phillips (A) 742 $275.00
Porto Rico Baltimore 1823 11.5 X 14.5 Ex-atlas HC engraving *From A General Atlas* Phillips (A) 742 $225.00
Rhode Island Baltimore 1823 14.5 X 11.5 Ex-atlas HC engraving *From A General Atlas* Phillips (A) 742 $225.00
South Carolina Baltimore 1823 11.5 X 14.5 Ex-atlas HC engraving *From A General Atlas* Phillips (A) 742 $225.00
St. Christophers Baltimore 1823 11.5 X 14.5 Ex-atlas HC engraving *From A General Atlas* Phillips (A) 742 $225.00
St. Lucia Baltimore 1823 11.5 X 14.5 Ex-atlas HC engraving *From A General Atlas* Phillips (A) 742 $150.00
St. Vincent Baltimore 1823 14.5 X 11.5 Ex-atlas HC engraving *From A General Atlas* Phillips (A) 742 $225.00
Tennessee Baltimore 1823 14.5 X 20.5 Ex-atlas HC engraving *From A General Atlas* Phillips (A) 742 $275.00
Tobago Baltimore 1823 14.5 X 11.5 Ex-atlas HC engraving *From A General Atlas* Phillips (A) 742 $175.00
Trinidad Baltimore 1824 14.5 X 11.5 Ex-atlas HC engraving *From A General Atlas* Phillips (A) 742 $225.00
United States Baltimore 1823 14.5 X 20.5 Ex-atlas HC engraving *From A General Atlas* Phillips (A) 742 $295.00
Vermont Baltimore 1823 14.5 X 11.5 Ex-atlas HC engraving *From A General Atlas* Phillips (A) 742 $225.00
Virgin Islands Baltimore 1823 11.5 X 14.5 Ex-atlas HC engraving *From A General Atlas* Phillips (A) 742 $175.00
Virginia Baltimore 1823 14.5 X 20.5 Ex-atlas HC engraving *From A General Atlas* Phillips (A) 742 $275.00
West Indies Baltimore 1823 11.5 X 14.5 Ex-atlas HC engraving *From A General Atlas* Phillips (A) 742 $225.00

Melish, J.

Ballston & Saratoga Springs...Albany and Adjacent country Phila 1822 6.5 x 4 Ex-atlas Engraving *from Description of the United States* $75.00
Baltimore, Annapolis and Adjacent Country Phila 1834 7 x 5 Ex-atlas HC engraving $85.00
Boston and Adjacent Country Phila 1818-22 7 x 4 Ex-atlas HC engraving *Engraved for J. Melish's Description of the United States* $85.00
Charleston and Adjacent Country Phila 1834 7 x 5 Ex-atlas HC engraving $85.00
Map of Dauphin and Lebanon Counties...Pennsylvania Phila 1818 17 x 23 Folding Map HC engraving $275.00
District of Columbia Phila 1834 7 x 5 Ex-atlas HC engraving $85.00
View of the Country Round the Falls of Niagara Phila 1816 7 x 4 Ex-atlas HC engraving $85.00
Falls of Ohio Phila 1815 6 x 4 Ex-atlas Engraving $125.00
Kentucky Phila 1812 8 x 14 Ex-atlas HC engraving *From Travels Through the United States* Howes M496 $450.00
East End of Lake Ontario and River St. Lawrence Phila 1815 18 x 22 Ex-atlas HC engraving *From Military and Topographical Atlas of the United States* $275.00

A Map of the State ofLouisiana With Part of Mississippi Territory... Phila 1816 46 x 33 Folding Map HC engraving $2,500.00

Map of the National Road Between Cumberland and Wheeling Phila 1816-22 6 x 11 Ex-atlas HC engraving $150.00

New Orleans and Adjacent Countrry Phila 1816 7 x 4 Ex-atlas HC engraving $85.00

New York and Adjacent Country Phila 1822 7 x 4 Ex-atlas HC engraving $85.00

Map of the Seat of War in North America Phila 1817 15. x 21.5 Ex-atlas HC engraving $650.00

Map ofPennsylvania... Phila 1826 63 x 77 Folding Map HC engraving $1,500.00

Philadelphia and Adjacent Country Phila 1822 7 x 4 Ex-atlas HC engraving $85.00

Map of the River St. Lawrence and Adjacent Country... Phila 1815 17 x 25 Ex-atlas HC engraving *From Military and Topographical Atlas of the United States* $425.00

St. Louis and Adjacent Country Phila 1822 7 x 4 Ex-atlas HC engraving $85.00

Map of the U.S.A. Designed to Illustrate...Memoirs of Wm. McClure Phila 1817 14 x 17 Ex-atlas HC engraving *From Transactions of the American Philosophical Society* $800.00

Northern Section of the United States Phila 1816 16 x 20 Ex-atlas Engraving *Karpinski 53 & 76* $325.00

United States Phila 1816 16 x 20 Folding Map HC engraving Illustrated $600.00

A Map of the Southern Section of the United States Including the Floridas & Bahama Islands... Phila 1813 16 x 21 Sep. Iss. HC engraving *Separate issue. Engraved by Tanner* $1,250.00

Map of the United States of America Phila 1816 37 x 58 Folding Map HC engraving $3,500.00

United States of America Phila 1818 16 x 20 Folding Map Engraving $675.00

United States of America Phila 1818 16 x 19.5 Folding Map HC engraving $800.00

United States of America Phila 1820 17 x 21 Ex-atlas HC engraving $600.00

United States of America Phila 1820-22 16 x 20 Ex-atlas HC engraving *From Lavoisine's Genealogical, Historical and Chronological Atlas* $500.00

United States of America Phila 1821 17 x 21 Folding Map HC engraving *M. Carey & Son. B. Tanner, engr.* $600.00

Northern Section of the United States...Southern Section Including Florida Phila 1816 15 x 21 Ex-atlas HC engraving *Two sheets* $1,250.00

Mitchell, S. A.

Publishers of Mitchell's New Universal Atlas, New General Atlas, as well as wall maps and folding maps. See De Silver, Bradley, Thomas Cowperthwait

A New Map ofAlabama With its Roads and Distances Phila 1847 14 x 11 Ex-atlas HC engraving *From A New Universal Atlas* $95.00

Mitchell's National Map of the American Republic Phila 1843 34 x 24 Wall map HC engraving *First edition. Insets of 32 cities* $800.00

Arizona and New Mexico Phila 1867 11.5 x 14.5 Ex-atlas Lithograph after engraving *From A New General Atlas* Phillips (A) 850 $75.00

Arizona and New Mexico Phila 1867 11.5 x 14.5 Ex-atlas Lithograph after engraving *From A New General Atlas* Phillips (A) 850 $75.00

County and Township Map ofArizona and New Mexico Phila 1881 15 x 22 Ex-atlas Lithograph after engraving *From a New General Atlas* Phillips (A) 895 $85.00

A New Map ofArkansas With Its Canals, Roads Distances Phila 1848 15 x 12 Ex-atlas HC engraving *From A New Universal Atlas* $95.00

Plan ofBaltimore Phila 1860 9 x 11 Ex-atlas Lithograph after engraving *From A New General Atlas* Phillips (A)831 $60.00

Plan ofBoston Phila 1860 13 x 11 Ex-atlas Lithograph after engraving *From A New General Atlas* Phillips (A)831 $75.00

County Map of California Phila 1864 13.5 x 10.5 Ex-atlas Lithograph after engraving *From A New General Atlas* $95.00

County Map of the State of California Phila 1873 23 x 15 Ex-atlas Lithograph after engraving *From A New General Atlas* Phillips (A)870 $95.00

Map of the State ofCalifornia...Territories of Oregon and Utah...New Mexico Phila 1845-50 16 x 13 Ex-atlas HC engraving *From A New Universal Atlas* $375.00

Chicago Phila 1867 13 x 11 Ex-atlas Lithograph after engraving *From A New General Atlas* $85.00

Plan ofChicago Phila 1874 11 x 9 Ex-atlas Lithograph after engraving *From A New General Atlas* $85.00

Chicago Phila 1879 22 x 14 Ex-atlas Lithograph after engraving *First edition of this map. From a New General Atlas* $85.00

Plan of Cincinnati Phila 1860 10.5 x 11 Ex-atlas Lithograph after engraving *From A New General Atlas* $60.00

Plan of Cincinnati and Vicinity Phila 1874 10.5 x 11 Ex-atlas Lithograph after engraving *From A New General Atlas* $60.00

Colorado Phila 1878-87 12 x 15 Ex-atlas Lithograph after engraving *From A New General Atlas* $85.00

County Map of Colorado, Wyoming, Dakota, Montana Phila 1874-78 19.5 x 14 Ex-atlas Lithograph after engraving *From A New General Atlas* $95.00

Connecticut Phila 1848 12.5 x 15 Ex-atlas HC engraving *From A New Universal Atlas* $85.00

Territory of Dakota Phila 1879 14 x 12 Ex-atlas Lithograph after engraving *From A New General Atlas* $85.00

County and Township Map of Dakota Phila 1887 15 x 12 Ex-atlas Lithograph after engraving *From A New General Atlas* $85.00

County Map of Dakota, Wyoming, Kansas, Nebraska and Colorado Phila 1870 19.5 x 15 Ex-atlas Lithograph after engraving *From A New General Atlas* $95.00

County Map of Dakota, Wyoming, Kansas, Nebraska and Colorado Phila 1879 19.5 x 15 Ex-atlas Lithograph after engraving *From A New General Atlas* $95.00

Plan of Detroit Phila 1879 10 x 14 Ex-atlas Lithograph after engraving *From A New General Atlas* $60.00

Florida Phila 1846 14.5 x 11.5 Ex-atlas HC engraving *From A New Universal Atlas* $225.00

County Map of Florida Phila 1867 10.5 x 13.5 Ex-atlas Lithograph after engraving *From A New General Atlas* $75.00

County Map of Florida Phila 1869 10.5 x 13.5 Ex-atlas Lithograph after engraving *From A New General Atlas* $75.00

County Map of Florida Phila 1872 10.5 x 13.5 Ex-atlas Lithograph after engraving *From A New General Atlas* $75.00

County Map of Georgia and Alabama Phila 1860 12.5 x 15 Ex-atlas Lithograph after engraving *From A New General Atlas* $50.00

County Map of Georgia and Alabama Phila 1863 12.5 x 15 Ex-atlas Lithograph after engraving *From A New General Atlas* $50.00

County Map of the States of Georgia and Alabama Phila 1880 14 x 21.5 Ex-atlas Lithograph after engraving *From A New General Atlas* $60.00

A New Map of Georgia With Its Canals, Roads, Distances Phila 1847 14 x 12 Ex-atlas HC engraving *From A New Universal Atlas* $95.00

Territory of Idaho Phila 1880 14.5 x 10.5 Ex-atlas Lithograph after engraving *From A New General Atlas* $95.00

Territory of Idaho Phila 1885 15 x 12.5 Ex-atlas Lithograph after engraving *12 Counties shown. From A New General Atlas* $85.00

County Map of Illinois Phila 1874 13.5 x 10.5 Ex-atlas Lithograph after engraving *From A New General Atlas* $50.00

A New Map of Illinois With Its Proposed Canals, Roads and Distances Phila 1847 16 x 13 Ex-atlas HC engraving *From A New Universal Atlas* $95.00

Tourist's Pocket Map of the State of Illinois... Phila 1834 15 x 12.5 Folding Map HC engraving $600.00

Indian Territory Phila 1879-87 11 x 13.5 Ex-atlas Lithograph after engraving *From A New General Atlas* $75.00

Indiana Phila 1884 14 x 11 Ex-atlas Lithograph after engraving *From A New General Atlas* $50.00

A New Map of Indiana With Its Roads and Distances Phila 1847 14 x 11.5 Ex-atlas HC engraving *From A New Universal Atlas* $85.00

Iowa Phila 1845 16 x 13 Ex-atlas HC engraving *From A New Universal Atlas* $225.00

Iowa Phila 1847 16 x 13 Ex-atlas HC engraving *From A New Universal Atlas* $125.00

Iowa Phila 1848 16 x 13 Ex-atlas HC engraving *31 Counties. From a New Universal Atlas* $125.00

County Map of Iowa and Missouri Phila 1860 12.5 x 15 Ex-atlas Lithograph after engraving *From A New General Atlas* $65.00

County and Township Map of ... Kansas and Nebraska Phila 1878 15 x 23 Ex-atlas Lithograph after engraving *From A New General Atlas* $85.00

Map of Kansas, Nebraska and Colorado Phila 1860 11.5 x 14 Ex-atlas Lithograph after engraving *From A New General Atlas* $150.00

• **Map of Kansas, Nebraska and Colorado** Phila 1861 11 x 13 Ex-atlas Lithograph after engraving *Showing Also Eastern Portion of Idaho. From a New General Atlas* Illustrated $85.00

Map ofKansas, Nebraska and Colorado Phila 1867 11 x 14 Ex-atlas Lithograph after engraving *Showing Southern Portion of Dacotah. From a New General Atlas* $85.00

Map ofKansas, Nebraska and Colorado...Idaho Phila 1861 11 x 13 Ex-atlas Lithograph after engraving *From a New General Atlas* $85.00

County Map of Kansas, Nebraska, Colorado, Dakota, Wyoming Phila 1872 20 x 14 Ex-atlas Lithograph after engraving *From A New General Atlas* $125.00

County Map ofKentucky & Tennessee Phila 1873 13 x 20 Ex-atlas Lithograph after engraving *From A New General Atlas* Phillips (A) 870 $60.00

A New Map ofKentucky With Its Roads and Distances Phila 1843 11.5 x 13.5 Folding Map HC engraving *Cloth or leather covers* $400.00

A New Map ofKentucky With Its Roads and Distances Phila 1846 11.5 x 14 Ex-atlas HC engraving *From A New Universal Atlas* $125.00

A New Map ofLouisiana Phila 1850 13 x 16 Ex-atlas HC engraving *From A New Universal Atlas* $95.00

Map of the States ofLouisiana, Mississippi and Alabama Phila 1835 17.5 x 21.5 Folding Map HC engraving *Cloth or leather covers* $600.00

County Map of Louisiana, Mississippi and Arkansas Phila 1860 13.5 x 10.5 Ex-atlas Lithograph after engraving *From A New General Atlas* Phillips (A)831 $65.00

Map ofLouisiana, Mississippi and Arkansas Phila 1861 15 x 12.5 Ex-atlas Lithograph after engraving *From A New General Atlas* $50.00

A New Map ofMaine Phila 1850 16 x 13 Ex-atlas HC engraving *From A New Universal Atlas* $75.00

County Map of the State ofMaine Phila 1860 10.5 x 13.5 Ex-atlas Lithograph after engraving *From A New General Atlas* Phillips (A)831 $60.00

A New Map ofMaryland and Delaware Phila 1850 13 x 16 Ex-atlas HC engraving *From A New Universal Atlas* $75.00

Massachusetts and Rhode Island Phila 1850 13 x 16 Ex-atlas HC engraving *From A New Universal Atlas* $75.00

County Map of Massachusetts, Connecticut and Rhode Island Phila 1860 11.5 x 13.5 Ex-atlas Lithograph after engraving *From A New General Atlas* Phillips (A)831 $65.00

Map ofMexico, Central America and the West Indies Phila 1870 15 x 23.5 Ex-atlas Lithograph after engraving *From A New General Atlas* Phillips (A)859 $95.00

The Tourist's Pocket Map ofMichigan Phila 1835 12 x 15 Folding Map HC engraving Phillips (M) 425 $375.00

County Map of Michigan and Wisconsin Phila 1860 11 x 13.5 Ex-atlas Lithograph after engraving *From A New General Atlas* Phillips (A)831 $65.00

A New Map ofMichigan With Its Canals, Roads and Distances Phila 1846 14.5 x 11.5 Ex-atlas HC engraving *From A New Universal Atlas* $150.00

Plan ofMilwaukee Phila 1874 14 x 10.5 Ex-atlas Lithograph after engraving *From A New General Atlas* $60.00

County Map ofMinnesota Phila 1864 11 x 14 Ex-atlas Lithograph after engraving $75.00

Minnesota and Dacotah Phila 1860 10.5 x 13.5 Ex-atlas Lithograph after engraving *First edition of this map. From a New General Atlas* Phillips (A)831 $125.00

A New Map ofMississippi Phila 1850 16 x 13 Ex-atlas HC engraving *From A New Universal Atlas* Phillips (A) 800 $95.00

• **Map ofMissouri** Phila 1847 16 x 13 Ex-atlas HC engraving *From A New Universal Atlas* Illustrated $125.00

Map ofMissouri Phila 1850 16 x 13 Ex-atlas HC engraving *From A New Universal Atlas* Phillips (A) 800 $95.00

Territory ofMontana Phila 1879 11 x 14.5 Ex-atlas Lithograph after engraving *From A New General Atlas* Phillips (A)890 $85.00

County and Township Map of Montana, Idaho and Wyoming Phila 1887 15 x 22 Ex-atlas Lithograph after engraving *From A New General Atlas* $95.00

New Hampshire and Vermont Phila 1862 13 x 11 Ex-atlas Lithograph after engraving *From A New General Atlas* $60.00

County and Township Map of ...New Hampshire and Vermont Phila 1879 19 x 12 Ex-atlas Lithograph after engraving *From A New General Atlas* Phillips (A)890 $50.00

County Map of New Jersey Maryland and Delaware Phila 1860 11 x 13 Ex-atlas Lithograph after engraving *Three maps on one sheet. From A New General Atlas* $50.00

New Mexico and Arizona Phila 1874 13 x 11 Ex-atlas Lithograph after engraving *From A New General Atlas* $75.00

Plan ofNew Orleans Phila 1860-71 9 x 11 Ex-atlas Lithograph after engraving *From A New General Atlas* $60.00

City ofNew York Phila 185016 x 13 Ex-atlas HC engraving *From A New Universal Atlas* $95.00
County Map of the State ofNew York Phila 186014 x 21.5 Ex-atlas Lithograph after engraving *With five inset maps. From a New General Atlas*Phillips (A)831 $60.00
Plan ofNew York Phila 186013 x 11 Ex-atlas Lithograph after engraving *From A New General Atlas*Phillips (A)831 $75.00
New York and Brooklyn Phila 188113.5 x 21 Ex-atlas Lithograph after engraving *From A New General Atlas* Phillips (A) 895 $75.00
Map of the State ofNew York Compiled from the Latest Authorities Phila 183217 x 22 Folding Map HC engraving *Cloth or leather covers* $350.00
The Empire State ofNew York With Its Counties, Towns, Villages Phila 186439 x 48.5 Folding Map Lithograph after engraving *Cloth or leather covers*Phillips (M) 512 $600.00
County Map of the States ofNew York, New Hampshire, Vermont, Massachusetts Phila 186013.5 x 21 Ex-atlas Lithograph after engraving *Rhode Island and Connecticut. From a New General Atlas*Phillips (A)831 $50.00
Map ofNorth America Phila 186013 x 11 Ex-atlas Lithograph after engraving *From A New General Atlas* Phillips (A)831 $75.00
A New Map ofNorth Carolina Phila 185013 x 16 Ex-atlas HC engraving *From A New Universal Atlas*Phillips (A) 800 $85.00
North Carolina (and) South Carolina (and) Florida Phila 186013 x 11 Ex-atlas Lithograph after engraving *From A New General Atlas*Phillips (A)831 $50.00
(Alaska) Northwestern America ...Territory Ceded by Russia ... Phila 186711.5 x 14 Ex-atlas Lithograph after engraving *From A New General Atlas*Phillips (A)850 $100.00
County Map of Ohio and Indiana Phila 1860-6711 x 13 Ex-atlas Lithograph after engraving *From A New General Atlas*Phillips (A)850 $50.00
Map of the States ofOhio, Indiana and Illinois With the Settled Part of Michigan Phila 183518 x 22.5 Folding Map HC engraving *Cloth or leather covers* $675.00
Oklahoma and Indian Territory Phila 189011.5 x 14.5 Ex-atlas Lithograph after engraving *From A New General Atlas* $125.00
Oregon and Upper California Phila 1845-4916 x 13 Ex-atlas HC engraving *From A New Universal Atlas* $375.00
County and Township Map of Oregon and Washington Phila 188320 x 14.5 Ex-atlas Lithograph after engraving *From A New General Atlas* $60.00
Oregon, Upper California and New Mexico Phila 1849-5016 x 13 Ex-atlas HC engraving *From A New Universal Atlas* $375.00
Map ofOregon, Washington and Part of British Columbia Phila 1860-6210.5 x 13.5 Ex-atlas Lithograph after engraving *From A New General Atlas* $125.00
Map ofOregon, Washington, Idaho and Part of Montana Phila 1866-7711 x 13.5 Ex-atlas Lithograph after engraving *From A New General Atlas* $75.00
A New Map ofPennsylvania Phila 184811.5 x 14.5 Ex-atlas HC engraving *From A New Universal Atlas* $85.00
Map ofPennsylvania, New Jersey and Delaware Phila 183217 x 21 Folding Map HC engraving *Cloth or leather covers* $300.00
County Map of Pennsylvania, New Jersey, Maryland and Delaware Phila 186011x 13 Ex-atlas Lithograph after engraving *From A New General Atlas* $60.00
PhiladelphiaPhila 184816 x 13 Ex-atlas HC engraving *From A New Universal Atlas* $95.00
Plan ofPhiladelphia Phila 186013 x 11 Ex-atlas Lithograph after engraving *From A New General Atlas* $75.00
A New Map ofSouth Carolina Phila 185013 x 16 Ex-atlas HC engraving *From A New Universal Atlas*Phillips (A)831 $85.00
St. Louis Phila 187914 x11 Ex-atlas Lithograph after engraving *From A New General Atlas*Phillips (A)890 $50.00
State of Illinois Phila 186113 x 11 Ex-atlas Lithograph after engraving *From A New General Atlas* $60.00
A New Map ofTennessee With Its Roads and Distances Phila 184613 x 16 Ex-atlas HC engraving *From A New Universal Atlas* $125.00
County Map of Texas Phila 186010.5 x 13.5 Ex-atlas Lithograph after engraving *Also 1861, 1867. From a New General Atlas*Phillips (A)831 $150.00
Map ofTexas From the Most Recent Authorities Phila 185013 x 16 Ex-atlas HC engraving *From A New Universal Atlas*Phillips (A) 800 $350.00
County Map of the State of Texas...Showing Adjoining States and Territories Phila 187714 x 21 Ex-atlas Lithograph after engraving *With NM and Indian Territory. From a New General Atlas* $125.00
Map ofThe United States Phila 186013 x 21 Ex-atlas Lithograph after engraving *From A New General Atlas* Phillips (A)831 $125.00

Map of the United States Phila 1831 43.5 x 34.5 Folding Map HC engraving *Cloth or leather covers* **$750.00**
Mitchell's Traveller's Guide Through the United States Phila 1832 17.5 x 22 Folding Map HC engraving *With booklet & supplementary sheet* **$750.00**
Traveller's Guide Through the United States Phila 1833 21.5 x 22.5 Folding Map HC engraving **$500.00**
A New Map of the United States Phila 1833 52.5 x 78.5 Wall map HC engraving **$1,250.00**
Mitchell's Reference and Distance Map of the United States Phila 1834 52.5 x 66.5 Wall map HC engraving *First edition. 13 Inset maps* **$1,000.00**
Mitchell's New National Map Exhibiting...United States Phila 1859 54 x 55 Wall map HC engraving Wheat 896 **$800.00**
Map of United States and Territories Phila 1860 13.5 x 21 Ex-atlas Lithograph after engraving *Phillips (A) 3558, 7. From a New General Atlas* Phillips (A) 831 **$125.00**
Map of the United States by J. H. Young Phila 1831 43.5 x 34.5 Wall map HC engraving *Revised editions published to 1844* Ristow 309 **$1,000.00**
Reference and Distance Map of the United States by J. H. Young Phila 1835 54.5 x 69 Folding Map HC engraving *With inset Maps* **$1,500.00**
Railroad Map of the United States Showing...Atlantic to the Pacific Phila 1880 14 x 22.5 Ex-atlas Lithograph after engraving *From A New General Atlas* Phillips (A) 892 **$95.00**
County Map of Utah and Nevada Phila 1865 11.5 x 14 Ex-atlas Lithograph after engraving *Also 1867 and 1869. From a New General Atlas* **$125.00**
County and Township Map of Utah and Nevada Phila 1881 15 x 23 Ex-atlas Lithograph after engraving *From A New General Atlas* Phillips (A) 895 **$75.00**
Tourist's Pocket Map of the State of Virginia Phila 1839 12.5 x 14 Folding Map HC engraving **$300.00**
County Map of Virginia and North Carolina Phila 1860 10 x 12 Ex-atlas Lithograph after engraving *From A New General Atlas* Phillips (A) 831 **$60.00**
County Map of Virginia and West Virginia Phila 1863 11 x 14.5 Ex-atlas Lithograph after engraving *1st Mitchell map showing WV as state. From a New General Atlas* **$60.00**
A New Map of Virginia With Its Canals, Roads and Distances... Phila 1846 14.5 x 11.5 Ex-atlas HC engraving *From A New Universal Atlas* **$125.00**
City of Washington Phila 1850 13 x 16 Ex-atlas HC engraving *From A New Universal Atlas* Phillips (A) 800 **$100.00**
Plan of Washington Phila 1861 11 x 13 Ex-atlas Lithograph after engraving *From A New General Atlas* **$85.00**
Plan of the City of Washington...Capitol of the United States Phila 1870 11 x 13 Ex-atlas Lithograph after engraving *From A New General Atlas* Phillips (A) 859 **$85.00**
A Map of the World on Mercator's Projection Phila 1843 47 x 74 Wall map HC engraving *Independent Texas* **$1,000.00**
Territory of Wyoming Phila 1879 11 x 14 Ex-atlas HC engraving *From A New General Atlas* Phillips (A) 890 **$95.00**
Territory of Wyoming Phila 1880 11 x 14 Ex-atlas Lithograph after engraving *From A New General Atlas* Phillips (A) 892 **$85.00**

Monk

Monk's New American Map Exhibiting North America, United States and Territories NY 1855 57.5 x 61 Wall Map HC engraving *Hoen & Co.* **$450.00**

Morse & Breese

Arkansas NY 1844-46 12 x 14.5 Ex-atlas Cerographic prtd color *From North American Atlas* Phillips (A) 1383 **$100.00**
Connecticut NY 1846 11 x 14 Ex-atlas Cerographic prtd color *From North American Atlas* Phillips (A) 1228,8 **$100.00**
• **Indiana** NY 1842 14 x 11 Ex-atlas Cerograph Illustrated **$175.00**
Mexico NY 1842 12 x 16 Ex-atlas Cerographic prtd color *From Cerographic Atlas* **$250.00**
Missouri NY 1844-46 12.5 x 15 Ex-atlas Cerographic prtd color *From North American Atlas* Phillips (A) 1228,32 **$125.00**
City of New York NY 1842 14 x 11 Ex-atlas Cerographic prtd color *From Cerographic Atlas* **$175.00**
Wisconsin, Southern Part NY 1844-46 12.5 x 15.5 Ex-atlas Cerographic prtd color *From North American Atlas* Phillips (A) 1228,31 Karrow 6, 1663 **$175.00**

Morse & Gaston

Alabama NY 1857 6.5 x 5 Ex-atlas Cerograph *From Diamond Atlas* Phillips (A) 824 **$60.00**
Kansas and Nebraska NY 1857 6 x 5 Ex-atlas Cerograph *From Diamond Atlas* Phillips (A) 824 **$60.00**
New Map of Our Country ...United States NY 1856 55 x 64 Wall map Lithograph after engraving **$600.00**

Utah & New Mexico NY 1857 5 x 6 Ex-atlas Cerograph *From Diamond Atlas* Phillips (A)824 $75.00
Virginia NY 1857 5.5 x 7 Ex-atlas Cerograph *From The World In Miniature* $60.00
Washington & Oregon Territories NY 1857 5 x 6 Ex-atlas Cerograph *From Diamond Atlas* Phillips (A)824 $75.00

Morse, J.

A Correct Map of the Georgia Western Territory Phila 1797 7 x 6 Ex-atlas Engraving Wheat & Brun 618 $250.00
Map of the States of Maryland and Delaware by J. Denison Phila 1796 7 x 9.5 Ex-atlas Engraving $200.00
A General Map of North America from the Best Authorities Phila 1796 7 x 9 Ex-atlas Engraving *From American Universal Geography* Wheat & Brun 55 $250.00
A Map of North America from the latest Discoveries 1806 Phila 1807 6 x 7 Ex-atlas Engraving *From Geography Made Easy* Phillips (M) 597 $200.00
Map of the Northern Part of the United States of America Phila 1797 8.5 x 15.5 Ex-atlas Engraving *From The American Gazeteer. Shows proposed NW Terr. states* See NW Terr $350.00
Pennsylvania Drawn from the Best Authorities Phila 1796 7.5 x 13 Ex-atlas Engraving *From American Universal Geography* Wheat & Brun 446 $175.00
Map of the Southern Parts of the United States of America Phila 1797 8 x 15.5 Ex-atlas Engraving *By Abraham Bradley* Phillips (M) 872 $275.00
Virginia Phila 1796 5.5 x 7.5 Ex-atlas Engraving *From American Universal Geography* Wheat & Brun 571 $125.00
West Indies According to the Best Authorities Phila 1793 8 x 12 Ex-atlas Engraving *From American Universal Geography* Wheat & Brun 686 $175.00

Page

Indexed Township Map of Michigan Showing...Railroad Stations, Post Offices 1881 25 x 16.5 Folding Map Lithograph after engraving *Stiff wraps* $325.00
Page's Indexed Township Map of Montana Showing ...Railroad Stations, Post offices... 1883 16 x 24 Folding Map Lithograph after engraving *Stiff wraps* $675.00

Peck, J.

A New Sectional Map of the State of Illinois 1854 35.5 x 26.5 Folding Map HC engraving *Cloth or leather folder* $1,250.00

Phelps

Phelps National Map of the United States NY 1849-54 20.5 x 26 Folding Map HC engraving *Cloth or leather folder* $500.00

Phelps & Ensign

Phelps & Ensign's Travellers Guide ...United States NY 1842 17 x 22 Folding Map HC engraving *Cloth or leather folder* $650.00
Phelps & Ensign's Travellers Guide ...United States NY 1843 26 x 40.5 Wall Map HC engraving $875.00
Phelps & Ensign's Travellers Guide ...United States NY 1845 17 x 21.5 Folding Map HC engraving *Cloth or leather folder* $600.00

Phelps & Watson

Phelps New National Map of the United States NY 1859 26.5 x 36.5 Wall Map HC engraving $700.00

Railroad Maps

NY Central & Hudson River RR...Hudson River Map NY 1876 90.5 x 4.5 Folding Map Lithograph *Binder* $200.00
Map of Michigan, S. & N... Indiana Railroad With Their ... NY 1851 16.5 x 56.5 Folding Map HC engraving *Connections from Council Bluffs to New York* $175.00

Railway Map Publishing Co.

Map of Boston Boston 1877 26 x 20 Folding Map Lithograph $95.00

Rand McNally & Co.

Official 24 x 36 Map of Alaska Chicago 1897 24 x 36 Folding Map Wax engraving $200.00
Arizona Chicago 1887 19 x 13 Ex-atlas Wax engraving *From Indexed Atlas of the World* $85.00
Map of the Atchison, Topeka & Santa Fe Railroad System Chicago 1884 16 x 33 Folding Map Wax engraving *Schedules and ads on verso* $350.00
Map of the Chicago & Northwest'n Railway... Chicago 1880 9 x 12 Folding Map Wax engraving $75.00
A Correct Map of the Chicago, Burlington & Quincy RR... Chicago 1883 26 x 44.5 Folding Map Wax engraving $300.00

Colorado Chicago 1883 19 x 13 Ex-atlas Wax engraving *From Indexed Atlas of the World* $75.00
Indexed County and Township Map of Colorado Chicago 1901 19 x 26 Folding Map Wax engraving $95.00
Indexed County and Township Map of Dakota Chicago 1882 28 x 22 Folding Map Wax engraving $95.00
Denver and Rio Grande Railroad System Chicago 1887 14.5 x 17.5 Folding Map Wax engraving *From Tourist's Handbook issued by the RR* $125.00
New Business Map of Florida Chicago 1898 21.5 x 27.5 Folding Map Wax engraving $85.00
Florida Railroads Chicago 1895 19 x 27 Ex-atlas Wax engraving $85.00
Maryland and D. C. Delaware Chicago 1888 12 x 18.5 Ex-atlas Wax engraving *From Indexed Atlas of the World* $75.00
Indexed County and Township Map of Maryland and Delaware Chicago 1890 13 x 19.5 Folding Map Wax engraving $85.00
Indexed Map of Michigan Chicago 1877 12.5 x 9 Folding Map Wax engraving *On two sheets. Wraps* $175.00
Montana Chicago 1882 12.5 x 19.5 Ex-atlas Wax engraving *From Indexed Atlas of the World* $85.00
Nebraska Chicago 1882 12.5 x 20 Ex-atlas Wax engraving *From Indexed Atlas of the World* $85.00
Nevada Chicago 1882 19.5 x 13 Ex-atlas Wax engraving *From Indexed Atlas of the World* $85.00
New Mexico Chicago 1882 19.5 x 13 Ex-atlas Wax engraving *From Indexed Atlas of the World.* $85.00
Pocket Map and Shipper's Guide of New York Chicago 1892 19 x 25.5 Folding Map Wax engraving $75.00
Oklahoma and Indian Territory Chicago 1894 13 x 20 Ex-atlas Wax engraving *From Indexed Atlas of the World. 2 sheets* $85.00
A Geographically Correct County Map of ... Traversed by St. Louis, Iron Mountain & Southern RR Chicago 1876 16.5 x 15.5 Folding Map Wax engraving *On Broadside with ads* $450.00
New Railroad & County Map of the United States and Canada Chicago 1876 52.5 x 96 Folding Map Wax engraving $375.00
Utah Chicago 1882 19.5 x 13 Ex-atlas Wax engraving *From Indexed Atlas of the World.* $75.00
Virginia Chicago 1889 18.5 x 25.5 Ex-atlas Wax engraving *From Indexed Atlas of the World* $75.00
Indexed County and Railroad Pocket Map... Virginia Chicago 1893 19 x 26 Folding Map Wax engraving $95.00
Indexed Map of Virginia and West Virginia Chicago 1877 11 x 20 Folding Map Wax engraving *Cloth folder* $175.00

Randel, John

The City of New York NY 1821 26 x 37 Folding Map HC engraving $2,000.00

Reid

The State of Virginia from the Best Authorities NY 1796 16 x 19.5 Sep.Iss. Engraving $600.00
• **The State of Virginia from the Best Authorities** NY 1796 16 x 19.5 Ex-atlas $600.00

Rice, G. J.

Rice's Sectional Map of Dakota St. Paul 1874-78 32 x 26 Folding Map Lithograph after engraving *Cloth folder* $750.00

Robinson, L.

Map of Ohio Compiled from the Latest Authorities Akron 1840 26 x 22.5 Wall Map HC Engraving $2,000.00
Improved Map of Vermont 1834 24 x 17.5 Wall Map HC Engraving $750.00

Rockwell

Map of Part of the Thousand Islands of the St. Lawrence River NY 1883 17.5 x 23 Folding Map Lithograph $500.00

Ross, E. H.

New Railroad and Sectional Map of Kansas St. Louis 1872 23.5 x 38 Folding Map Lithograph $1,000.00

Scott

Massachusetts Phila 1795 6 x 7 Ex-atlas Engraving *From the United States Gazeteer. Wheat & Brun 216* $125.00
N. W. Territory Phila 1795 7.5 x 6 Ex-atlas Engraving *From the United States Gazeteer* $350.00
Pennsylvania Phila 1795 6 x 7.5 Ex-atlas Engraving *From the United States Gazeteer* Illustrated $125.00
Rhode Island Phila 1795 7 x 6.5 Ex-atlas Engraving *From the United States Gazeteer. Wheat & Brun 252* $125.00
South Carolina Phila 1795 6 x 7 Ex-atlas Engraving *From the United States Gazeteer. Wheat & Brun 602* $125.00
Virginia Phila 1795 6 x 7 Ex-atlas Engraving *From the United States Gazeteer* $200.00

Sherman & Smith

Map ofMilwaukee Milw185740 x 27.5 Folding Map Engraving $350.00

Sidney

Sidney's Map of Twelve Miles AroundNew York, With Names of Property Owners Phila184933 diam 2 Sheets Engraving $700.00

Smith, J. C.

Also see Colton

Map ofLong Island With the Environs of New York and...ConnecticutNY185437 x 55.5Wall MapHC Engraving $750.00

Guide Through the States ofOhio, Michigan, Indiana, Illinois, Missouri, Wisconsin & IowaNY 185417.5 x 22 Folding MapHC Engraving*From Colton, The Western Tourist and Emigrant's Guide...* $175.00

Guide Through the States ofOhio, Michigan, Indiana, Illinois, Missouri, Wisconsin & IowaNY 185417.5 x 22 Folding MapHC Engraving*From Colton, The Western Tourist and Emigrant's Guide...* $175.00

New Map for Travellers Through theUnited States NY184921.5 x 25.5 Folding MapHC Engraving*234pp text* $750.00

Snow & Co.

Map of the Railways inNew England and Part of New YorkNY18498.5 x 7 Folding Map Engraving*From Pathfinder Railway Guide for the New England States* $100.00

Taintor Bros. & Merrill

Map of the State ofGeorgiaNY187421.5 x 16.5 Ex-atlas Lithograph after engraving $95.00

Map of the State ofMissouri 187417 x 21.5 Ex-atlas Lithograph after engraving $95.00

Tanner, H. S.

Publisher of A New Universal Atlas, A New American Atlas, folding maps and wall maps.

A New Map ofAlabama With its Roads and Distances Phila1833-3610.5 x 13.5 Ex-atlasHC engraving*From A New Universal Atlas*Phillips (A)774 $225.00

A New Map ofArkansas With Its Canals, Roads... Phila184214 x 11.5 Ex-atlasHC engraving*From A New Universal Atlas* $150.00

A Map of the Roads Leading to ... Britania...Susquehanna County Penn'a. Phila1819 Sep. issue Engraving*From The Portfolio* $225.00

ConnecticutPhila183611 x 14 Ex-atlasHC engraving *One railroad shown*Phillips (A)774 $150.00

Map ofFlorida Phila182327 x 21 Ex-atlasHC engraving *From A New American Atlas* $975.00

• **Florida**Phila183316 x 13 Ex-atlasHC engraving*From The Universal Atlas* Illustrated $275.00

Georgia and Alabama Phila1819-2320 x 27 Ex-atlas HC Engraving*From American Atlas* $850.00

• **A New Map ofGeorgia With Its Roads and Distances**Phila1833-3613 x 10.5 Ex-atlasHC engraving *From A New Universal Atlas*Phillips (A)774 Illustrated $175.00

Illinois and Missouri Phila182328 x 22.5 Ex-atlasHC engraving*From A New American Atlas* See Phillips (M)327 $975.00

A New Map ofIllinois With Its Proposed Canals, Roads... Phila184114 x 11.5 Ex-atlasHC engraving*From A New Universal Atlas* $175.00

A New Map ofIndiana With Its Roads and Distances Phila183613 x 10.5 Ex-atlasHC engraving*From A New Universal Atlas*Phillips (A)774 $175.00

• **Iowa**Phila184116 x 13 Ex-atlasHC engraving*From A New Universal Atlas* Illustrated $175.00

A New Map ofKentucky With Its Roads and Distances Phila184613.5 x 16 Ex-atlasHC engraving *From A New Universal Atlas* $175.00

Louisiana and Mississippi Phila182529 x 23 Ex-atlas HC engraving*From A New American Atlas*Phillips (A)774 $850.00

A New Map ofLouisiana With Its Canals, Roads... Phila184211.5 x 14.5 Ex-atlasHC engraving*From A New Universal Atlas* $150.00

A New Map ofMaine Phila1833-3914 x 11 Ex-atlasHC engraving*From A New Universal Atlas*Phillips-A-6086, 5 $150.00

Map of the States ofMaine, New Hampshire, Vermont, Massachusetts... Phila182327 x 22 Ex-atlas HC engraving*From A New American Atlas* $750.00

A New Map ofMaryland and Delaware With Their Canals, Roads... Phila183611 x 14 Ex-atlasHC engraving*From Universal Atlas*Phillips (A)774 $175.00

Mexico and Guatemala Phila183412 x 15 Ex-atlasHC engraving*Texas not part of Mexico* $250.00

Mexico and Guatemala Phila1834-4511.5 x 14.5 Ex-atlasHC engraving*Carey & Hart Publishers*Phillips (A)774 $400.00

The Traveller's Pocket Map of Michigan With Its Canals, Roads and Distances Phila183210.5 x 13 Folding MapHC engraving Phillips (M)424 $375.00

A New Map ofMichigan With Its Canals, Roads and Distances Phila 1841 15 x 12 Ex-atlas HC engraving *From A New Universal Atlas* $185.00
A New Map ofMississippi With Its Roads and Distances... Phila 1841 14.5 X 11.5 Ex-atlas HC engraving *From A New Universal Atlas (Tanner's Universal Atlas)* $175.00
A New Map ofMississippi Phila 1836-45 14 x 11.5 Ex-atlas HC engraving *Carey & Hart Publishers* $175.00
• **A New Map of Missouri...** Phila 1841 16 x 13 Ex-atlas HC engraving *From A New Universal Atlas* Illustrated $150.00
New Hampshire and Vermont Phila 1833-36 14 x 11 Ex-atlas HC engraving *From A New Universal Atlas* Phillips-A-774, 6 $125.00
New York Phila 1819-23 22 x 26 Ex-atlas HC engraving *From A New American Atlas* $750.00
A Map ofNorth America Phila 1822 42.5 x 57.5 Wall Map HC engraving $4,750.00
North America Phila 1836-42 14.5 x 12 Ex-atlas HC engraving *From A New Universal Atlas* Phillips-A-788,2 $225.00
Map ofNorth Carolina and South Carolina by H. S. Tanner Phila 1825 23 x 29 Ex-atlas HC engraving *From American Atlas 2d Edition* $850.00
Ohio and Indiana Phila 1819-23 21 x 26 Ex-atlas HC engraving *From A New American Atlas* $650.00
A New Map ofOhio... Phila 1833 15 x 11 Ex-atlas HC engraving *From The Universal Atlas* Illustrated
Map ofPennsylvania and New Jersey Phila 1823 21 x 28 Ex-atlas HC engraving *From American Atlas* $750.00
A Map of the Canals and Railroads of Pennsylvania and New Jersey Phila 1850 21 x 27.5 Sep. issue HC engraving *Separately issued* $650.00
A New Map ofPennsylvania With It Canals, Railroads... Phila 1840 11 x 13.5 Ex-atlas HC engraving *Shows 58 counties* $175.00
Plan of the City ofPhiladelphia Phila 1836 16 x 13 Folding Map HC engraving $250.00
A New Map ofTennessee With Its Roads and Distances Phila 1836 11 x 15 Ex-atlas HC engraving *From A New Universal Atlas* $175.00
• **United States** Phila 1839-46 15 x 12 Ex-atlas HC engraving *From A New Universal Atlas* $200.00
United States of America Phila 1829 50 x 62.5 Wall Map HC engraving $1,800.00
A Map of the United States of Mexico Phila 1826 25 x 30.5 Folding Map HC engraving *2d edition* Wheat-TM-529 $3,500.00
A New Map ofVirginia With Its Canals, Roads and Distances Phila 1836 11 x 13 Ex-atlas HC engraving *From A New Universal Atlas* Phillips (A)774 $175.00
Virginia, Maryland and Delaware Phila 1820 20.5 x 29 Ex-atlas HC engraving *From American Atlas* $875.00
City ofWashington Phila 1836-44 11.5 x 14.5 Ex-atlas HC engraving *Carey & Hart Publishers* Phillips (A)774 $200.00
City ofWashington Phila 1846 12.5 x 15.5 Ex-atlas HC engraving *Phila: S. A. Mitchell* $150.00
West Indies 1834 11.5 x 14.5 Ex-atlas HC engraving *Carey & Hart Publishers* $125.00
Wisconsin Phila 1846 16 x 13.5 Ex-atlas HC engraving *From A New Universal Atlas* $175.00
World on Mercator's Projection Phila 1823 23 x 29 Ex-atlas HC engraving *From American Atlas 2d Edition* $600.00

Tanner, T. R.

Strangers' New York City Guide NY 1842 18 x 24 Folding Map HC engraving Illustrated $500.00

Taylor, Benjamin

A New & Accurate Plan of the City ofNew York NY 1797 24.5 x 38 Wall Map HC engraving $18,000.00

Thomas, Cowperthwait & Co

Publishers of (Mitchell's) New Universal Atlas

A New Map ofAlabama With Its Roads and Distances Phila 1850-55 14.5 x 12 Ex-atlas HC engraving *From A New Universal Atlas* $95.00
A New Map ofArkansas With Its Canals, Roads... Phila 1854 14.5 x 12 Ex-atlas HC engraving *From A New Universal Atlas* Phillips (A)813 $95.00
A New Map ofCalifornia...Oregon, Washington, Utah & New Mexico Phila 1850-52 15.5 x 12.5 Ex-atlas HC engraving *From A New Universal Atlas* Phillips (A) 807 $375.00
Map ofFlorida Phila 1850-55 16 x 13 Ex-atlas HC engraving *From A New Universal Atlas* Phillips (A) 807 $100.00
A New Map of Georgia With Its Roads and Distances Phila 1850 14 x 11.5 Ex-atlas HC engraving *From A New Universal Atlas* Phillips (A)800 $95.00
A New Map of the State ofIllinois With Its Proposed Canals, Roads... Phila 1851-54 15.5 x 13.5 Ex-atlas HC engraving *From A New Universal Atlas* Phillips (A) 807 $95.00

A New Map of Indiana With Its Roads and Distances Phila 1850 12.5 x 10 Ex-atlas HC engraving *From A New Universal Atlas* Phillips (A)800 $95.00
A New Map of the State of Iowa Phila 1854 13.5 x 16 Ex-atlas HC engraving *From A New Universal Atlas* Phillips (A)814 $85.00
A New Map of Louisiana With Its Canals, Roads and Distances... Phila 1853 11.5 x 14.5 Ex-atlas HC engraving *A New Universal Atlas* Phillips (A)809 $85.00
A New Map of Maryland and Delaware Phila 1850-54 10 x 13.5 Ex-atlas HC engraving *From A New Universal Atlas* Phillips (A)800 $95.00
A New Map of Michigan With Its Canals, Roads and Distances Phila 1850 15 x 11.5 Ex-atlas HC engraving *Also 1854* Phillips (A)800 $125.00
Map of Minnesota Territory Phila 1850 13 x16 Ex-atlas HC engraving *9 Counties shown* Phillips (A)800 $175.00
Map of Minnesota Territory Phila 1854 13 x16 Ex-atlas HC engraving *From A New Universal Atlas* Phillips (A)813 $125.00
A New Map of Mississippi With Its Roads and Distances Phila 1850 14.5 x 11.5 Ex-atlas HC engraving *From A New Universal Atlas* Phillips (A)800 $95.00
A New Map of the State of Missouri Phila 1854 13.5 x 16 Ex-atlas HC engraving *From A New Universal Atlas* Phillips (A)813 $85.00
Map of New Jersey Reduced from...Gordon's Map Phila 1850 15 x 12.5 Ex-atlas HC engraving *20 Counties shown* Phillips (A)800 $95.00
A New Map of New York With Its Canals, Roads and Distances Phila 1850 12 x 14.5 Ex-atlas HC engraving *From A New Universal Atlas* Phillips (A)800 $85.00
A New Map of Nth Carolina With Its Canals, Roads and Distances... Phila 1850-55 15 x 12.5 Ex-atlas HC engraving *A New Universal Atlas* Phillips (A)800 $95.00
A New Map of the State of Ohio Phila 1854 16 x 13.5 Ex-atlas HC engraving *From A New Universal Atlas* Phillips (A)813 $85.00
A New Map of Pennsylvania Phila 1851 12 x 14.5 Ex-atlas HC engraving *From A New Universal Atlas* Phillips (A)805 $85.00
Philadelphia Phila 1851 15.5 x 12.5 Ex-atlas HC engraving *A New Universal Atlas* Phillips (A)805 $85.00
A New Map of South Carolina With Its Canals, Roads... Phila 1850-55 11.5 x 14 Ex-atlas HC engraving *From A New Universal Atlas* Phillips (A)800 $85.00
A New Map of Tennessee With Its Roads and Distances... Phila 1850-55 11.5 x 15.5 Ex-atlas HC engraving *A New Universal Atlas* Phillips (A)800 $95.00
Map of Texas from the Most Recent Authorities Phila 1851 12 x 15 Ex-atlas HC engraving *From A New Universal Atlas* Phillips (A)805 $325.00
• **A New Map of the United States of America** Phila 1850-52 16 x 26.5 Ex-atlas HC engraving *From A New Universal Atlas* Phillips (A)800 Illustrated $275.00
A New Map of Virginia With Its Canals, Roads... Phila 1854 11.5 x 14 Ex-atlas HC engraving *From A New Universal Atlas* Phillips (A)813 $85.00
City of Washington Phila 1851 12 x 15 Ex-atlas HC engraving *From A New Universal Atlas* Phillips (A)805 $175.00
Map of the State of Wisconsin Phila 1850-55 16 x 13 Ex-atlas HC engraving *From A New Universal Atlas* Phillips (A)800 Illustrated $125.00

Walling

Map of the State of Maine Portland 1862 61 x 63 Wall Map HC Engraving $600.00
Map of the State of Vermont NY 1859 62 x 59 Wall Map HC Engraving *Published by Johnson & Browning* $600.00

Watson

New Railroad and Distance Map of Minnesota & Iowa Chicago 1877-83 16 x 12.5 Ex-atlas Wax engraving *From New Indexed Family Atlas* $75.00
Watson's New Railroad and Distance Map ...United States and Canada Chicago 1871 35.5 x 46.5 Folding Map Wax engraving *Cloth folder* $1,000.00
Watson's New Map of the Western States, Territories, Mexico and Central America Chicago 1869 36.5 x 27.5 Folding Map Wax engraving *Cloth folder* $1,250.00

Weishampel

New and Enlarged Map of Baltimore City... Baltimore 1872 24.5 x 28.5 Folding Map Lithograph $500.00
West & Johnston **Map of the State of Virginia Containing the Counties...Towns...** Richmond 1864 22.5 x 34.5 Folding Map HC engraving $3,500.00

Whitman and Searl

Map of Eastern Kansas Boston 1856 27 x 21 Folding Map HC engraving $650.00

Wilson & Co.

Indexed Sectional Map of Southern California SF 1895 22 x 38.5 Folding Map Lithograph $500.00

Young, J. H.

The Tourist's Pocket Map of Indiana Phila 1833 15.75 x 13.25 Folding Map HC engraving $275.00

FOLDING MAPS, WALL MAPS & SEPARATELY ISSUED MAPS

Listed by Publisher

• *Illustrated*

Aschbach

Pocket Map Showing the Probable Theatre of War Phila 1861 15 x 13 Folding Map HC engraving $800.00

Asher & Co.

The Historical War Map Baltimore 1862 24 x 33 Folding Map HC engraving *Imprint of E. F. Hazelton, Baltimore* $600.00

The Historical War Map Baltimore 1863 24 x 33 Folding Map HC engraving *Imprint of Barnitz, Cincinnati. With 72p text* $600.00

Aspin

North and South America Phila 1823 13.5 x 17 Sep. Issue HC engraving *From Abbe Gaultiers Geographical Game. Shows Franklinia in eastern TN* $275.00

Barnes, R. L.

County, Township and Railroad Map of ... Pennsylvania Phila 1857 32.5 x 49 Wall Map HC engraving $500.00

12 Miles Around Philadelphia Phila 1858 21 x 21 Folding Map HC engraving *Cloth folder* $400.00

Barnes Driving Map of Phildelphia and Surroundings Phila 1874 24.5 x 28.5 Folding Map HC engraving *Cloth folder* $250.00

Map of Venango County, Pennsylvania Phila 1865 24 x 32.5 Folding Map HC engraving *Cloth folder* $750.00

Bradley

Railroad Map of the United States Phila 1886 14 x 23 Folding Map Lithograph $175.00

Bradley, A.

Map of the United States Exhibiting the Post Roads... Phila 1796 34.5 x 37.5 Folding Map Hand colored engraving $17,500.00

Map of the United States Exhibiting the Post Roads... Phila 1804 38 x 52.5 Folding Map Hand colored engraving *Schwarz & Ehrenberg 222* $12,500.00

Britton & Rey

Map of San Francisco from the latest Surveys SF 1872 17 x 19.5 Folding Map UC engraving *Cloth Folder. "A Map and Street Directory of San Francisco"* $300.00

Burr, David H.

Map of Florida Washington 1839 50 x 35 Folding Map HC engraving $1,500.00

Map of Kentucky and Tennessee Washington 1839 36 x 50 Folding Map HC engraving $1,500.00

Map of New Jersey & Pennsylvania Washington 1839 36 x 50 Folding Map HC engraving $1,500.00

Map of New Jersey and Pennsylvania Washington 1839 37.5 x 50.5 Folding Map HC engraving *2 sheets* $800.00

Map of the State of New York Ithaca 1839 19 x 24 Folding Map HC engraving *Leather covers* $350.00

Carleton, Osgood

Map of Massachusetts Proper Boston 1832 32 x 47 Folding Map HC engraving $2,250.00

Chapman

Chapman's Sectional Map of Illinois Milwaukee 1857 38.5 x 23 Folding Map HC engraving *Cloth folder* $750.00

Chapman's Township Map ofIllinois Milwaukee 1857 17 x 13.5 Folding Map HC engraving *Cloth folder* $450.00

Colby

Map of the State ofMaine Houlton 1889 33.5 x 25 Folding Map Lithograph *Cloth folder* $325.00

Colton **Map of the State ofAlabama** NY 1885 36 x 27 Folding Map Lithograph after engraving *Cloth folder. Separately issued.* $325.00

Colton

Map of the City of Brooklyn...City of Williamsburgh...Part of the City of New York NY 1855 32.5 x 46 Wall Map HC engraving $425.00

California NY 1854 15.5 x 12 Folding Map HC engraving *Cloth folder* $1,250.00

Colton's California & Nevada NY 1873 25 x 17 Folding Map Lithograph after engraving *Cloth or leather folder* $500.00

City ofChicago, Illinois NY 1856 12.5 x 8.5 Folding Map HC engraving *Cloth folder* $850.00

Map ... Thirty Three Miles Around City of New York NY 1879 24.5 x 23.5 Circular Map Lithograph after engraving $600.00

Colton's Georgia NY 1864 14 x 11 Folding Map Lithograph after engraving *Cloth or leather folder* $300.00

Colton's Map of the State of Georgia NY 1866 38 x 24.5 Folding Map Lithograph after engraving *Cloth or leather folder* $850.00

Map ofGeorgia Central RR and Connections NY 1859 10 x 14.5 Folding Map Lithograph after engraving *Lang & Lang imprint* $200.00

New Sectional Map of the State ofIllinois NY 1852 30 x 25 Folding Map HC Engraving *Cloth or leather folder* $500.00

Map ofIllinois NY 1854 14 x 11 Folding Map HC Engraving *Cloth folder* $325.00

Colton's Map of the State ofIndiana Compiled from...United States Surveys... NY 1877 40 x 26 Folding Map Lithograph after engraving *Cloth or leather folder* $500.00

New Railroad Map ofIndiana, Ohio and Part of Illinois NY 1875 16 x 28 Folding Map Lithograph after engraving $75.00

New Railroad Map ofIndiana, Ohio and Part of Illinois NY 1875 16 x 28 Folding Map Lithograph after engraving $75.00

Map ofIowa NY 1854 12.5 x 14.5 Folding Map HC Engraving *Cloth or leather folder* $325.00

Colton's Township Map of ... Iowa NY 1863-66 16 x 22 Folding Map Lithograph after engraving *Cloth folder* $275.00

Colton's New Sectional Map of ... Kansas NY 1869 29 x 56 Folding Map Lithograph after engraving *Cloth folder* $650.00

Lake Superior and the Northern Part of Michigan NY 1854 13 x 16 Folding Map Lithograph after engraving *Cloth folder* $350.00

Colton's Map ofLake Superior and Upper Peninsula of Michigan... NY 1868 16.5 x 24.5 Folding Map Lithograph after engraving *Cloth folder. "Showing...Portage Lake...Canal...Iron Lands...Separate issue"* $350.00

Colton's Map of the State of Louisiana and Eastern Part of Texas NY 1871 30 x 39.5 Folding Map Lithograph after engraving *Cloth folder* $650.00

Colton's Maine NY 1877 17 x 13 Folding Map Lithograph after engraving *Cloth or leather folder* $150.00

Massachusetts & Rhode Island NY 1854 12 x 16 Folding Map HC Engraving *Cloth folder* $175.00

Massachusetts & Rhode Island NY 1854 12 x 16 Folding Map HC Engraving *Cloth folder* $175.00

Colton's Massachusetts & Rhode Island NY 1867 15 x 15 Folding Map Lithograph after engraving *Cloth or leather folder* $150.00

Colton's Mexico NY 1861 11 x 14 Folding Map Lithograph after engraving *Cloth folder* $450.00

Colton's New Sectional Map of the State of Minnesota NY 1873 20 x 25 Folding Map Lithograph after engraving *Cloth folder. 2 maps* $400.00

Colton's New Map of Missouri NY 1869 21 x 27 Folding Map Lithograph after engraving *Cloth folder* $250.00

Sectional Map ofNebraska and Part of Dakota NY 1872 33 x 40 Folding Map Lithograph after engraving *Cloth or leather folder* $400.00

Sectional Map ofNebraska and Part of Dakota NY 1872 33 x 40 Folding Map Lithograph after engraving *Cloth or leather folder* $400.00

Colton's New Sectional Map ofNebraska and Part of Dakota NY 1870 28 x 37 Folding Map Lithograph $300.00

Colton's Map ofNew Mexico and Arizona NY 1877 20 x 24 Folding Map Lithograph after engraving *Cloth or leather folder* $450.00

New York NY 1833 17 x 21 Folding Map HC Engraving *Cloth folder. First Colton publication* $600.00

Colton's Map ofNew York NY 1850 20 x 20 Folding Map HC Engraving $275.00

Colton's Railroad and Township Map of ... New York NY 1853-60 28 x 24 Folding Map Lithograph after engraving *Cloth folder* $275.00

New York NY 1854 11 x 14 Folding Map Lithograph after engraving *Cloth folder* $250.00

Map ... Thirty Three Miles Around New York City NY 1855 24.5 x 23 Folding Map HC Engraving *Cloth folder* $500.00

Colton's New York City, Brooklyn, Jersey City, Hoboken.. NY 1873 22.5 x 15 Folding Map Lithograph after engraving *Cloth folder* $375.00

New York, Brooklyn, Williamsburgh, Jersey City & the Adjacent.. NY 1853 25 x 51 Wall Map HC Engraving $650.00

Map of the State ofNew York....Embracing Plans of the Cities...by David A. Burr NY 1834 46 x 56 Wall Map HC Engraving $800.00

Colton's North Carolina NY 1869-71 14 x 16 Folding Map Lithograph after engraving *Cloth folder* $350.00

Colton's Railroad and Township Map ofOhio NY 1867 20 x 24 Folding Map Lithograph after engraving $250.00

Guide Through Ohio, Michigan, Indiana, Illinois NY 1857 20 x 27 Folding Map HC Engraving *Cloth folder stamped "Map of the Western States"* $400.00

Guide Through Ohio, Michigan, Indiana, Illinois, Missouri, Wisconsin & Iowa NY 1855 20.5 x 25.5 Folding Map HC Engraving *Bound with Colton's Western Tourist and Emigrant's Guide* $450.00

Guide Through Ohio, Michigan, Indiana, Illinois, Missouri, Wisconsin & Iowa NY 1855 20.5 x 25.5 Folding Map HC Engraving *Bound with Colton's Western Tourist and Emigrant's Guide* $450.00

Colton's New Township Map of ... Pennsylvania NY 1866 17 x 27 Folding Map Lithograph after engraving *Cloth folder* $175.00

Colton's Map ofPennsylvania NY 1871 14 x 18 Folding Map Lithograph after engraving $225.00

Portsmouth on the Ohio River NY 1836 21 x 30 Folding Map HC Engraving *Cloth or leather folder. Bound with Burr's map of Ohio* $1,250.00

Map of the Richmond and Louisville RR Connecting...Virginia...Kentucky... NY 1882 30 x 40 Folding Map Lithograph after engraving *Cloth folder* $350.00

South Carolina NY 1853 11 x 14 Folding Map HC Engraving *Cloth folder* $425.00

J. H. Colton's Map of the Southern States, Including Maryland, Delaware NY 1864 38 x 54 Folding Map Lithograph after engraving *Cloth folder. Map in two sections* $1,500.00

Colton's Map of the State of Tennessee NY 1871 20 x 25 Folding Map Lithograph after engraving *Cloth or leather folder. 2 maps* $450.00

• **Texas** NY 1856 16 x 25 Folding Map Lithograph after engraving *Illustrated* $500.00

New Railroad and County Map of the United States NY 1860-62 33 x 40 Folding Map Lithograph after engraving *Cloth or leather folder* $600.00

New Guide Map of the United States and Canada with Railroads, Counties NY 1862-66 36 x 31 Folding Map Lithograph after engraving *Cloth or leather folder* $500.00

G. W. Colton's New Guide Map of the United States and Canada With Railroads, Counties, etc. NY 1861 30 x 36 Folding Map Lithograph after engraving *Cloth or leather folder* $600.00

Colton's Map of the United States of America NY 1850 20 x 24 Folding Map Lithograph after engraving *Cloth or leather folder. J. H. Colton 86 Cedar St., New York* $300.00

United States of America NY 1855 18 x 27 Folding Map HC Engraving *Imprint J. H. Colton...172 William St., NY. Separately issued* $350.00

G. W. & C. B. Colton's United States of America NY 1872-76 16 x 28 Folding Map Lithograph after engraving *Cloth folder* $250.00

Map of the United States of America, British Provinces, Mexico... NY 1854 34 x 43 Folding Map HC Engraving *Cloth or leather folder* $1,000.00

Map of the United States of America, The British Provinces, Mexico... NY 1851 36 x 46 Wall Map HC Engraving $600.00

Burr's Map of the United States Published by J. H. Colton NY 1833 17 x 21 Folding Map HC Engraving *J. H. Colton & Co. 9 Wall Street* $750.00

Map of the United States Showing Routes of U.S. Mail Steam Packets NY 1849 Folding Map HC Engraving $1,500.00

Map of the United States, British Provinces... NY 1853 47 x 54 Wall Map HC Engraving $800.00

Colton's Map of the United States, the Canadas, &c.... NY 1854 24 x 29 Folding Map Lithograph after engraving *Cloth or leather folder* $325.00

Colton's New Railroad and County Map ... United States... NY 1869-71 32 x 34 Folding Map Lithograph after engraving *Cloth or leather folder* $450.00

Colton's Map of the Oil District of Venango, Crawford, and Warren Counties, Pennsylvania NY 1865 31 x 37 Folding Map Lithograph after engraving *Cloth or leather folder* $600.00

Map of Vermont NY 1859 14 x 11 Folding Map Lithograph after engraving *Cloth folder* $200.00

Colton's Map of Virginia NY 1872 11 x 15 Folding Map Lithograph after engraving *Cloth folder* $200.00

Map of the Virginia, Kentucky and Ohio Railroad.... NY 1881 28.5 x 41.5 Wall Map Lithograph after engraving $275.00

Colton's... Map of the Seat of War in Virginia, Maryland, &c. NY 1862 26.5 x 19 Folding Map Lithograph after engraving *Cloth or leather folder* $1,000.00

Colton's New Topographical Map of ... Virginia, West Virginia, Maryland & Delaware... NY 1870 28 x 42 Folding Map Lithograph after engraving *Cloth folder* $450.00

Colton's New ...Map of the States of Virginia. Maryland and Delaware... NY 1862 30.5 x 44.5 Folding Map Lithograph after engraving *Cloth or leather folder* $750.00

Colton's New Topographical Map of ... Virginia. Maryland and Delaware...East Tennessee...Military Sta.. NY 1862 30.5 x 44.5 Folding Map Lithograph after engraving *Cloth or leather folder* $750.00

Topographical Map of the West Indies and Adjacent Coasts by John Pinkerton NY 1852 19 x 27 Folding Map HC Engraving *Cloth or leather folder.* $750.00

Colton's Map of the States & Territories West of the Mississippi...to the Pacific Ocean... NY 1867 28 x44 Folding Map Lithograph after engraving *Cloth or leather folder.* $700.00

Colton's Map of the States & Territories West of the Mississippi...to the Pacific Ocean... NY 1871 28 x44 Folding Map Lithograph after engraving *Cloth or leather folder.* $700.00

Colton's Map of the State ofWest Virginia & Portions of Adjoining States NY 1873 23 x 25.5 Folding Map Lithograph after engraving *Cloth or leather folder* $450.00

Colton's Map of the Oil District ofWest Virginia and Ohio NY 1865 31 x 36 Folding Map Lithograph after engraving *Cloth or leather folder* $600.00

Colton **Map of the Western States** NY 1854 17.5 x 22 Folding Map HC Engraving *Cloth or leather folder* $350.00

Colton's Railroad & Township Map ...Western States NY 1856 43 x 43 Folding Map HC Engraving *Cloth or leather folder* $600.00

Railroad & Township Map Western States NY 1856 33 x 40 Folding Map HC Engraving *Cloth or leather folder* $600.00

Wisconsin NY 1854 15 x 12 Folding Map HC Engraving *Separately issued* $350.00

Colton's New Illustrated Map of the World NY 1849 31 x 42 Folding Map HC Engraving *Cloth or leather folder. First edition.* $950.00

Colton's New Illustrated Map of the World NY 1851 31 x 42 Folding Map HC Engraving *Cloth or leather folder. Title moved to top* $875.00

Disturnell

Routes Between New York and Washington Phila 1837 23.4 x 4.5 Folding Map HC engraving *Cloth folder* $800.00

Army Map of the Seat of War in Virginia, Showing Battlefields, Fortifications... Phila 1861 27 x 25 Folding Map HC engraving *Cloth folder* $850.00

Duncan & Co.

Plan of the City and Environs ofNew Orleans... Phila 1865 15.5 x 18.5 Folding Map HC engraving $700.00

Entwhistle

Entwhistle's Handy Map ofWashington and Vicinity... Wash 1876 16 x 21 Folding Map Lithograph $175.00

Farmer

An Improved ... Map of the Surveyed Part of... Michigan NY 1835 21 x 31 Folding Map HC engraving *Cloth or leather folder. Second Issue Phillips (M) 425* $1,500.00

An Improved ... Map of the Surveyed Part of... Michigan NY 1836 21 x 31 Folding Map HC engraving *Cloth or leather folder. Second Issue* $1,500.00

Map of the Territories ofMichigan and Ouisconsin Detroit 1830 40 x 34 Folding Map HC engraving *Phillips (M)424* $1,250.00

Improved Map of the Territories ofMichigan and Ouisconsin Albany 1835 20 x 34 Folding Map HC engraving *Phillips (M)424* $1,000.00

Map of the Surveyed Part ...Territory ofMichigan on a Scale of 8 miles... Detroit 1826 20 x 21 Folding Map HC engraving *Phillips (M)424* $1,250.00

Finley, A.

Alabama Phila 1829 8.5 x 11 Folding Map HC engraving *Cloth or leather folder Phillips (A)752* $600.00

Map ofFlorida According to the Latest Authorities (with) West Indies Phila 1827 na Folding Map HC engraving *Leather folder* $1,000.00

Map ofLouisiana, Mississippi, and Alabama... Phila 1827 17 x 20 Folding Map HC engraving $850.00

. **Maine** Phila 1828 11.5 x 8.5 Folding Map HC engraving $225.00

Massachusetts Phila 1826 9 x 11 Folding Map HC engraving *Leather folder* $375.00

Map of Ohio and the Settled Parts of Michigan Phila 1834 19 x 13 Folding Map HC engraving *Leather folder* $750.00

Map of the United States Phila 1826 17 x 21 Folding Map HC engraving *Leather folder* $650.00

Virginia Phila 1825 8.5 x 11 Folding Map HC engraving *Leather folder* $500.00

Frey, A. C.

Topographical Railroad & County Map of ... California and Nevada NY 1868 38.5 x 30.5 Folding Map Lithograph after engraving $850.00

Gaston & Johnson

A New Map of Our Country NY 1854 55 x 62 Wall Map HC engraving $750.00

Goodrich

Map of the Hudson Between Sandy Hook & Sandy Hill... NY 1820 47 x 9 Folding Map Engraving *Half leather folder* $1,500.00

Gray

Map of Cayuga and Seneca Counties, New York...by O. W. Gray NY 1859 58 x 58 Wall Map HC engraving $375.00

Map of Orleans & Niagara Counties, New York...by O. W. Gray Phila 1860 60 x 60 Wall Map HC engraving *Phila: A. R. Z. Dawson* $375.00

Greenleaf, J.

Map of the State of Maine with the Province of New Brunswick Brattleboro 1844 50 x 42 Wall Map HC engraving $2,000.00

Ide

Ide's Map of Montana Helena 1891 21 x 38 Folding Map Lithograph $800.00

Keeler, W. J.

National Map of the United States Washington 1867 50 x 60 Folding Map $800.00

Lapham

The State of Wisconsin Milwaukee 1852 31.5 x 48 Folding Map HC engraving *Phillips (M) 1077* $600.00

Lawson, J. T

Lawson's Map... of the Gold Regions of Upper California NY 1849 15 x 21 Folding Map HC engraving $2,000.00

Lloyd

Lloyd's New Political Chart...map of the United States Showing Free States, Border Slave States... NY 1861 34.5 x 25.5 Folding Map Lithograph after engraving $450.00

New Military Map of the Border & Southern States NY 1862 30 x 41.5 Wall Map Lithograph after engraving $650.00

Lucas, Fielding

- **Plan of Baltimore** Baltimore 1823 14.5 X 20.5 Folding Map HC engraving Illustrated $475.00

Melish, J.

Map of Dauphin and Lebanon Counties...Pennsylvania Phila 1818 17 x 23 Folding Map HC engraving $275.00

A Map of the State of Louisiana With Part of Mississippi Territory... Phila 1816 46 x 33 Folding Map HC engraving $2,500.00

Map of Pennsylvania... Phila 1826 63 x 77 Folding Map HC engraving $1,500.00

United States Phila 1816 16 x 20 Folding Map HC engraving *Illustrated* $600.00

A Map of the Southern Section of the United States Including the Floridas & Bahama Islands... Phila 1813 16 x 21 Sep. Iss. HC engraving *Separate issue. Engraved by Tanner* $1,250.00

Map of the United States of America Phila 1816 37 x 58 Folding Map HC engraving $3,500.00

United States of America Phila 1818 16 x 20 Folding Map Engraving $675.00

United States of America Phila 1818 16 x 19.5 Folding Map HC engraving $800.00

United States of America Phila 1821 17 x 21 Folding Map HC engraving *M. Carey & Son. B. Tanner, engr.* $600.00

Mitchell, S. A.

Mitchell's National Map of the American Republic Phila 1843 34 x 24 Wall map HC engraving *First edition. Insets of 32 cities* $800.00

Tourist's Pocket Map of the State of Illinois... Phila 1834 15 x 12.5 Folding Map HC engraving $600.00

A New Map of Kentucky With Its Roads and Distances Phila 1843 11.5 x 13.5 Folding Map HC engraving *Cloth or leather covers* $400.00

Map of the States of Louisiana, Mississippi and Alabama Phila 1835 17.5 x 21.5 Folding Map HC engraving *Cloth or leather covers* $600.00

The Tourist's Pocket Map of Michigan Phila 1835 12 x 15 Folding Map HC engraving *Phillips (M) 425* $375.00

Map of the State of New York Compiled from the Latest Authorities Phila 1832 17 x 22 Folding Map HC engraving *Cloth or leather covers* $350.00

The Empire State of New York With Its Counties, Towns, Villages Phila 1864 39 x 48.5 Folding Map Lithograph after engraving *Cloth or leather covers Phillips (M) 512* $600.00

Map of the States of Ohio, Indiana and Illinois With the Settled Part of Michigan Phila 1835 18 x 22.5 Folding Map HC engraving *Cloth or leather covers* $675.00

Map of Pennsylvania, New Jersey and Delaware Phila 1832 17 x 21 Folding Map HC engraving *Cloth or leather covers* $300.00

Map of the United States Phila 1831 43.5 x 34.5 Folding Map HC engraving *Cloth or leather covers* $750.00

Mitchell's Traveller's Guide Through the United States Phila 1832 17.5 x 22 Folding Map HC engraving *With booklet & supplementary sheet* $750.00

Traveller's Guide Through the United States Phila 1833 21.5 x 22.5 Folding Map HC engraving $500.00

A New Map of the United States Phila 1833 52.5 x 78.5 Wall map HC engraving $1,250.00

Mitchell's Reference and Distance Map of the United States Phila 1834 52.5 x 66.5 Wall map HC engraving *First edition. 13 Inset maps* $1,000.00

Mitchell's New National Map Exhibiting United States Phila 1859 54 x 55 Wall map HC engraving *Wheat 896* $800.00

Map of the United States by J. H. Young Phila 1831 43.5 x 34.5 Wall map HC engraving *Revised editions published to 1844 Ristow 309* $1,000.00

Reference and Distance Map of the United States by J. H. Young Phila 1835 54.5 x 69 Folding Map HC engraving *With inset Maps* $1,500.00

Tourist's Pocket Map of the State of Virginia Phila 1839 12.5 x 14 Folding Map HC engraving $300.00

A Map of the World on Mercator's Projection Phila 1843 47 x 74 Wall map HC engraving *Independent Texas* $1,000.00

Monk

Monk's New American Map Exhibiting North America, United States and Territories NY 1855 57.5 x 61 Wall Map HC engraving *Hoen & Co.* $450.00

Morse & Gaston

New Map of Our Country ... United States NY 1856 55 x 64 Wall map Lithograph after engraving $600.00

Page

Indexed Township Map of Michigan Showing...Railroad Stations, Post Offices 1881 25 x 16.5 Folding Map Lithograph after engraving *Stiff wraps* $325.00

Page's Indexed Township Map ofMontana Showing ...Railroad Stations, Post offices... 1883 16 x 24 Folding Map Lithograph after engraving *Stiff wraps* $675.00

Peck, J.

A New Sectional Map of the State ofIllinois 1854 35.5 x 26.5 Folding Map HC engraving *Cloth or leather folder* $1,250.00

Phelps

Phelps National Map of theUnited States NY 1849-54 20.5 x 26 Folding Map HC engraving *Cloth or leather folder* $500.00

Phelps & Ensign

Phelps & Ensign's Travellers Guide ...United States NY 1842 17 x 22 Folding Map HC engraving *Cloth or leather folder* $650.00

Phelps & Ensign's Travellers Guide ...United States NY 1843 26 x 40.5 Wall Map HC engraving $875.00

Phelps & Ensign's Travellers Guide ...United States NY 1845 17 x 21.5 Folding Map HC engraving *Cloth or leather folder* $600.00

Phelps & Watson

Phelps New National Map of the United States NY 1859 26.5 x 36.5 Wall Map HC engraving $700.00

Railroad Maps

NY Central & Hudson River RRHudson River Map NY 1876 90.5 x 4.5 Folding Map Lithograph *Binder* $200.00

Map ofMichigan, S. & N... Indiana Railroad With Their ... NY 1851 16.5 x 56.5 Folding Map HC engraving *Connections from Council Bluffs to New York* $175.00

Railway Map Publishing Co.

Map ofBoston Boston 1877 26 x 20 Folding Map Lithograph $95.00

Rand McNally & Co.

Official 24 x 36 Map ofAlaska Chicago 1897 24 x 36 Folding Map Wax engraving $200.00

Map of theAtchison, Topeka & Santa Fe Railroad System Chicago 1884 16 x 33 Folding Map Wax engraving *Schedules and ads on verso* $350.00

Map of theChicago & Northwest'n Railway... Chicago 1880 9 x 12 Folding Map Wax engraving $75.00

A Correct Map of theChicago, Burlington & Quincy RR... Chicago 1883 26 x 44.5 Folding Map Wax engraving $300.00

Indexed County and Township Map of Colorado Chicago 1901 19 x 26 Folding Map Wax engraving $95.00

Indexed County and Township Map of Dakota Chicago 1882 28 x 22 Folding Map Wax engraving $95.00

Denver and Rio Grande Railroad System Chicago 1887 14.5 x 17.5 Folding Map Wax engraving *From Tourist's Handbook issued by the RR* $125.00

New Business Map ofFlorida Chicago 1898 21.5 x 27.5 Folding Map Wax engraving $85.00

Indexed County and Township Map of Maryland and Delaware Chicago 1890 13 x 19.5 Folding Map Wax engraving $85.00

Indexed Map of Michigan Chicago 1877 12.5 x 9 Folding Map Wax engraving *On two sheets. Wraps* $175.00

Pocket Map and Shipper's Guide of New York Chicago 1892 19 x 25.5 Folding Map Wax engraving $75.00

A Geographically Correct County Map of ... Traversed by St. Louis, Iron Mountain & Southern RR Chicago 1876 16.5 x 15.5 Folding Map Wax engraving *On Broadside with ads* $450.00

New Railroad & County Map of the United States and Canada Chicago 1876 52.5 x 96 Folding Map Wax engraving $375.00

Indexed County and Railroad Pocket Map...Virginia Chicago 1893 19 x 26 Folding Map Wax engraving $95.00

Indexed Map of Virginia and West Virginia Chicago 1877 11 x 20 Folding Map Wax engraving *Cloth folder* $175.00

Randel, John

The City of New York NY 1821 26 x 37 Folding Map HC engraving $2,000.00

Reid

The State of Virginia from the Best Authorities NY 1796 16 x 19.5 Sep.Iss. Engraving $600.00

Rice, G. J.

Rice's Sectional Map of Dakota St. Paul 1874-78 32 x 26 Folding Map Lithograph after engraving *Cloth folder* $750.00

Robinson, L.

Map of Ohio Compiled from the Latest Authorities Akron 1840 26 x 22.5 Wall Map HC Engraving $2,000.00

Improved Map of Vermont 1834 24 x 17.5 Wall Map HC Engraving $750.00

Rockwell

Map of Part of the Thousand Islands of the St. Lawrence River NY 1883 17.5 x 23 Folding Map Lithograph $500.00

Ross, E. H.

New Railroad and Sectional Map of Kansas St. Louis 1872 23.5 x 38 Folding Map Lithograph $1,000.00

Sherman & Smith

Map of Milwaukee Milw 1857 40 x 27.5 Folding Map Engraving $350.00

Sidney

Sidney's Map of Twelve Miles Around New York, With Names of Property Owners Phila 1849 33 diam 2 Sheets Engraving $700.00

Smith, J. C.

Map of Long Island With the Environs of New York and...Connecticut NY 1854 37 x 55.5 Wall Map HC Engraving $750.00

Guide Through the States of Ohio, Michigan, Indiana, Illinois, Missouri, Wisconsin & Iowa NY 1854 17.5 x 22 Folding Map HC Engraving *From Colton, The Western Tourist and Emigrant's Guide...* $175.00

New Map for Travellers Through the United States NY 1849 21.5 x 25.5 Folding Map HC Engraving *234pp text* $750.00

Snow & Co.

Map of the Railways in New England and Part of New York NY 1849 8.5 x 7 Folding Map Engraving *From Pathfinder Railway Guide for the New England States* $100.00

Tanner, H. S.

A Map of the Roads Leading to ... Britania...Susquehanna County Penn'a. Phila 1819 Sep. issue Engraving *From The Portfolio* $225.00

The Traveller's Pocket Map of Michigan With Its Canals, Roads and Distances Phila 1832 10.5 x 13 Folding Map HC engraving *Phillips (M)424* $375.00

A Map of North America Phila 1822 42.5 x 57.5 Wall Map HC engraving $4,750.00

A Map of the Canals and Railroads of Pennsylvania and New Jersey Phila 1850 21 x 27.5 Sep. issue HC engraving *Separately issued* $650.00

A Map of the Canals and Railroads of Pennsylvania and New Jersey Phila 1850 21 x 27.5 Sep. issue HC engraving *Separately issued* $650.00

Plan of the City of Philadelphia Phila 1836 16 x 13 Folding Map HC engraving $250.00

United States of America Phila 1829 50 x 62.5 Wall Map HC engraving $1,800.00

A Map of the United States of Mexico Phila 1826 25 x 30.5 Folding Map HC engraving *2d edition Wheat-TM-529* $3,500.00

Tanner, T. R.

- **Strangers' New York City Guide** NY 1842 18 x 24 Folding Map HC engraving *Illustrated* $500.00

Taylor, Benjamin

A New & Accurate Plan of the City of New York NY 1797 24.5 x 38 Wall Map HC engraving $18,000.00

Walling

Map of the State of Maine Portland 1862 61 x 63 Wall Map HC Engraving $600.00

Map of the State of Vermont NY 1859 62 x 59 Wall Map HC Engraving *Published by Johnson & Browning* $600.00

Watson

Watson's New Railroad and Distance Map ...United States and Canada Chicago 1871 35.5 x 46.5 Folding Map Wax engraving *Cloth folder* $1,000.00

Watson's New Map of the Western States, Territories, Mexico and Central America Chicago 1869 36.5 x 27.5 Folding Map Wax engraving *Cloth folder* $1,250.00

Weishampel

New and Enlarged Map of Baltimore City... Baltimore 1872 24.5 x 28.5 Folding Map Lithograph $500.00

West & Johnston

Map of the State of Virginia Containing the Counties...Towns... Richmond 1864 22.5 x 34.5 Folding Map HC engraving $3,500.00

Whitman and Searl

Map of Eastern Kansas Boston 1856 27 x 21 Folding Map HC engraving $650.00

Wilson & Co.

Indexed Sectional Map of Southern California SF 1895 22 x 38.5 Folding Map Lithograph $500.00

Young, J. H.

The Tourist's Pocket Map of Indiana Phila 1833 15.75 x 13.25 Folding Map HC engraving $275.00

ATLASES

Listed by Publisher

We have not included price information for some atlases because of the infrequency of availability. Please consult auction records or a specialist dealer

Arrowsmith, A. & Lewis, S.

A New and Elegant General Atlas Phila 1804 4to Phillips (A)702 *63 maps* $650.00

A New and Elegant General Atlas Boston 1805 4to Phillips (A)708 *Second edition. 63 maps* $650.00

A New and Elegant General Atlas Boston 1812 4to Phillips (A)718 *63 maps* $600.00

A New and Elegant General Atlas Boston 1819 4to Phillips (A)734 *63 maps* $650.00

Asher & Adams

New Commercial Statistical and Topographical Atlas NY 1872 Folio Phillips (A)1272 *39 maps* $400.00

New Commercial Statistical and Topographical Atlas NY 1874 Folio Phillips (A)1273 *41 maps* $400.00

Bradford, T. G.

A Comprehensive Atlas Boston 1835 4to $1,500.00

An Illustrated Atlas Boston 1838 Folio $3,250.00

Burr. David

A New Universal Atlas NY 1833 Folio Phillips (A)771 *63 maps. See Phillps 1379a* $3,500.00

Carey, H.C. & Lea, I.

A Complete Historical, Chronological and Geographical ... Atlas Phila 1822 Folio Phillips (A)1373a *First edition. 46 maps* $6,000.00

A Complete Historical, Chronological and Geographical ... Atlas Phila 1827 Folio Phillips (A)1177 *Third edition. 46 maps* $6,000.00

A Complete Historical, Chronological and Geographical ... Atlas Phila 1823 Folio Phillips (A) 762 *Second edition. 46 maps* $6,000.00

Carey, Matthew

American Atlas Phila 1795 Folio Phillips (A)1172 *21 American maps. First American atlas* $12,500.00

American Atlas Phila 1809 Folio Phillips (A) 1173 *Second edition. 26 maps* $7,500.00

A General Atlas for the Present War Phila 1794 *16 maps of American states****

The General Atlas for Carey's Edition of Guthrie's Geography Phila 1795 ***

Carey's General Atlas Phila 1796 Folio Phillips (A)683 *45 maps* $7,500.00

Carey's General Atlas Phila 1814 Folio Phillips (A)722 *58 maps* $6,000.00

Carey's General Atlas Phila 1811 Folio *58 maps* $6,000.00

Carey's General Atlas Phila 1814 Folio Phillips (A)1372 *58 maps* $5,500.00

Carey's General Atlas Phila 1818 Folio Phillips (A) 732 *58 maps* $4,500.00

American Pocket Atlas Phila 1796 16mo Phillips (A)1364 *First edition. 19 maps* $2,500.00

American Pocket Atlas Phila 1801 12mo $1,500.00

Carey, Matthew **American Pocket Atlas** Phila 1805 12mo (Phillips (A) 1368 *20 maps* $1,500.00

American Pocket Atlas Phila 1813 12mo $1,500.00

American Pocket Atlas Phila 1814 12mo Phillips (A) 1370 *23 maps* $1,500.00

Colles, C.

The Geographical Ledger and Systematized Atlas NY 1794 8vo *Ristow 163. Impossibly rare****

Colton

Colton's Octavo Atlas of the World NY 1856 8vo *47 maps* $475.00

Colton, G. W. **Colton's Atlas of the World** NY 1856 Folio Phillips (A)816 *58 maps 2 vols* $1,750.00

Colton, G. W. **Colton's Atlas of the World** NY 1857 Folio $1,500.00

Colton's General Atlas NY 1857 Folio Phillips (A) 827 *96 maps* $800.00
Colton's General Atlas NY 1858 Folio Phillips (A) 827 *Ristow 313-326* $800.00
Colton's General Atlas NY 1859 Folio $800.00
Colton's General Atlas NY 1861 Folio $800.00
Colton's General Atlas NY 1866 Folio $1,500.00
Colton's General Atlas NY 1868 Folio $750.00
Colton's General Atlas NY 1870 Folio Phillips (A) 856 *101 maps* $750.00
Colton's General Atlas NY 1873 Folio Phillips (A) 866 *104 maps* $750.00
Colton's General Atlas NY 1876 Folio Phillips (A) 879 *106 maps* $750.00
Colton's General Atlas NY 1877 Folio $750.00
Colton's General Atlas NY 1878 Folio Phillips (A) 886 *106 maps* $750.00
Colton's General Atlas NY 1881 Folio $750.00
Colton's General Atlas NY 1882 Folio Phillips (A) 911 *104 maps* $750.00

Finley, A.

A New General Atlas Phila 1824 Folio Ristow 268 *60 maps.* $6,000.00
A New American Atlas Phila 1826 Folio Phillips (A) 1378 *First state of two. 15 maps Howes F140* $6,000.00
A New General Atlas Phila 1829 Folio Phillips (A) 752 *58 maps* ***
A New General Atlas Phila 1831 4to Phillips (A) 752 *60 maps* $3,750.00

Gray

Gray's Atlas of the United States Phila 1873 Folio Phillips (A) 1390 *65 maps* $750.00
Gray **Gray's Atlas of the United States** Phila 1874 Folio $750.00
Gray **Gray's Atlas of the United States** Phila 1878 Folio $750.00

Greenleaf, J.

A New Universal Atlas Brattleboro 1842 Folio Phillips (A) 784 *65 maps* $2,250.00
A New Universal Atlas Brattleboro 1848 Folio $2,000.00

Johnson & Browning

Johnson's New Illustrated (Steel Plate) Family Atlas... NY 1860-61 Folio *Successors to J. H. Colton & Co." Ristow 325* $850.00

Johnson & Ward

Johnson's New Illustrated (Steel Plate) Family Atlas... NY 1862 Folio Phillips (A) 837 *59 maps Ristow 325* $850.00
Johnson's New Illustrated (Steel Plate) Family Atlas... NY 1863 Folio Phillips (A) 840 *64 maps Ristow 325* $850.00
Johnson's New Illustrated (Steel Plate) Family Atlas... NY 1864 Folio Phillips (A) 843 *64 maps Ristow 325* $850.00
Johnson's New Illustrated (Steel Plate) Family Atlas... NY 1865 Folio *Ristow 325* $850.00
Johnson's New Illustrated (Steel Plate) Family Atlas... NY 1866 Folio *Ristow 325* $850.00
Johnson's New Illustrated (Steel Plate) Family Atlas... NY 1867 Folio *Ristow 325* $850.00
Johnson's New Illustrated (Steel Plate) Family Atlas... NY 1869 Folio *Ristow 325* $850.00
Johnson's New Illustrated (Steel Plate) Family Atlas... NY 1872 Folio *Ristow 325* $750.00

Lucas, Fielding

A General Atlas Baltimore 1823 Folio Phillips (A) 742 *104 Maps. Ristow267.* $6,000.00
A New and Elegant General Atlas... Baltimore 1816? Folio Ristow 266 ***

Melish, John

Travels in the United States Phila 1812 12mo Howes M496 *8 maps* $500.00
Travels in the United States Phila 1815-18 12mo Howes M496 $400.00
A Geographical Description of the United States Phila 1815 12mo Howes M490 *Ristow 166. 3 maps* $600.00
A Geographical Description of the United States Phila 1816 8vo Howes M490 *5 maps* $600.00
A Geographical Description of the United States Phila 1822 8vo Howes M490 *12 maps* $600.00
A Geographical Description of the United States NY 1826 8vo Howes M490 *12 maps* $500.00
A Military and Topographical Atlas of the United States Phila 1813 8vo Phillips (A) 1346 *8 maps* $3,500.00
A Military and Topographical Atlas of the United States Phila 1815 8vo Phillips (A) 1347 *12 maps* $4,000.00

Mitchell, S. A.

New American Atlas Phila 1831 ***
Mitchell, S. A. **A New Universal Atlas** Phila 1846 Folio *First edition* $2,500.00

A
General Atlas
CONTAINING DISTINCT
MAPS
Of all the known Countries in the
WORLD
Constructed from the Latest Authority.

BALTIMORE:
Published by Fielding Lucas, Junr.

Nº 138, Market Street.

Contents.

Title page and contents page from Fielding Lucas' General Atlas...Baltimore, 1823.
Maps from this atlas are illustrated on pgs 57 & 74

A New Universal Atlas Phila 1846 Folio *Second edition* $2,000.00
A New Universal Atlas Phila 1847 Folio $2,000.00
Mitchell, S. A. **A New Universal Atlas** Phila 1848 Folio $2,000.00
A New Universal Atlas Phila 1849 Folio Phillips (A) 797 *72 maps. Philadelphia: S. A. Mitchell* $2,000.00
A New Universal Atlas Phila 1850 Folio Phillips (A)800 *Philadelphia: Thomas, Cowperthwait. 72 maps* $2,000.00
A New Universal Atlas Phila 1851 Folio Phillips (A)805 *Philadelphia: Thomas, Cowperthwait. 73 maps* $2,000.00
A New Universal Atlas Phila 1852 Folio Phillips (A)807 *Philadelphia: Thomas, Cowperthwait. 73 maps* $2,000.00
A New Universal Atlas Phila 1853 Folio Phillips (A)809 *Philadelphia: Thomas, Cowperthwait. 73 maps* $2,000.00
A New Universal Atlas Phila 1854 Folio Phillips (A)813 *Philadelphia: Cowperthwait, Desilver & Butler. 71 maps* $2,000.00
A New Universal Atlas Phila 1854 Folio (Phillips (A)814 *Philadelphia: Cowperthwait, Desilver & Butler. 72 maps* $2,000.00
A New Universal Atlas Phila 1857 Folio Phillips (A)823 *Philadelphia: Desilver. 75 maps* $2,000.00
A New General Atlas Phila 1860 Folio Phillips (A)831 *Philadelphia: S. A. Mitchell, jr.* $800.00
A New General Atlas Phila 1865 Folio Phillips (A)846 *Philadelphia: S. A. Mitchell, jr. 51 Maps, numerous revisions and additions* $800.00
A New General Atlas Phila 1866 Folio Phillips (A)848 *Philadelphia: S. A. Mitchell, jr. 52 maps Utah and Nevada added* $800.00
A New General Atlas Phila 1867 Folio Phillips (A)850 *Philadelphia: S. A. Mitchell, jr. 53 maps 3 Maps added* $950.00
A New General Atlas Phila 1870 Folio Phillips (A) 859 *Philadelphia: S. A. Mitchell, jr. 57 maps Numerous revisions* $800.00
A New General Atlas Phila 1873 Folio Phillips (A)870 *Philadelphia: S. A. Mitchell, jr. 58 maps* $650.00
A New General Atlas Phila 1876 Folio Phillips (A)880 *Philadelphia: S. A. Mitchell, jr. 63 maps* $650.00
Mitchell, S. A. **A New General Atlas** Phila 1878 Folio Phillips (A) 888 *Philadelphia: S. A. Mitchell, jr. 67 maps* $650.00
A New General Atlas Phila 1879 Folio Phillips (A)890 *Philadelphia: S. A. Mitchell, jr. 72 maps Western Territories Added* $800.00
A New General Atlas Phila 1880 Folio Phillips (A) 892 *Philadelphia: Bradley & Co. 73 maps* $450.00
A New General Atlas Phila 1881 Folio Phillips (A)895 *Philadelphia: Bradley & Co.* $450.00
A New General Atlas Phila 1882 Folio Phillips (A)906 *Philadelphia: Bradley & Co. 72 maps* $450.00
A New General Atlas Phila 1884 Folio Phillips (A) 920 *Wm. Bradley & Bro. 72 maps* $450.00
A New General Atlas Phila 1893 Folio Phillips (A)983 *A. R. Keller. 68 maps* $450.00
Mitchell's New Reference Atlas... Phila 1865 Folio Phillips (A)847 *E. H. Butler & Co. 56 maps* $850.00

Morse, J.

The American Gazetteer Boston 1797 8vo *7 maps* $450.00
The American Geography Elizabethtown 1789 8vo *2 folding maps* $2,000.00
The American Universal Geography Boston 1796 8vo *18 maps* $650.00

Morse, S. E.

A New Universal Atlas New Haven 1822 4to $450.00
An Atlas of the United States on an Improved Plan New Haven 1823 8vo *Ristow 154* $650.00

Morse & Breese

Cerographic Atlas of the United States NY 1842 Folio Phillips (A)1383 *32 maps* $1,250.00
Morse's North American Atlas NY 1842-45 Folio Phillips (A)1228 *36 maps* $1,250.00

Morse & Gaston

The Diamond Atlas NY 1857 12mos Phillips (A)824 *2 vols. 31 maps 54 & 31 maps Phillips (A) 824* $300.00

Phillips & Hunt

The People's Atlas NY 1883 4to *51 maps* $125.00

Rand McNally & Co.

Rand-McNally's New Standard Atlas of the World NY 1899 Folio Phillips (A)1043 $250.00
Business Atlas Chicago 1876-77 Folio Phillips (A)1397 *First atlas published by Rand McNally. 27 maps Ristow 473* $500.00

A COMPLETE

HISTORICAL, CHRONOLOGICAL, AND GEOGRAPHICAL

AMERICAN ATLAS,

BEING

A GUIDE TO THE HISTORY

OF

NORTH AND SOUTH AMERICA,

AND THE

WEST INDIES:

EXHIBITING

AN ACCURATE ACCOUNT

OF THE

DISCOVERY, SETTLEMENT, AND PROGRESS OF THEIR VARIOUS KINGDOMS,

STATES, PROVINCES, &c.

TOGETHER WITH THE

WARS, CELEBRATED BATTLES, AND REMARKABLE EVENTS,

TO THE YEAR 1822.

ACCORDING TO THE PLAN OF LE SAGE'S ATLAS,

AND INTENDED AS A COMPANION TO

LAVOISNE'S IMPROVEMENT OF THAT CELEBRATED WORK.

PHILADELPHIA:

H. C. CAREY AND I. LEA,—CHESNUT STREET.

1823.

Title page and contents page from the second edition of Carey & Lea's ...American Atlas. Philadelphia, 1823.
Maps from this atlas are illustrated on pgs 19, 39, & 55

CONTENTS.

INDEX.

A

NEW UNIVERSAL ATLAS

Containing Maps of the various

Empires, Kingdoms, States and Republics

OF THE

WORLD

With a special map of each of the United States, plans of Cities &c.
Comprehended in seventy sheets and forming a series of

ONE HUNDRED AND SEVENTEEN MAPS

PLANS AND SECTIONS.

FIRST LANDING OF COLUMBUS IN THE NEW WORLD.

"Columbus and his followers landed and kneeling they all kissed the ground they had so long desired to see. they next erected a Crucifix and prostrating themselves before it returned thanks to God for conducting their voyage to such an happy issue."
Herrera's life of Columbus

PHILADELPHIA

PUBLISHED BY S. AUGUSTUS MITCHELL,
N.E. corner of Market & 7th Streets.
1848.

Title page from Mitchell's New Universal Atlas. Phila, 1848. Editions of this atlas were issued by various publishers, including Desilver and Thomas, Cowperthwait, from 1846-1856. Mitchell purchased the copyright from Tanner in 1845. A map from the 1847 edition of this atlas is illustrated on pg 63.

Scott

The United States Gazeteer...Illustrated with Nineteen Maps Phila 1795 8vo *First edition* $2,750.00

Tanner, H. S.

A New Universal Atlas Phila 1836 Folio Phillips (A)774 *68 maps* $3,250.00

(Carey & Hart) **A New Universal Atlas** Phila 1843 Folio Phillips (A)788 *70 maps* $2,500.00

(Carey & Hart) **A New Universal Atlas** Phila 1844 Folio $2,500.00

(Carey & Hart) **A New Universal Atlas** Phila 1845 Folio $2,500.00

Atlas of the United States Phila 1826 Folio *11 maps Howes T25* $6,000.00

Atlas of the United States Phila 1835 Folio Phillips (A)1380 *24 maps* $4,500.00

A New American Atlas Phila 1823 Folio Phillips (A)1374 *22 maps* $5,500.00

A New American Atlas Phila 1823 *Issued in 5 parts 1818-23 Howes T29****

A New American Atlas Phila 1823 *Issued in 3 parts 1819-23 Howes T29****

A New American Atlas Phila 1825 *Howes T29****

A New American Atlas Phila 1825-33 Phillips (A)1376 *With maps dated to 1833 Howes T29****

A New American Atlas Phila 1839 Phillips (A)1382 *Howes T29****

A New Pocket Atlas of the United States Phila 1828 24mo *Howes T30****

A New Universal Atlas Phila 1842 Folio Phillips (A)788 *70 maps* $3,500.00

Tunison

Tunison's Peerless Universal Atlas Jacksonville, IL 1886 4to $225.00

Winterbotham & Reid

The American Atlas Phila 1796 Folio *20 maps. Ristow 153****

COLTON'S

ATLAS OF THE WORLD,

ILLUSTRATING

PHYSICAL AND POLITICAL GEOGRAPHY.

BY GEORGE W. COLTON.

ACCOMPANIED BY DESCRIPTIONS

GEOGRAPHICAL, STATISTICAL, AND HISTORICAL,

BY RICHARD SWAINSON FISHER, M.D.

VOLUME I.—NORTH AND SOUTH AMERICA, ETC.

NEW YORK:

J. H. COLTON AND COMPANY,

No. 172 WILLIAM, CORNER BEEKMAN STREET.

LONDON: TRÜBNER AND COMPANY, NO. 12 PATERNOSTER ROW.

1856.

Title page and List of Maps from Colton's Atlas of the World. NY, 1856. Often considered the last of the elegant American atlases it was also one of the first mass produced atlases. Maps from this atlas are illustrated on pgs 23 & 65

LIST OF MAPS

CONTAINED IN

COLTON'S ATLAS OF THE WORLD.

VOLUME I.

JOHNSON'S

New Illustrated

(STEEL PLATE)

FAMILY ATLAS,

WITH DESCRIPTIONS,

GEOGRAPHICAL, STATISTICAL, AND HISTORICAL.

Compiled, Drawn, and Engraved

UNDER THE SUPERVISION OF

J. H. COLTON AND A. J. JOHNSON.

B. P. WARD, GENERAL AGENT.

NEW YORK:

JOHNSON AND BROWNING,

FORMERLY

(SUCCESSORS TO J. H. COLTON AND COMPANY,)

NO. 133 NASSAU STREET.

1861.

Title page and List of Maps from Johnson's New Illustrated Family Atlas. Improved lithographic techniques enabled this publisher to issue large editions of this atlas through the 1860's and 1870's. Maps from the 1861 and 1864 editions are illustrated on pgs 25, 27, 31 & 47

LIST OF MAPS

CONTAINED IN

JOHNSON'S FAMILY ATLAS.

MITCHELL'S

NEW GENERAL ATLAS,

CONTAINING MAPS OF THE

VARIOUS COUNTRIES OF THE WORLD,

PLANS OF CITIES, ETC.,

EMBRACED IN

FIFTY-THREE QUARTO MAPS,

FORMING A SERIES OF

EIGHTY-FOUR MAPS AND PLANS,

TOGETHER WITH

VALUABLE STATISTICAL TABLES.

PHILADELPHIA:
PUBLISHED BY S. AUGUSTUS MITCHELL, JR.,
No. 31 SOUTH SIXTH STREET.
1864.

Title page and List of Maps from Mitchell's New General Atlas
Editions of this atlas were issued by various publishers, including Mitchell and Bradley, through the 1880's
A map from this atlas is illustrated on pg 29

LIST OF MAPS.

1. THE WORLD — EASTERN AND WESTERN HEMISPERES.
2. THE WORLD — MERCATOR'S PROJECTION.
3. NORTH AMERICA.
4. NOVA SCOTIA, NEW BRUNSWICK, CAPE BRETON, AND PRINCE EDWARD'S ISLANDS.
5. CITY AND HARBOR OF HALIFAX.
6. CANADA EAST.
7. ENVIRONS OF MONTREAL.
8. CANADA WEST.
9. UNITED STATES AND TERRITORIES. (*Double Map.*)
10. HAMPTON ROADS AND NORFOLK HARBOR.
11. PENSACOLA BAY
12. MAINE.
13. PORTLAND HARBOR AND VICINITY.
14. NEW HAMPSHIRE AND VERMONT.
15. MASSACHUSETTS, CONNECTICUT, AND RHODE ISLAND.
16. NEW YORK, NEW HAMPSHIRE, VERMONT, MASSACHUSETTS, RHODE ISLAND, AND CONNECTICUT. (*Double Map.*)
17. HARBOR AND VICINITY OF NEW YORK.
18. HARBOR AND VICINITY OF BOSTON.
19. PLAN OF NEW YORK CITY, BROOKLYN, ETC.
20. PLAN OF THE CITY OF BOSTON.
21. PENNSYLVANIA, NEW JERSEY, MARYLAND, AND DELAWARE.
22. VICINITY OF PHILADELPHIA.
23. VICINITY OF BALTIMORE.
24. PLAN OF THE CITY OF PHILADELPHIA.
25. PLAN OF THE CITY OF BALTIMORE.
26. PLAN OF THE CITY OF WASHINGTON.
27. VIRGINIA.
28. KENTUCKY AND TENNESSEE.
29. GEORGIA AND ALABAMA.
30. NORTH CAROLINA, SOUTH CAROLINA, AND FLORIDA.
31. HARBOR OF CHARLESTON.
32. LOUISIANA, MISSISSIPPI, AND ARKANSAS.
33. PLAN OF NEW ORLEANS.
34. TEXAS.
35. VICINITY OF GALVESTON.
36. OHIO AND INDIANA.
37. PLAN OF CINCINNATI.
38. ILLINOIS.
39. PLAN OF CHICAGO.
40. MISSOURI AND IOWA.
41. MICHIGAN AND WISCONSIN.
42. MINNESOTA.
43. KANSAS, NEBRASKA, AND COLORADO.
44. OREGON, WASHINGTON TERRITORY, AND BRITISH COLUMBIA.
45. CALIFORNIA.
46. MAP OF THE SETTLEMENTS IN THE VALLEY OF THE GREAT SALT LAKE COUNTRY.
47. HARBOR OF SAN FRANCISCO.

UTAH TERRITORY,
NEW MEXICO TERRITORY, } *See Map of the United States.*
ARIZONA.

48. MEXICO, CENTRAL AMERICA, AND WEST INDIES. (*Double Map.*)
49. ISLAND OF CUBA.
50. ISLAND OF JAMAICA.
51. BERMUDA ISLANDS.
52. ROUTE OF THE PANAMA RAILROAD.
53. SOUTH AMERICA.
54. MAP OF THE PROPOSED ATRATO CANAL ROUTE TO CONNECT THE ATLANTIC AND PACIFIC OCEANS.
55. NEW GRENADA, VENEZUELA, AND GUIANA.
56. EQUADOR AND PERU.
57. ARGENTINE CONFEDERATION.
58. BRAZIL.
59. HARBOR OF RIO JANEIRO.
60. HARBOR OF BAHIA.
61. CHILI.
62. ISLAND OF JUAN FERNANDEZ.
63. EUROPE.
64. RUSSIA IN EUROPE, NORWAY AND SWEDEN.
65. DENMARK.
66. HOLLAND AND BELGIUM.
67. FRANCE, SPAIN, AND PORTUGAL.
68. SWITZERLAND.
69. ISLAND OF CORSICA.
70. ENGLAND AND WALES
71. SCOTLAND.
72. SHETLAND ISLANDS.
73. IRELAND.
74. PRUSSIA AND THE GERMAN STATES.
75. AUSTRIA, ITALY, TURKEY IN EUROPE, AND GREECE.
76. MALTESE ISLANDS.
77. ASIA.
78. PERSIA, TURKEY IN ASIA, AFGHANISTAN, AND BELOOCHISTAN.
79. PALESTINE, OR THE HOLY LAND.
80. HINDOOSTAN, FARTHER INDIA, CHINA, AND THIBET.
81. OCEANICA.
82. SANDWICH ISLANDS.
83. AFRICA.
84. ISLAND OF ST. HELENA.

SELECT BIBLIOGRAPHY

Brown, Ralph H. *Historical Geography of the United States* NY 1948
Brown, Lloyd C. *The Story of Maps* Boston 1949
Brown, Lloyd C. *Map Making* Boston 1960
Buisseret, David, ed. *From Sea Charts to Satellite Images* Chicago 1990 *Interpreting American History through Maps*
Ehrenberg & Schwarz *The Mapping of America* NY 1980
Goetzmann, W. H. *Army Exploration in the American West* New Haven 1959
Goss, John *The Mapping Of North America* London 1990
Howes, Wright *USIANA* NY 1962
Jolly, David C. *Maps of America in Periodicals Before 1800* Brookline 1989
Karpinski, Louis C. *Map Bibliography of Michigan and the Great Lakes* Lansing 1931
Phillips, P. Lee *A List of Maps of America in the Library of Congress...* Washington 1901
Phillips, P. Lee *A List of Geographical Atlases...* Washington 1909 *4 vols*
Potter, Jonathan *Country Life Book of Antique Maps* Secaucus 1988
Ristow, W. W. *American Maps and Mapmakers* Detroit 1985
Rosenthal & Jolly *Antique Map Price Record & Handbook* Brookline 1982-1994 *Annual volumes.*
Wheat, J. C. *Mapping the Transmississippi West* San Francisco 1957-63
Wheat, J. C. & Brun, C. F. *Maps and Charts Published in America Before 1800* New Haven 1969
Wilford, John Noble *The Mapmakers* NY 1981
Woodward, David *The All American Map* Chicago 1977 *Wax engraving's influence on cartography*